Christianity and the Culture of Relativism in the Anthropologies of Joseph Ratzinger and Stanley Hauerwas

Christianity and the Culture of Relativism in the Anthropologies of Joseph Ratzinger and Stanley Hauerwas

(Rediscovering the Truth of Christianity)

Charles Ssennyondo, STL, STD

Library of Congress Control Number: 2012920684
ISBN: Hardcover   978-1-4797-4444-2
                 Softcover   978-1-4797-4443-5
                 Ebook   978-1-4797-4445-9

This book was printed in the United States of America.

To order additional copies of this book, contact:
Xlibris Corporation
1-888-795-4274
www.Xlibris.com
Orders@Xlibris.com
114606

Dedication

To my parents
Mathias Kakooza and Bernadette Nakanwagi, without whom I would
not be. With their simple but robust Catholic faith, I am who I am.

Imprimatur

Francis Cardinal George, O.M.I., Ph.D.
Archbishop of Chicago

Nihil Obstat
Reverend Emery A. de Gaál
Reverend Raymond J. Webb
censores deputati

[Permission to publish is an official declaration of ecclesiastical authority that the material is free from doctrinal and moral error in accord with Canon 823. No legal responsibility is assumed by the grant of this permission.]

Given at Chicago this <u>12th day</u> of <u>September, 2012</u>.

Table of Contents

PART I
General Introduction

PART II
Joseph Ratzinger and Stanley Hauerwas
against the Culture of Relativism

Chapter One

Chapter Two

Chapter Three

Chapter Four

PART III
Toward a Christian Response to Relativism

Chapter Five

Chapter Six

Chapter Seven

Chapter Eight

PART IV:

Epilogue
Means by which Sub-Saharan African Culture can ward off Relativism

Chapter Nine

Introduction

Origin of the Hypothesis

In "Classics of the 20th Century," one of the first courses in the STL program, I read a book by Peter Berger, *A Rumor of Angels*, in which I found significant ideas that best describe the contemporary perception of religion in general and Christianity in particular. Peter Berger writes,

> The supernatural has departed from the modern society; God is dead; we are living in a post-Christian era; religion—a vanishing leftover from the dark ages of superstition; those to whom the supernatural is still a meaningful reality find themselves in the status of a minority—a cognitive minority—a group formed around a body of deviant knowledge.[1]

The talk of a post-Christian era and the proliferation of antireligious ideas precipitated my search for a possible response. Second, the reality of religious pluralism also led me to wonder if we can still speak of *the Christian* truth that is one and indivisible. The prevalent pluralism seemed to me to be also the result of a relativistic view of reality. This culture of relativism threatens to *erode* completely my own centuries-old Ganda culture in Uganda. One motivation for me to write this book is to assist in combating this threat to my people as priest and theologian.

I wrote my STL thesis on Ratzinger's theology, whose remarkable contemporary theology attempts an answer to the contemporary relativistic culture. My doctoral project is an expansion of that thesis. In addition, the doctoral

---

[1] Peter Berger, *A Rumor of Angels* (New York: Doubleday and Company, Inc., 1970), 1–6.

1

project aimed at making a comparison between a Catholic perspective and a valiant Protestant attempt to address the same issues.

1. Relevance of the Topic: The Culture of Relativism

The reality of relativism is not new but in fact a very old phenomenon whose origins have been traced back to the well-known Greek philosopher Protagoras who famously stated, "Everything is relative. There are two sides to everything. Man is the measure of all things, of those being that they are, of those not being, that they are not."[2] Relativism can be described as a state of absoluteness of the individual, where the individual is source and summit of the truth, the good and bad, and the right and wrong. Joseph Ratzinger defined it as "allowing oneself to be led here and there by any wind of doctrine."[3] He also notes that this trend defines our times today—that today "we are witnessing the 'dictatorship of relativism' which does not recognize anything as absolute and leaves as the ultimate measure only the measure of each one and his own desires."[4] According to him, in "an un-reflected, uncritical and naïve way, the modern world has been ensnared into relativism."[5]

Like Ratzinger, Hauerwas also envisions a world where absolute truth, norms, and values, are being sacrificed, replacing them with subjective/relative ones and systematically ensuring that the objective ones never come back into play. For Hauerwas, relativism means "democratic policing of Christianity."[6] According to him, relativism is a result of extreme liberalism which emasculated Christianity in the name of societal peace. Evidently, Hauerwas' greatest pain is that

> Christians have learned to police their convictions in the name
> of sustaining such social orders. They cannot appear in public
> using explicit Christian language since that would offend other
> actors in our allegedly pluralist polity. But if this is genuinely a
> pluralist society, why should Christians not be able to express
> their most cherished convictions in public? If we are in an age

---

[2] Protagoras in *Great Philosophers*, http://oregonstate.edu/instruct/phl201/modules/ Philosophers/Protagoras/protagoras.html (accessed on April 30, 2012).

[3] Ibid.

[4] John F. Thornton and Susan B. Varenne, eds., *The Essential Pope Benedict XVI: His Central Writings and Speeches* (New York: HarperCollins Publishers, 2007), 22.

[5] Gediminas T. Jankunas, *The Dictatorship of Relativism: Pope Benedict XVI's Response* (New York: St. Paul's Press, 2011), 337 (Back cover).

[6] Stanley Hauerwas, *Dispatches from the Front: Theological Engagements with the Secular* (Durham, NC: Duke University Press, 1995), 93.

of identity-politics, why does the identity of Christians need to be suppressed?[7]

2. Ratzinger's and Hauerwas' Anthropological Discourses

Both Ratzinger and Hauerwas agree that relativism is a result of a defective anthropology which in the end results into a crisis of faith. Therefore, to revert it, the anthropological nuance must be corrected.

a. Joseph Ratzinger

In very general terms, Ratzinger's anthropology is a "doctrine" of *relationality* and *creatureliness*. His anthropology accrues from his relational theology. It stems from the fact of creation, from which follows logically, that a creature automatically depends and relies on a creator for its life and sustainability. He is opposed to the ideology of *makability* and *relationlessness* prevailing in today's society. His theology reaffirms that man is a creature of God and not just a creature, but the *imago Dei*. Therefore, by acting without God, man disassociates himself from his creator and denies that he is a creature. He ceases to be the *imago Dei*. Ratzinger illustrates this by observing,

> The mentality of "*makability*" tells us that we must free ourselves from every requirement to receive, from all dependency. We must stand on our own, independent of others and of God. Ratzinger counters: *relationlessness* is not our own; cut off from relationships, our truth is denied—and, with it, our freedom—for freedom and truth go together. God is not the enemy of our freedom but its ground. When people deny their creatureliness, they end up replacing God with a capital "G" with a whole host of exploitative small "g" gods, such as commercial forces, greed, public opinion, etc. the tyranny of these is an enslavement far greater.[8]

As a remedy, Ratzinger proposes a rebuilding of the relationship with the Creator—a communion with the Lord. He suggests a reversal of what happened

---

[7] Ibid.
[8] James Corkery, *Joseph Ratzinger's Theological Ideas: Wise Cautions and Legitimate Hopes* (New York: Paulist Press, 2009), 40–41. (Cf. Gen. 3:3—Original Sin).

at the tower of Babel.[9] Ratzinger's anthropology is a response to modern culture's denial of truth. The theologian from Bavaria summarizes,

> It is obvious that the concept of truth has become suspect . . .
> people are afraid when someone says, "This is the truth," or
> even "I have the truth." We never have it; at best it has us.
> No one will dispute that one must be careful and cautious in
> claiming the truth. But simply to dismiss it as unattainable is
> really destructive. A large proportion of contemporary phi-
> losophies, in fact, consist of saying that man is not capable
> of ethical values, either. Then he would have no standards.
> Then he would only have to consider how he arranged things
> reasonable for himself, and then at any rate the opinion of the
> majority would be the only criterion that counted.[10]

Ratzinger believes that uncoupled from truth, humanity dies. Why? Because,

> As human beings, we receive a dialogical, relational essence
> and are called to live this in history in an existence that is at
> once gift and task. We have a responsibility to shape our lives,
> always in fidelity to what we have received as created beings.
> We have no freedom of our own. Our freedom is a normed
> freedom—not blind and directionless, but guided by the light
> of what is given to us with our creation.[11]

b. Stanley Hauerwas

Hauerwas' theological dialogue seems to be a retelling of the story of Jesus Christ, the story of a Christian, the story of God's creation.[12] He suggests recourse to the rhetoric of creation—man situating himself in the story of creation as one of the creatures. The story of creation is manifested and fulfilled in the story of Christ. Therefore, a Christian is one who situates himself or herself in this story of creation. But this story is not only a story for a Christian but for all humanity, for we are all God's creatures.

Hauerwas proposes a union in Christ in whom we become one with God our Creator. This union in Christ is fully realized in the Eucharist. In an

---

[9] Joseph Ratzinger, *Pilgrim Fellowship of Faith: The Church as Communion* (San Francisco: Ignatius Press, 2002), 61.
[10] Benedict XVI, *Light of the World*, trans. Michael Miller and Adrian Walker (San Francisco: Ignatius Press, 2010), 50–51.
[11] Corkery, *Joseph Ratzinger's Theological Ideas*, 41–42.
[12] Stanley Hauerwas, *Christian Existence Today: Essays on Church, World, and Living in Between* (Durham, NC: Labyrinth Press, 1988), 40.

interview, Hauerwas asserts that the Eucharist is "a rite in which we become part of the body of Christ."[13] Therefore, according to Hauerwas, unity in Christ is key in theology and Christian living.

Hauerwas is critical of an *implicit* denial of "creation"—being made synonymous with "nature."[14] He worries that the prevailing culture wants to impose on humanity: that the idea of creation is mythical. It denies that there is a force above nature and in which nature finds meaning and fulfillment.

Hauerwas teaches a fallen nature of man and insists that this is the reason for the world order thereafter. He wants the fact of original sin to be retold as a basic truth. He is acutely conscious of humanity's fallenness and envisages God's dealings with us as being converting and transformative, creating a new language.[15] He is opposed to the prevailing culture which downplays the notion of sin and punishment.

3. Their Respective Anthropological Strengths and Weaknesses

Anthropological Themes	Joseph Ratzinger's Position	Stanley Hauerwas' Position
Man: His Life and Origin	Man is a creation of God and cannot be fully defined separate from Jesus of Nazareth. The incarnate person of God fulfills humanity. Jesus/Logos is the perfect *imago Dei* in whom this image is fulfilled in humankind. The incarnation is the basis for anthropology. At the center of human life is the paschal mystery, which is the full manifestation of God's love.	Man is a creation of God, defined by the community—the church. Humankind is realized and fulfilled in the mystery of Pentecost, in which a new language was created. Apart from Christianity, human life, according to Hauerwas, is more of a humanism based on social consensus[16] and action other than on the *Logos* who lives and perfects the *imago Dei* in humankind.

[13] This was in an *Interview with Hauerwas* on January 28, 2011, at Duke University Divinity School (Cf. appendix).

[14] Stanley Hauerwas, *In Good Company: The Church as Polis* (Notre Dame, IN: University of Notre Dame Press, 1995), 181.

[15] Stanley Hauerwas, *The Church as God's New Language*, http://jeremyberg.wordpress.com/2010/01/05/essay-stanley-hauerwas-the-Church-as-gods-new-language (accessed on October 19, 2010).

[16] "Hauerwas has a pragmatic criterion of truth, making a community the justification of Christian convictions. Scripture, then, does not have any inherent meaning." In Stephen Webb, "The Very American Stanley Hauerwas," *First Things* (June/July 2002): 14–17.

God, Humankind, and the World	For Ratzinger, man is relational; he cannot live without God and the world. These three are all relational and derive their meaning in as far as they live in these relationships. His anthropology is essentially one of communion.	While Hauerwas believes in a relational nature of man, he, at the same time, envisages a separateness of living, a *resident alienism*. In as long as Hauerwas encourages Christians to be resident aliens, living in an "alternative polis," he implicitly encourages and may lead to the medieval Puritanism—fashioning an isolated "holy" society within a larger evil society. This again may lead man to disconnect from one another.[17]
The Fall and Redemption	Ratzinger believes in the *fallenness* of man and in his need for redemption. However, this redemption is not achievable without Christ. Fullness of redemption is possible through the sacraments as channels of grace.	For Hauerwas, redemption is possible by faith in Jesus Christ alone. But man ascends to it directly without sacramental mediation.

4. Synthesis

Ratzinger makes the following conclusion:

Gratia praesupponit naturam is correct and fully biblical in saying that grace does not destroy what is truly human in man but, salvages and fulfills it. This genuine humanity of man, the created order "man," is completely extinguished in no man; it lies at the basis of every single human person and in many different ways continuously has its effects on man's concrete existence, summoning and guiding him. But of course in no man is it present without warping or falsification; instead, in every individual it is caked with the layer of filth.[18]

---

[17] This, as a result, can lead to separation from God, which puts Hauerwas in the position of a Christian existentialist who can appropriately be christened "the Kierkegaard of America."

[18] Joseph Ratzinger: Pope Benedict XVI, *Dogma and Preaching: Applying Christian Doctrine to daily Life* (San Francisco: Ignatius Press, 2011), 158.

Therefore, Ratzinger elucidates that the "second man" is the channel/the way of grace to mankind, breaking open the hard shell of *vainglory* that covers the divine glory within him. This means that there is no grace without the cross. On the basis of a robust Chalcedonian Christology, Ratzinger is able to affirm: only the humanity of the Second Adam is fully true humanity. The Cross is not the "crucifixion of man" at all, as Nietzsche thought, but rather his true healing. "The humanity of God is indeed the true humanity of man, the grace that fulfills nature."[19]

Hauerwas holds quite a different position. First and foremost, he rejects natural theology (and therefore rejects natural law as well). His emphatic thesis is that "natural theology is impossibly abstracted from a full doctrine of God."[20] According to him, natural theology would equate to a natural science without reference to or reliance on any supposed special exceptional or miraculous revelation.[21] Insofar as Hauerwas objects to the use of reason alone to describe the nature of God, he is right. Revelation is the indispensable basis for knowing God. However, this does not mean that nature is devoid of grace. For, as Ratzinger illustrates above, also *postlapsarian* human nature is endowed with grace—with the desire to seek God. Thus, the second nature of humankind fulfills that to which human nature is ordered toward from the beginning, namely, God. Further, Hauerwas does not seem to be consistent with his position as he later tends to base his ecclesiology on political and existential arguments.

Despite his critique of natural theology, rendering it a mere humanism, Hauerwas' ecclesiology tragically betrays his anthropology because in it, he portrays an "acting" church, i.e., a people who live by acting, fighting, and resisting evil, a community within a community—"resident aliens"—very much like the great humanists, such as Henry David Thoreau or Mahatma Gandhi have advocated. Rather than one allowing God's strength and grace to work through Christians, Hauerwas' Christians resort to their own human devices. Such people would be little different from agnostic or atheistic humanists who struggle for only establishing "a kind and caring society." But the psalmist says, "Unless the Lord guards the city, the guard keeps watch in vain" (Ps 127:1). This makes Hauerwas a tragic figure: a Christian existentialist à la Kierkegaard whose anthropology actually contradicts his revelational and theological concerns.

---

[19] Ibid., 159–161.
[20] Stanley Hauerwas, *With the Grain of the Universe: The Church's Witness and Natural Theology* (Grand Rapids, MI: Brazos Press, 2001), 10.
[21] Ibid., 26.

5. Conclusions

Anthropology hinges on Christology. If Chalcedon teaches that Jesus became fully human,[22] then it means that it is only in Jesus that we learn to be fully human. In ultimate analysis, if Gen 1:26 and the incarnation of the Lord are ignored, human rights remain hollow. A godless world appears to be the most palatable and convenient idea to an economy-driven humanity today, as it frees people from the promptings of the law and a divine lawgiver. The greatest craving for man, it so seems, is to be a *solipsistic* self-legislator. However, the end result of this is a replacement of the truth with servitude to horizontal pragmatism (for true freedom lies in the truth) and the good with the bad, the wrong, the evil, the unjust and at the end of the line, self-willed death.

The following words from Ratzinger sum up our project:

> Once more, we have to say: How far we are from a world in which people no longer need to be taught about God because he is present within us! It has been asserted that our century is characterized by an entirely new phenomenon: the appearance of people incapable of relating to God. We have reached the stage where a kind of person has developed in whom there is no longer any starting point for the knowledge of God. Our distance from God—the obscurity and the dubiousness surrounding him today—is greater than ever before; indeed, that even we who are trying to be believers often feel as if the reality of God is being withdrawn from between our hands.[23]

---

[22] ND 614, Council of Chalcedon, AD 451: "Our Lord Jesus Christ, the same perfect in divinity and perfect in humanity, the same truly God and truly man." Cf. Vatican II Council: "He who is the 'image of the invisible God' (Col 1:15), is himself the perfect man who has restored in the children of Adam that likeness to God which had been disfigured ever since the first sin. Human nature, by the very fact that it was assumed, not absorbed, in him, has been raised in us also to a dignity beyond compare." GS 22.

[23] Joseph Ratzinger, *What It Means to be a Christian* (San Francisco: Ignatius Press, 2006), 24–25.

List of Abbreviations

AG	*Ad Gentes*, Decree on the Missionary Activity of the Church, Vatican II
BD	Bachelor of Divinity
BBC	British Broadcasting Corporation
CCC	*Catechism of the Catholic Church*
CMS	Church Missionary Society
DH	Denzinger/Hűnermann, *Enchiridion Symbolorum Definitinum et Declarationum de Rebus Fidei et Morum*
LG	*Lumen Gentium*, Dogmatic Constitution on the Church, Vatican II
LUMSA	*Libera Università Maria Santissima Assunta*
ND	Neuner and Dupuis, *The Christian Faith*
SC	*Sacrosanctum Concilium*, The Constitution on Sacred Liturgy, Vatican II

Acknowledgement

The Psalmist says, "The Lord is our God, He made us, we belong to Him, we are His people, the flock He shepherds" (Ps 100:3). And the Lord Jesus told us, "Without me you can do nothing" (Jn 15:5). I therefore wish to express my sincere gratitude to Almighty God, for his goodness to me—his love and care, his providence and protection, his wisdom and the gift of faith. As I write this, on my lips is the song of the psalmist: "What return to Yahweh can I make for his goodness to me? I will lift the cup of salvation and call on the name of the Lord" (Ps 116:12).

Second, I would like thank my parents who have been so supportive of me, even in very difficult moments. In my mother tongue, we have a saying, *"Batenda enswa okuwooma, beerabira enkuyege ezaazimba ekiswa,"* literally translated, "They praise the ants and forget the termites who build the anthill." All my studies have been through hardships, but my parents did the harder part. They went without food that I may eat; without good clothing that I may go to school; without fun that I may have a good life. I have no doubt my success is theirs. Together with them, I acknowledge with gratitude, the sacrifices and love from siblings. Many of them did not take their studies beyond grade school because I required all the funds; they lead a very humble life because they sacrificed a good life for me. My relatives and friends too contributed a great deal. Mentioning one by one would make another chapter. I would like to include all of you who helped me in my studies in these two words: Thank you!

Academic successes can enjoy much supported from home but can yield nothing if there is no one at school. I would like to sincerely thank all my teachers—right from grade school through to university. They did a great job turning me into a human being—different from what my parents gave birth to. To these I add all my classmates and contemporaries in all the schools I attended. You have been a great company and support. Alone, I would learn nothing. Thank you so much and may God reward you!

I would like to express my gratitude toward my bishop, Rt. Rev. Paul

Ssemogerere and my diocese of Kasana-Luweero, for the financial and moral support they have accorded me throughout all my studies. I particularly thank them for allowing me undertake graduate studies here in the States. They could do nothing greater. Thank you for putting such trust in me.

Many thanks go the Archdiocese of Chicago for granting me a scholarship for my STL. I had never imagined such could happen to me. I thank the University of St. Mary of the Lake for admitting me and supporting me during my studies. I thank you all from the president to the last staff. You have always been there for me. God bless you. In a like manner, I would like to acknowledge the goodness of Our Lady of Humility Parish Community. I was supposed to return to my country after my STL, and they offered to send me back to school for my doctorate; I could not believe my ears. Not only that, they gave me a home as well; I was homeless, and they helped me find a home! I can't thank you enough. It all started with Fr. Dr. David Mulvihill, the pastor emeritus, welcomed and embraced by the current pastor, Fr. Tom Hoffman, and accepted by the entire community. May God shower you all with his abundant blessings!

I can hardly find appropriate words to thank my supervisor and director, Rev. Fr. Emery de Gaál Gyulai. Fr. Emery, thank you for your wise guidance. With all humility, you accepted me and we worked and walked together through my STL and doctoral programs. I did not know what you do, and you helped me find it. I was afraid to undertake anything, and you gave me courage. I was many times hopeless and confused, and you gave me hope. You have been an angel to me. With heartfelt gratitude, I express my gratitude, and please accept my humble thanks. God reward your efforts!

Also, I would like to express my gratitude to Fr. Raymond Webb, the second reader. His meticulous reading of the manuscript greatly enhanced the quality of the text. Great appreciation to you, Fr. Webb!

I was privileged to get a chance of meeting one of my major reference theologians, Professor Stanley Hauerwas, PhD. I think this was an opportunity of its own nature to have firsthand information from the person behind the formation of this paper. I never expected to access him in the first place given his busy schedule. In addition, the welcome and attention he accorded me gave me the confidence that I was doing something of value. But most importantly, I appreciate the knowledge and wisdom Stanley exposed during our ecumenical, academic interview. Thank you, Dr. Hauerwas, for your kindness and your firm Christian faith.

And finally, last but not least, I thank Mari Johnson, Sheila Pope, and Diane Rizzio for proofreading my paper. Thank you for enduring my terrible English. I cannot count how many grammatical mistakes I made and how bad my sentence constructions were. But you diligently spent time to look at each of them and advised me—and corrected me. Thank you for giving me your time and for being so patient with me. I now know better English. Thank you for teaching me.

Preface

As the world gets more and more democratic, there is a widespread feeling among peoples of almost all cultures that universals are things of the past. In post modernity, many people have developed a bitter resentment to anything coherent and unified—system or idea or set of values that claim to be universal. In most cases, such is claimed to be a dogmatic and enslaving mentality—an intolerant perspective toward life or worse still, fascism at work. The world seems to suggest that it is fashionable to be tolerant because it makes us humans who are loving and free. No wonder the Catholic Church is resented and hated by many, because it holds on to things. It has doctrines that are lasting and consistent (which many term as conservative). It also claims, as it is in the name, to be universal. The prevailing contemporary culture feels that such doctrines, and institutions that hold them, have lived beyond their time. They so think, therefore, that the church has no more relevance in today's world, and therefore, the pope and his clergy "better pack up their bags and go home."

Under such circumstances, one wonders if the church indeed still has any place in this world. Is Christianity still relevant today; what remains of its doctrines if each individual decides on what is right and wrong, good and bad? Can God still talk to his people and if so, through which media? Is God's word and covenant still everlasting, or is the God idea simply an outdated one?

In this book, we will try to explore the gravity and magnitude of this new culture and find out how far it has gone. We shall narrow and base our research and deliberations on the theological and anthropological discourses of both Joseph Ratzinger and Stanley Hauerwas. By limiting our findings on only them, they will be the main driving wheel of our research. We shall begin with the reaffirming, in an apologetic manner, of the mandate of the church to evangelize to all ages and nations to the end of times. This will be included in the foreword.

We shall then go to the main body of our paper, beginning with the main elements that inform the theologies and anthropologies of both Ratzinger and Hauerwas. This will be contained in part one of the paper. Part two will treat the analysis of this monster called "culture of relativism" by both Joseph Ratzinger and Stanley Hauerwas. In the same section, we shall have recourse to other main protagonists of relativism especially in the modern times where this culture remotely originated. We shall also examine the remedies these theologians Ratzinger and Hauerwas offer against relativism.

Part three will attempt to find what we can refer to as the Christian response to relativism—putting together both Catholic and Protestant discourses, marking carefully the differences, many of which are actually relativistic, between Catholic and Protestant theologies and anthropologies. We shall conclude this part with the contributions of our main theologians, Ratzinger and Hauerwas, toward a recovery of a Christian Formation of Culture. In the very last chapter, however, we shall illustrate that the root cause of relativism is an anthropology gone bad. To reverse the trend there is need to get our theological anthropology right. This will be brought out clearly in this chapter.

Foreword

**(By Fr. Emery de Gaál, director of
Dr. Ssennyondo's Doctoral Dissertation)**

It is Fr. Ssennyondo's achievement to compare two noted theologians' anthropologies as both address the rapidly spreading phenomenon of relativism. He does this as a postgraduate student of theology, but most importantly as a priest who is deeply worried about the future of his own people, the Baganda, who are torn between their rich ancestral heritage, Catholic and Protestants faiths on the one hand and more recently militant Moslem proselytizing in Uganda and secularized modernity ever more forcefully asserting itself on the other.

On 275 pages, he lays out a rich tapestry of insights, positions, and arguments. He supports his arguments with over 650 footnotes. In the appendix, he added an instructive interview he had conducted with Stanley Hauerwas at Duke University. Roughly 200 different titles are integrated into his study.

The first theologian he selected is Joseph Ratzinger. He is a widely published and celebrated theologian and now Pope Benedict XVI. He earned a prize already when penning his own doctoral dissertation in 1953. He is a member of the much-respected foreign section of the French Academie, succeeding the Russian human rights activity and nuclear physicist Andrei Sakharov. Some consider him the most significant theologian on the throne of Peter since Leo the Great. In many ways, his views reflect the cumulative wisdom of the church: of scripture, the councils, the saints, the church fathers, and theologians to this day.

The interlocutor he chose for him is most different: in his Christian faith, in temperament, in style, in language, and in what solutions he offers. While a committed Christian himself, he originates in the Methodist Church and now worships in an Episcopalian parish at Duke University. His views are not grounded in tradition or church or sacraments. While Ratzinger's language can be hauntingly beautiful at times, Hauerwas speaks the talk of Texan upbringings. His language is that of a prophetic John the Baptist. Hauerwas is a graduate from Yale University. Before joining the faculty at Duke Divinity School, he had been teaching at Notre Dame University. The 2001 *Time Magazine* nominates him "America's best theologian." He had been invited to give the distinguished Gifford Lectures at St. Andrews in Scotland. He has been vaguely associated with narrative theology and post-liberalism and thereby attached to such respected theologians as Brevard Childs, under whom he had studied, Hans Frei, and George Lindbeck. Not in a spirit-sustained tradition, nor in a, as sacrament apprehended church, but in the "timeless" à la John Howard Yoder, does he locate his as witnessed to by scripture. Significantly, he claims "the first task of the church is to make the world the world, not to make the world more just. . . . Creation names God's continuing unrelenting desire for us to want to be loved by that love manifest in Christ's life, death, and resurrection." While Ratzinger uses the coherence of the Catholic faith as expressed also in dogma, Hauerwas, this American Kierkegaard, employs frequently deontological argumentation to overcome a utilitarian rationalization of the human person.

He introduces us to the topic by stating the call *ad gentes* for all Christians. Subsequently, using a number of sources, he acquaints the reader with the varied lives and remarkable achievements of Ratzinger and Hauerwas. This sets the stage to discuss in what ways the two Christian thinkers of his choice analyze the phenomenon of relativism and what remedies they suggest to overcome this malaise. His study makes out the different remedies they offer in their respective anthropologies. His methodological analysis shows convincingly that their respective understandings of the deleterious consequences of original sin are planets apart. Likewise, their understanding of justification and sacraments are thematized. He develops the historical, intellectual genealogy Hauerwas is indebted to: Martin Luther, Fredrich Schleiermacher, and Søren Kierkegaard. As a result, he maintains it is only logical for Hauerwas to insist on Christian ethics as lived discipleship to be the remedy he offers a world losing at an ever-accelerating speed its compass. Yet he also poses the question how such an ethos of Christian living can be sustained if the ecclesial ambiance in which it is to prosper remains vague. As to Hauerwas, so also to the mind of Ratzinger the remedy is lived discipleship of Jesus Christ. However, discipleship is not one of a lonesome volition, but one based on a sacramental life rooted in an ecclesial community. This ecclesial reality is perceived as sacramental itself. The remedy Ratzinger offers must be a radically different one. He accentuates the differences by correlating nature and grace, *imago Dei* and *similitudo Dei*. He contrasts Augustinianism vis-à-vis Thomism to bear out the specifically Ratzingerian position within the Catholic vision.

Father Ssennyondo has brought into dialogue two significant theological minds, most unlikely ever to meet in real life. Both minds are concerned with a future where the human race might be completely subservient to economic, political, or ideological interests; where poetry and philosophy are pointless exercises, of a world not furthering an understanding of the human person and of his or her supernatural goal; of a global community no longer capable of articulating the hope for a *visio beatifica*.

He diligently crafts his thesis around two terms: anthropology and relativism. He demonstrates that Christian anthropology is the basis for overcoming a solipsistic exercise condemning the individual to his or her own generation of values and insights. With Augustine, Ratzinger reminds us God is *"Tu autem eras interior intimo meo et superior summon meo"* (*Confessiones* III, 6:II). It is the human heart which realizes that God is more intimate to myself than to myself. It is only the human being who suffers when denied a relationship to the origin of and calling of his own being, by relativism preaching the only prima facie flattering message: develop your own values and ethics, as everything outside your self is relative. However, valiant his scholarly efforts are, his study demonstrates how very much less convincing Hauerwas' rhetoric is in overcoming a relativistic culture.

The academia is indebted to Fr. Ssennyondo for embarking on this interesting comparison.

Prologue

Biblical Foundations for the Ageless Mission of the Church to Evangelize

The Second Vatican Council's Dogmatic Constitution of the Church, *Lumen Gentium*, helps us to understand the mystery of the church. The Council Fathers understood the church, not as some human institution, but as an institution commissioned by Christ himself who is the head of the church.[24] They also understood Christ's mission as universal and ageless—traversing the threshold of both time and geographical divide. They made it clear that the church is the body of Christ to which this mission was entrusted—to go and be light to the world by proclaiming Christ's Gospel.[25] The council states,

> Christ is the Light of humanity; and it is, accordingly, the heart-felt desire of this sacred Council . . . that by proclaiming his Gospel to every creature (Mk 16:15), it may bring to all men that light of Christ which shines out visibly from the Church. Since the Church, in Christ, is in the nature of sacrament—a sign and instrument, that is, of communion with God and of unity among all men—she here proposes, for the benefit of the faithful and of the whole world, to set forth, as clearly as pos-

---

[24] "He is the head of the body, the Church; he is the beginning, the firstborn from the dead, so that he might come to have first place in everything" (Col 1:18).

[25] "And He said to them, 'Go into all the world and proclaim the good news to the whole creation.'" (Mk 16:15).

sible, and in tradition laid down by earlier Councils, her own nature and universal mission.[26]

The Council Fathers based the text on the biblical command of Christ to the apostles to go to the whole world and preach to every creature. It is important to note here that the mission is universal and Christ did not apply any frontiers or life span to it—it has no cut-off date. In addition, if the mission is to preach to every creature and to all the earth, then it must be limitless in terms of time, because creatures live in different generations and times. The creatures that lived during Christ's time are not the creatures living today, and will not be the same creatures living in the years to come. And yet, the Gospel is to be preached to all creation.[27] This is the reason Christ chose apostles and entrusted them with the duty of continuing his mission while he is physically away. This mission will continue until he comes again to judge the living and the dead.

Therefore, the church's mission is an ongoing sacramental-sociological phenomenon until Jesus comes back to separate between the sheep and the goats (Mt 25:31–46). It is in line with this that the church also understands herself as missionary by nature. This missionary activity is on until the end. Fortunately or unfortunately, the time for this end is unknown to her (Mt 24:44) and unknown to the Son himself (Mt 24:36), but to the Father alone. The council stated further:

> The Church on earth is by its very nature missionary since, according to the plan of the Father, it has its origin in the mission of the Son and the Holy Spirit . . . This universal plan of God for salvation is not carried out solely in a secret manner . . . What was once preached by the Lord, or fulfilled in him for the salvation of mankind, must be proclaimed and spread to the ends of the earth (Acts 1:8), starting from Jerusalem (Lk 24:27), so that what was accomplished for the salvation of all men may, in the course of time, achieve its universal effect.[28]

---

[26] "Lumen gentium cum sit Christus, haec Sacrosancta Synodus, in Spiritu Sancto congregata, omnes homines claritate Eius, super faciem Ecclesiae resplendente, illuminare vehementer exoptat, omni creaturae Evangelium annuntiando (Mc 16:15). Cum autem ecclesiae sit in Christo veruti sacramentum seu signum et instrumentum intimae cum Deo unionis totiusque generis humani unitatis, naturam missionemque suam universalem, praecedentium Conciliorum argumento instans, pressius fidelibus suis et mundo universe declarare intendit." LG 1, in DH 4101.

[27] "Go into all the world and proclaim the good news to the whole creation" (Mk 16:15).

[28] "Ecclesia peregrinans natura sua missionaria est, cum ipsa ex missione Filii missioneque Spiritus Sancti originem ducat secundum Propositum Dei Patris. Hoc autem Propositum ex «fontali amore» seu caritate Dei Patris profluit, qui, cum sit Principium sine Principio,

In the *Dogmatic Constitution on Divine Revelation, Dei Verbum*, the Council Fathers made it patent that God creates and conserves all things by his word. This makes reference to John 1:3. In Genesis, God creates this world with his word. The word who creates all things also sustains them. Without the word, nothing can exist, for in him all things came to be (Jn 1:3). This creative word of God is the one the fourth evangelist refers to as the word made flesh and dwelt among us (Jn 1:14). The word made incarnate is Jesus Christ who is among us as creator and protractor of creation. Therefore, God continues to create and sustain the universe through Jesus who dwells among us as the Council Fathers stated,

> After God had spoken many times and in various ways through the prophets, in these last days he has spoken to us by a Son (Heb 1:1-2). For he sent his Son, the eternal Word who enlightens all men, to dwell among men and to tell them about the inner life of God. Hence, Jesus Christ, sent as a man among men, speaks the words of God (Jn 3:34), and accomplishes the saving work which the Father gave him to do (Jn 5:36). As a result, he himself—to see whom is to see the Father (Jn 14:9)—completed and perfected Revelation and confirmed it with divine guarantees.[29]

---

ex quo Filius gignitur et Spiritus Sanctus per Filium procedit, ex nimia et misericordi benignitate sua libere creans et insuper gratiose vocans nos ad Secum communicandum in vita et gloria, bonitatem divinam liberaliter diffudit ac diffundere non desinit, ita ut qui conditor est omnium, tandem fiat «omnia in omnibus» (1 Cor 15:28), gloriam suam simul et beatitudinem nostram procurando. Placuit autem Deo homines non tantum singulatim, quavis mutua connexione seclusa, ad vitae Suae participationem vocare, sed eos in populum constituere, in quo filii sui, qui erant dispersi, in unum congregarentur. Hoc universale Dei propositum pro salute generis humani perficitur non solum modo quasi secreto in mente hominum vel per incepta, etiam religiosa, quibus ipsi multipliciter Deum quaerunt, «si forte attrectent eum aut inveniant quamvis non longe sit ab unoquoque nostrum» (Acts 17:27): haec enim incepta indigent illuminari et sanari, etsi, ex benigno consilio providentis Dei, aliquando pro paedagogia ad Deum verum vel praeparatione evangelica possint haberi. Deus autem ad pacem seu communionem Secum stabiliendam fraternamque societatem inter homines, eosque peccatores, componendam, in historiam hominum novo et definitivo modo intrare decrevit mittendo Filium suum in carne nostra, ut homines per Illum eriperet de potestate tenebrarum ac Satanae et in Eo mundum Sibi reconciliaret. Illum ergo, per quem fecit et saecula, constituit haeredem universorum, ut in Illo omnia instauraret." AG 2-3, http://www.vatican.va/archive/hist_councils/ii_vatican_council/documents/vat-ii_decree_19651207_ad-gentes_en.html (accessed on January 11, 2012).

[29] "Postquam vero multifariam multisque modis Deus locutus est in Prophetis, "novissime diebus istis locutus est nobis in Filio" (Heb 1:1-2). Misit enim Filium suum, aeternum

The Fathers continue to assert that "the Christian economy, since it is the new and definitive covenant, will never pass away."[30] This is attested in Jesus's own words after entrusting the leadership of the church to Peter: "And I tell you, you are Peter, and on this rock I will build my Church, and the gates of Hades will not prevail against it" (Mt 16:18). These words of Jesus point to a church that will stand the challenges of time. The mission of the church is identical in nature to the church herself, that is to say, the church and her mission are continuous. And this mission is not carried out by the church in isolation, but with her founder guiding and leading her, for he promised to be with his church until the end of time (Mt 28:20). Jesus did not stipulate when this mission will end, and so, no one has the legitimacy to determine the end of the church's mission. The Lord said, "But about that day and hour no one knows, neither the angels of heaven, nor the Son, but only the Father" (Mt 24:36). The church's mission goes on until that day which only the Father knows.

In chapter 4 of *The 2008 Synod of Bishops*, the bishops discussed the word of God as the life-giving element of the church. The Synod states that the Word of Scripture is a word personally addressed by God, like a letter, to each one, in the concrete circumstances of life.[31] They outlined three major functions of the word of God in the church, namely, the church is born from the word of God and lives by it, the word of God sustains the church throughout her history, and the word of God permeates and animates the entire life of the church.[32]

The threefold dimensions of scripture demonstrate evidently that devoid of the word of God, the church cannot exist; and without the word of God, the church cannot be sustained; and without the word of God, the life of the church is moribund—completely lifeless. Therefore, the church's mission is dependent upon the scriptures that unmistakably avow her continuity.

At the great commissioning, Jesus commanded his disciples to "go therefore and make disciples of all nations" (Mt 28:19). He also promised to be with

---

scilicet Verbum, qui omnes homines illuminat, ut inter homines habitaret iisque intima Dei enarraret (cf. Io 1,1–18). Iesus Christus ergo, Verbum caro factum, "homo ad homines" missus (3), "verba Dei loquitur" (Io 3,34), et opus salutare consummat quod dedit ei Pater faciendum (cf. Io 5,36; 17,4). Quapropter Ipse, quem qui videt, videt et Patrem (cf. Io 14, 9), tota Suiipsius praesentia ac manifestatione, verbis et operibus, signis et miraculis, praesertim autem morte sua et gloriosa ex mortuis resurrectione, misso tandem Spiritu veritatis, revelationem complendo perficit ac testimonio divino confirmat, Deum nempe nobiscum esse ad nos ex peccati mortisque tenebris liberandos et in aeternam vitam resuscitandos." DV 4, DH 4198.

[30] DV 4.

[31] "The Synod of Bishops 2008," http://www.vatican.va/roman_curia/synod/documents/rc_synod_doc_20080511_instrlabor (accessed November 3, 2009).

[32] "The Synod of Bishops 2008," http://www.vatican.va/roman_curia/synod/documents/rc_synod_doc_20080511_instrlabor (accessed November 3, 2009).

them always, "to the end of the age" (Mt 28:20). This is the basis for the church's mission to the world. There are three key positions in this great commissioning that will be our center of attention:

i. "Go Therefore and Make All Disciples" (Mt 28:19)

Jesus commissioned the apostles to "make disciples" of Jesus. Just as Jesus first called them to follow him so that he might make them fishers of men (Lk 5:10), he likewise sends them to the ends of the earth to make all people his disciples. This mission to make disciples is a mission to evangelize. John Paul II accentuates this mission with great precision and clarity:

> The Lord Jesus sent his apostles to every person, people and place on earth. In the apostles, the Church received a universal mission-one which knows no boundaries-which involves the communication of salvation in its integrity according to that fullness of life which Christ came to bring (Jn 10:10). The Church was "sent by Christ to reveal and communicate the love of God to all people and nations." This mission is one and undivided, having one origin and one final purpose; but within it, there are different tasks and kinds of activity. First, there is the missionary activity which we call *mission ad gentes,* in reference to the opening words of the Council's decree on this subject. This is one of the Church's fundamental activities: it is essential and never-ending. The Church, in fact, cannot withdraw from her *permanent mission of bringing the Gospel* to the multitudes the millions and millions of men and women-who as yet do not know Christ the Redeemer of humanity. In a specific way this is the missionary work which Jesus entrusted and still entrusts each day to his Church.[33]

The apostles' responsibility was to be fishers of men, fishing them for the Lord. As John Paul II stated above, there are multitudes of people far from the Lord that need to be brought to him. He reechoes Jesus's words: "The harvest is plentiful, but the laborers are few" (Mt 9:37). This abundance is also symbolized in the great catch of fish that Peter and his friends had at the command of the Lord (Lk 5:6–7). Jesus intended to teach the apostles that the catch is so enormous, so overwhelming, so vast—like the fish in the sea—and yet lost in deep

---

[33] John Paul II, *On the Permanent Validity of the Church's Missionary Mandate "Redemptoris Missio,"* Encyclical Letter (December 7, 1990), 52.

waters. This mission demands total commitment and surrender to Jesus, or else it would be a total failure, for it is not by man's power. Peter confessed to Jesus that they had spent the whole night and caught nothing (Jn 21:3). However, at Jesus's word, they were able to catch many fish (Jn 21:6). This serves to illustrate that the mission of making disciples was not going to be an easy one for the apostles, but nevertheless, with Jesus they would succeed.

The instruction for the disciples to become fishers of men "denotes the beginning of a new period of salvation: Catching human beings and in so being bringing them new life."[34] Peter and the eleven's assignment was to catch men and women with the inducement of God's word and thereby bringing them new life.[35] In other words, making disciples means transforming people's lives into new lives. This was the mission of Peter and is the mission of all of Jesus's disciples. The twelve were the first company of preachers. Their mission is the same mission of the church today.

i. "Of All Nations" (Mt 28:19)

The mission of the apostles and of the church was not restricted to those living in the native place of Jesus. It was not just for the Jews only, nor even just for Israel as the chosen race. Rather, it is to all nations. It is a universal mission. At his ascension, Jesus said to his disciples, "you will be my witnesses in Jerusalem, in all Judea and Samaria, and to the ends of the earth" (Acts 1:8). Mark's version of the great commissioning is even more captivating. While Matthew uses the term "nations," Mark uses "creation." According to him, Jesus said to his disciples, "go into all the world; proclaim the good news to the whole creation" (Mk 16:15). In other words, the mission of the church is not only for human beings but goes beyond and includes all creation, as St. Paul says, "for the creation is waits with eager longing for the revealing of the children of God; . . . , the whole creation has been groaning in labor pains until now" (Rom 8:19, 22).

Thus, the mission of the church is for all segments of creation: social, political, economic, and religious. The church is sent to bring the good news to all creation, to transform all creation, and to bring new life to all creation. In our argument about and against the secularism and relativism of the contemporary world,[36] we will deal with the negations of those who accuse religion of

---

[34] Raymond E. Brown, et al., eds., *The New Jerome Biblical Commentary* (Garden City, NY: Prentice Hall, Inc., 1990), 692.

[35] Brown, et al., eds., *The New Jerome Biblical Commentary*, 692.

[36] Of course, secularism and relativism are old realities. However, it has come to reality more in today's society as Jankunas states, "the origin of relativism has been traced back to the famous Greek Philosopher Protagoras, but Pope Benedict XVI's claims that in an

imposing itself on society. The modern world claims that the tenure for religion, and Christianity in particular, expired and is no longer germane to today's world, or that Christianity was only meant for the people of Israel. However, this is at odds with Jesus's proclamation and the commissioning of the church to proclaim the Gospel to all creation.

ii. "To the End of the Age" (Mt 28:20)

The church's mission is ageless. Some sociologists like Peter Berger argue that we are now living in a post-Christian era, and that the modern age is one in which the divine has receded into the background of human concern and consciousness.[37] In other words, they are claiming that Christianity has outlived its day. Therefore, following such claims, the mission of the church is also supposed to have ended with the Christian era. Peter Berger says, "Today the supernatural as a meaningful reality is absent or remote from the horizons of everyday life of large numbers. Those to whom the supernatural is still a meaningful reality find themselves in the status of a minority, a cognitive minority—a group formed around a body of deviant knowledge."[38] Berger sounds similar to Nietzsche, for whom religion is the opium of the people, when he states that religious belief relates to religious need as orgasm does to lust.[39]

Perhaps the raison d'être these sociologists and atheists attach no use for religion today is because religion, and Christianity in particular, is becoming less influential in society. But this does not mean that it is no longer useful, nor does it mean that its mission has been accomplished. The Lord Jesus instituted the church and commissioned her with a mission—a mission that will last forever. He prophesied that forces of the netherworld would antagonize it, but they would never prevail over it. He thus said, "And I tell you, you are Peter, and on this rock I will build my church, and the gates of Hades will not prevail against it" (Mt 16:18).

The challenges and the failures experienced by and in the church can, by no means, refer to the end of the church's mission. Her mission goes on until the end of time (Mt 28:18–20). Jesus promised a second coming when he will come to judge the living and the dead (Mt 24:30). Until that time, this mission of Christ and of the church still continues.

The two theologians whose perspectives we will discuss in this paper attach

---

unreflected, uncritical and naïve way, the modern world has been ensnared into relativism." in Gediminas Jankunas, *The Dictatorship of Relativism*, 337.

[37] Peter L. Berger, *A Rumor of Angels: Modern Society and the Rediscovery of the Supernatural* (New York: Doubleday & Company, Inc., 1970), 5.

[38] Ibid., 5–6.

[39] Ibid., 25.

to scriptures a great importance in their theological writings. And so, while disputing those who want to terminate the church's mission in this world, they support their arguments with pertinent texts from the scriptures. To begin with, Joseph Ratzinger believes that the scriptures are the basis for theology. He appreciated the scriptures from his earliest days.[40] He recounts his early days in the seminary as being influenced by the scriptures. He thus states,

The Bible spoke to us with new immediacy and freshness. But those things that in the liberal method that were arbitrary and tended to flatten out the Bible could be compensated for by obedience to dogma. A characteristic fruitfulness came from that balance between liberalism and dogma. So it was that, for the six semesters of my theological studies, I listened to and assimilated all of Maier's lectures with the greatest attention. Exegesis has always remained for me the center of my theological work. Maier is to be thanked for the fact that, for us, Sacred Scripture was "the soul of our theological studies."[41]

From this testimony, Ratzinger makes it patent that all his theology is deep-rooted in the scripture as its source and soul. Therefore, his critique of the modern culture is a theological response to relativism and a reaffirmation of the church's relevance and continuity of her mission in the modern world. Asked whether the church belongs to God himself, Ratzinger responded, "the Church has been appropriated by God to be his particular possession in the world, something that especially belongs to him, the living temple. God does not live in stone but is alive. Those people in whom he is alive and who belong to him, accordingly form his true temple."[42] If God is alive in this world, and the temple he lives in is alive, it must logically imply that the mission of this temple (which is the church), is alive as well. As long as God lives, his temple will live and its mission will continue.

Elsewhere, Ratzinger discusses the nature of the church as follows:

The Church is first of all fixed to the historical origin in the eleven men whom Jesus chose [eleven were left, plus Matthias, who was elected to the office]. This is not some mythology or other, an invented piece of ideology, but is truly anchored in the historical events concerned with Jesus Christ and can always at any time be renewed from these apostolic origins. At the same time, this expresses not only fidelity to the witness, to the faith of the apostles, but also a sacramental dimension. Because of this, we cannot simply rethink the Church whenever we like;

---

[40] Joseph Ratzinger, *Milestones: Memoirs 1927–1977* (San Francisco: Ignatius Press, 1998), 52.

[41] Ratzinger, *Milestones*, 52–53.

[42] Ibid., 63.

she stands rather in unbroken relationship with her origins, in constant continuity with them. The sacrament of ordination to the priesthood expresses this relationship to something we have not ourselves invented and, at the same time, refers to the Holy Spirit as guarantor of this continuity.[43]

Above is an elucidation Ratzinger uses to demonstrate that the church and her mission are biblical and incessant with the Holy Spirit as her principal mover.

The second vital theologian in this paper is Stanley Hauerwas. He, like Ratzinger, bases his theology on the scriptures and acknowledges that the church and her mission must be moved by and according to the word of God.

Hauerwas believes that Christian theology should not be the display of abstract ideas, but must be a form of discourse that is meant to help us live more faithfully as Christians who are part of that community called church.[44] He says that "to the extent that we abandon Scripture as integral to the theological enterprise, we allowed the Scripture to be separated from Church-centered practice."[45] Therefore, Hauerwas recognizes the scriptures as the foundation for the existence of the church and the fountain for theology. According to Hauerwas, there is no church and no theology without the scriptures.

Hauerwas' concept of the church and her mission is scripture-based. On this basis, he critiques the contemporary society which is moving toward the rejection of the scriptures, the church and her mission. Instead, he maintains that Christians must be a people who have their lives constituted scripturally.[46] He situates the beginning of the church and its mission at the biblical Pentecost where he articulates that this was the creation of a new people with a new language. He states that at Pentecost, "God created a new language, a language that is more than words, but a people whose very differences contribute to their unity."[47] He continues to illustrate that the church is not only a new people with a new language, but it is also a community that has continuity.

According to Hauerwas,

The Church has a story to tell in which God is the main character. But the Church cannot tell that story without becoming

---

[43] Joseph Ratzinger, *God and the World: Believing and Living in Our Time* (San Francisco: Ignatius Press, 2000), 349–350.

[44] Stanley Hauerwas, *Unleashing the Scriptures* (Nashville, TN: Abingdon Press, 1993), 8.

[45] Hauerwas, *Unleashing the Scriptures*, 9.

[46] Ibid., 40.

[47] Stanley Hauerwas, *Christian Existence Today: Essays on Church, World, and Living in Between* (Grand Rapids, MI: Brazos Press, 1988), 53.

part of the tale. The Church, Catholic and apostolic, is not our but God's creation. Moreover, it is not a creation that God did at one point in time and does not need to do again. Rather, it is our belief that what God did at Pentecost he continues to do to renew and sustain the presence of the Church.[48]

This indicates that according to Hauerwas, the church and its mission are first and foremost biblical, having been commissioned by the Holy Spirit on Pentecost (Acts 2:1–13), and second, have a continuous nature, being sustained by the Holy Spirit.

---

[48] Ibid., 54.

PART I

General Introduction

Joseph Ratzinger and Stanley Hauerwas: Biographies and Elements Influencing their Anthropologies

a. Joseph Ratzinger

Joseph Ratzinger was born on Holy Saturday, April 16, 1927, in Marktl am Inn.[49] His father was a policeman. In 1929, the family moved to Tittmoning on the border with Austria. In 1932, they moved in a new home in Aschau am Inn—a well-to-do agricultural village. In 1937, when his father retired, they moved into their house (in Traunstein) which his parents had bought in 1933, an old, inexpensive farmhouse with no running water. There he entered the first class in the humanistic gymnasium (for classical languages). He learned Latin and Greek. At the same time, he was an altar server.

On Easter Sunday of 1939, Joseph Ratzinger joined the Minor Seminary.[50] This was the year when the Second World War began. The seminary was turned into a military hospital, and he began to live at home and walk to school. He studied Greek, Latin, mathematics, and literature. He started writing with great zeal, translating the liturgical texts. In 1941, the schools were closed due to war and he and his brother came home.

In 1943, Ratzinger was serving as a helper at an antiaircraft (AA) battery in Munich. He recalls,

> We lived in barracks like the regular soldiers . . . Our first

---

[49] "Biography of His Holiness, Pope Benedict XVI," in http://www.vatican.va/holy_father/benedict_xvi/biography/documents/hf_ben-xvi_bio_20050419_short-biography_en.html (accessed on October 20, 2009).
[50] Ibid.

location was Ludwigsfeld, north of Munich, where we had to protect a branch of the Bavarian Motor Works (BMW) . . . Then we went to Unterföhring, to Innsbruck . . . finally transferred to Gilching.[51]

On September 10, 1944, they were freed from serving at the AA batteries. Then on September 20, he was taken with other friends to Burgenland. After the death of Hitler, Ratzinger escaped from the camp at the end of April 1945 and went home. He arrived unhurt. But while at home, he was taken as a prisoner of war by American soldiers. On June 19, 1945, he was released. This marked the end of the war reality for him.

In November 1945, he joined the seminary at Freising,[52] where he studied philosophy. He was very interested in liturgical celebrations. In 1947, he went to study theology in Munich. He also was very much interested in the Bible. He stated, "Exegesis has always remained for me the center of my theological work. . . . Sacred Scripture was the 'soul of our theological studies.'"[53]

He was ordained a priest on the Feast of Sts. Peter and Paul (June 29, 1951) by Cardinal Faulhaber in the cathedral at Freising. On August 1, 1951, he began his first appointment as assistant pastor in the Parish of the Precious Blood in Munich. On October 1, 1952, he was assigned to the seminary in Freising. Meanwhile, he was writing his doctoral dissertation, and on July 1953, he received his doctorate in theology with the thesis: *"Volk und Haus Gottes in Augustins Lehre von der Kirche"* (People and House of God in St. Augustine's Doctrine of the Church).[54] Four years later, he qualified for university teaching with a dissertation on *"Die Geschichtstheologie des Heiligen Bonaventura"* (The Theology of History in St. Bonaventure).[55] He went to lecture in the University of Munich in 1958, and soon after that, he was named professor of fundamental theology and dogma at the College of Philosophy and Theology in Freising. On April 15, 1959, he started lecturing at the University of Bonn.

When the Second Vatican Council opened in Rome in October 1962, Fr.

---

[51] Ratzinger, *Milestones*, 31.

[52] "Biography of His Holiness, Pope Benedict XVI," in http://www.vatican.va/holy_father/benedict_xvi/biography/documents/hf_ben-xvi_bio_20050419_short-biography_en.html (accessed on October 20, 2009).

[53] Ratzinger, *Milestones*, 52–53.

[54] Pope Benedict XVI, *Volk und Haus Gottes in Augustins Lehre von der Kirche* (München: K. Zink, 1954). Cf. cover page. This dissertation is not translated into English.

[55] Joseph Ratzinger, *The Theology of History in St. Bonaventure*, trans. Zachary Hayes (Chicago, IL: Franciscan Herald Press, 1971). Cf. cover page.

Joseph Ratzinger was appointed by Cardinal Joseph Frings, archbishop of Cologne, as his theological adviser.[56] There, he contributed specifically to the debate about the "Sources of Revelation," that is, scripture and tradition. He worked with Karl Rahner in this task. In the summer of 1963, he took up the post of lecturing in Münster, dividing his time between Münster and Rome to attend the council's discussions. Then in the summer of 1966, he started lecturing at Tübingen. In 1969, he received an invitation to take an appointment as the chair for dogma at Regensburg. While at Regensburg, he was appointed to the International Papal Theological Commission. This is where he became acquainted with Henri de Lubac and Hans Urs von Balthasar.

On the vigil of Pentecost, May 28, 1977, he was consecrated as archbishop of Munich and Freising.[57] His episcopal motto was "Coworker of the truth," from the third letter of John (3 Jn 8), and his symbols were the shell, as a sign of Christian existence as pilgrimage, and the bear, expressing both the burden and the hope of life. Pope Paul VI made him cardinal on June 27 of the same year. He was appointed prefect of the Sacred Congregation for the Doctrine of the Faith by John Paul II on November 25, 1981. On February 15, 1982, he resigned the pastoral governance of the Archdiocese of Munich and Freising. On November 6, 1998, he was elected as vice dean of the College of Cardinals, and on November 30, 2002, he became its dean. He became pope on April 19, 2005, and took on the name Benedict VXI.

> In the Roman Curia he has been a member of the Council of the Secretariat of State for Relations with States; of the Congregations for the Oriental Churches, for Divine Worship and the Discipline of the Sacraments, for Bishops, for the Evangelization of Peoples, for Catholic Education, for Clergy and for the Causes of the Saints; of the Pontifical Councils for Promoting Christian Unity, and for Culture; of the Supreme Tribunal of the *Apostolic Signatura*, and of the Pontifical Commissions for Latin America, "Ecclesia Dei," for the Authentic Interpretation of the Code of Canon Law, and for the Revision of the Code of Canon Law of the Oriental Churches.[58]

---

[56] Ratzinger, *Milestones*, 54.

[57] "Biography of His Holiness, Pope Benedict XVI," Libreria Edtrice Vaticana, 2005, http://www.vatican.va/holy_father/benedict_xvi/biography/documents/hf_ben-xvi_bio_20050419_short-biography_en.html (accessed on October 20, 2009).

[58] "Biography of His Holiness, Pope Benedict XVI," Libreria Edtrice Vaticana, 2005, http://www.vatican.va/holy_father/benedict_xvi/biography/documents/hf_ben-xvi_bio_20050419_short-biography_en.html (accessed on October 20, 2009).

i. His Works and Theological Contributions

Among Joseph Ratzinger's many publications special mention should be made of his *Introduction to Christianity*, a compilation of university lectures on the Apostolic Creed published in 1968 and *"Dogma and Preaching"* (1973), an anthology of essays, sermons, and reflections dedicated to pastoral arguments. Another is his address to the Catholic Academy of Bavaria on "Why I Am Still in the Church." It had a wide resonance. In it he stated with his usual clarity: "one can only be a Christian in the Church, not beside the Church."

His many publications are spread out over a number of years and constitute a point of reference for many people, especially those interested in entering deeper into the study of theology. In 1985, he published his interview-book, *The Ratzinger Report*, on the situation of the faith and *Salt of the Earth* in 1996. On the occasion of his seventieth birthday, the volume *At the School of Truth* was published, containing articles by several authors on different aspects of his personality and publications.

He has received numerous *honoris causa* doctorates, in 1984 from the College of St. Thomas in St. Paul, Minnesota; in 1986 from the Catholic University of Lima; in 1987 from the Catholic University of Eichstätt; in 1988 from the Catholic University of Lublin; in 1998 from the University of Navarre; in 1999 from the LUMSA (Libera Università Maria Santissima Assunta) of Rome; and in 2000 from the Faculty of Theology of the University of Wrocław in Poland.[59]

Fr. Emery de Gaál describes Joseph Ratzinger as "the anti-Nietzsche."[60] Fr. De Gaál explicates that

> Benedict XVI is challenging modernity to a revision of the suppositions and assumptions Nietzsche instilled in it in such a sustained manner. A loss of purpose and values has become the norm for many people. Nihilism has become the practical worldview of today. While Nietzsche claimed that "Christianity is the greatest misfortune that had befallen humankind," Benedict XVI responds that "Jesus Christ is the greatest fortune imaginable for humankind."[61]

Thus, Ratzinger's key contribution to theology and to humankind is his

---

[59] Ibid.

[60] Emery de Gaál Gyulai, *The Theology of Pope Benedict XVI: The Christocentric Shift* (New York: Palgrave Macmillan, 2010), 6.

[61] Ibid.

recuperation of Christian roots—bringing Christ back to his rightful position in the church and in society.

Joseph Ratzinger, now Pope Benedict XVI, has so broadly contributed to theology that it is difficult to situate an area in theology upon which he has not pronounced himself. Emery de Gaál appropriately comments thus: "Pope Benedict is not part of a movement or school of theology, but rather committed to the whole of the faith as expressed in Scripture, the liturgy, the Church fathers, the saints, and the teaching office of the Church."[62] Ratzinger has not only contributed to the development of a fundamental or foundational Christian theology but has also been a disciple of the truth. He is faithful to the truth and seeks it steadfastly. De Gaál continues to explicate this:

> For Ratzinger, one criterion of a healthy Christian spirituality is the willingness to suffer a lack of understanding and appreciation, and even malice, with good humor and without resistance, very much like Our Lord. . . . Much in the vein of Augustine, the inner logic of creation by God and that of sin allow the opposing, sinful person [the other] full well to recognize truth. No matter how many words lies might employ, the sovereign reality of truth cannot be denied.[63]

Ratzinger's theological contributions are principally Christological. In all his works, he is striving to engender in the reader, a personal encounter with Jesus. Fr. De Gaál recapitulates this:

> It is a commonly held opinion that Ratzinger's theological contributions are essentially ecclesiological in nature. While it is true that he dedicated his dissertation and *Habilitationsschrift* [habilitation, i.e., his postdoctoral thesis] to ecclesiological themes, the inner motivation and fulcrum of his theology is supremely Christological. His concern is not primarily an academic or cerebral one but is rather the result of a personal encounter with Jesus Christ as a believer living the sacramental life of the Catholic Church. For Ratzinger, God is the reality of charity that constitutes a human being in freedom.[64]

Ratzinger subscribes to a personalist Christology.[65] For him, every distance

---

[62] Ibid., 7.
[63] Ibid., 10.
[64] de Gaál, *The Theology of Pope Benedict XVI*, 15.
[65] Ibid., 16.

from Christ is a detachment from the source of meaning and unity.[66] Thus, Ratzinger calls for a personal relationship with Christ which he envisions as a journey that takes us from this life to the next. In accord with Bonaventure, Ratzinger argues that Christian hope is not stagnant but organizes the here and now in preparation for the kingdom of God.[67] "He thereby makes clear that Christian hope rests not on a state or condition but on a person. . . . If, however, people lose sight of God's standard, the standard of eternity, then all that remains as guiding thread is nothing but egoism."[68]

It is on this rationale that Ratzinger admonishes the modern culture of relativism which he indicts as being based on the vanity of this world. He also accuses modern technology and sciences of having suppressed[69] an appreciation for meditation and contemplation, making natural revelation inaccessible to the postmodern human being.[70]

> Inevitably, the consequence is a loss of access to the natural law. The *lex divinum* (divine law) and the *lex naturalis* (natural law) no longer meet as the *desiderium natural ad videndum Deum* (the natural desire for the vision of God) is lost sight of amid the constant fleeting impressions and satisfactions of a consumerist society.[71]

Fr. Emery de Gaál makes a conclusive summary statement about Ratzinger's theological contribution as follows:

> It is a joy reading Pope Benedict XVI's vast opus because of his sovereign command of the Western heritage and his genuine theological concern, which is characterized by being humble, non-polemical, and removed from the slightest suspicion of vanity. It is doubtful whether our age will produce anyone similarly educated and erudite.[72]

---

[66] Ibid.
[67] Ibid.
[68] Ibid., 18.
[69] Joseph Ratzinger refers to this suppression of Christian values as the "dictatorship of relativism," in Benedict XVI, *Light of the World: The Pope, the Church, and the Signs of the Times* (San Francisco, CA: Ignatius Press, 2010), 50.
[70] de Gaál, *The Theology of Pope Benedict XVI*, 18.
[71] Ibid., 22.
[72] Ibid., 14.

b. Stanley Hauerwas

Stanley Hauerwas was born on July 24, 1940, in Texas. He obtained his BA at Southwestern University; BD, MD, MPhil, and his PhD at Yale University; and a DD at the University of Edinburgh.[73] At Yale Divinity School, Hauerwas came under the influence of James Gustafson. With James Gustason, Hauerwas studied and assimilated Reinhold Neibuhr. While teaching at Notre Dame University, Hauerwas came across the work of a Mennonite theologian—John Howard Yoder, who criticized the work of his former hero at Yale, Reinhold Neibuhr. He thus developed an inclination toward Yoder's theology, especially with questions regarding the modern philosophical foundations for just-war thinking. However, behind all his assimilations and inclinations, Hauerwas' real hero is Dietrich Bonhoeffer, especially his work, *The Cost of Discipleship*.[74] Hauerwas' emphasis on discipleship and his nonviolence attitude comes directly from the influence of Bonhoeffer.

Hauerwas was also influenced by a Catholic philosopher, Alasdair MacIntyre, who uses Thomist thought regarding virtue ethics to critique modern and postmodern culture.[75] Also, the fourteen years he spent at Notre Dame University created a big impact on his theology. Arne Rasmusson admits that Hauerwas' heritage is close to Catholicism than Protestantism. He says that Hauerwas has strong Catholic sympathies. He, however, notes that Hauerwas believes that the most nearly faithful form of Christian witness is most exemplified by the often unjustly ignored people called "Anabaptists" or "Mennonites."[76]

It is surprising that despite his admiration and similarities in theology with the Catholic theology or Mennonites, Hauerwas remains a Methodist Christian. However, Hauerwas does not seem to care to which church (denomination) he belongs. He believes that a theologian should not be confined to any single denomination, but rather write theology that is "universally Catholic."[77] He actually refers to himself as a theologian of the Church Catholic. In his own

---

[73] Stanley Hauerwas, *Hannah's Child: A Theologian's Memoir* (Grand Rapids, MI: William B. Eerdmans Publishing Company, 2010), 47–72.

[74] Ibid.

[75] Ibid.

[76] Arne Rasmusson, *The Church as Polis* (Notre Dame, IN: University of Notre Dame Press, 1995), 24.

[77] Hauerwas applies the terms "Catholic" here in the same way St. Ignatius of Antioch used it. St. Ignatius was the first to use the term Catholic to refer to the church of Christ. Thus, "Καθολικός, Catholic" in both St. Ignatius and Hauerwas refers to the entire community of believers, Cf. Milton P. Brown, *The Authentic Writings of Ignatius* (Durham, NC: Duke University Press, 1963), 30.

words he states, "I stand in the Catholic tradition that both affirms the universality of the Church and confess God's Trinitarian nature."[78] He also says, "I am a Texan Methodist who went to Yale, came under the influence of Barth and Wittgenstein, taught two years with the Lutherans at Augustana College [Rock Island, Illinois], fourteen with the Catholics at Notre Dame, and finally have ended up with the Methodists at Duke."[79]

Hauerwas' experience with different denominations notwithstanding and despite the influence they exerted on him, Hauerwas is reluctant to commit himself to any of them. True, he belongs to the Methodist Church, but as far as his theological work is concerned, he detaches himself from Methodist theology in the same way he distances himself from any other denomination. He states that the position he represents cuts across divisions from the past because according to him, "the basis of those divisions no longer matters."[80]

According to Hauerwas, theologians are now identified by positions, such as Bultmannians, Barthians, Process, Liberal, Post-Liberal, etc. He believes his bearing helps by not serving a particular small community. He is comfortable in that position and insists that he was trained "to engage in the activity of theology as a tradition-determined activity without ever being determined by any one tradition."[81] He believes *foundationism* (absolutizing a denomination as institution) is a mistake. He makes a confession: "I like to think of myself as Mennonite camp follower, but as Yoder eloquently argues in *The Priestly Kingdom*, he is not a Mennonite theologian, but a theologian of the Church Catholic—an ambition I also share."[82]

i. His Works and Theological Contributions

Stanley Hauerwas can be described as a theological ethicist whose job is to write about what is right. He is very well known for his work in medical ethics, especially in regard to the mentally handicapped. His works cover practically every single issue one can think of. He is a very comprehensible writer and a very prolific one as well. The key themes in Hauerwas' theological writings are "How Christian communities must sustain themselves in the modern world as a 'diaspora religion' (resident aliens), the value of narrative in these communities, the problems caused by a liberal society, the necessity of remaining faithful to one's creed; and pacifism."[83]

---

[78] Stanley Hauerwas, *Christian Existence Today* (Durham, NC: The Labyrinth Press, 1988), 3.
[79] Hauerwas, *Dispatches from the Front*, 19.
[80] Ibid., 21.
[81] Ibid.
[82] Ibid., 22.
[83] Stanley Hauerwas, *The Hauerwas Reader* (Durham, NC: Duke University Press, 2001), 557

His major works include *The Peaceable Kingdom, Resident Aliens: Life in the Christian Colony; Dispatches from the Front: Theological Engagements with the Secular; In Good Company: The Church as Polis; Prayer Plainly Spoken; With the Grain of the Universe: The Gifford Lectures for 2001; After Christendom: How the Church Is to Behave if Freedom, Justice, and a Christian Nation Are Bad Ideas; Christian Existence Today; Naming the Silence: God, Medicine, and the Problem of Suffering, and Suffering Presence: Theological Reflections on Medicine, the Mentally Handicapped, and the Church.*[84]

In his career, Hauerwas has attempted to resuscitate the importance of virtue and character within the church. He, as a theologian and a moralist, believes that virtue is central in Christian life. He lays emphasis on the importance of the recovery of the integrity of the church as an alternative political community.[85] Hauerwas states, "I have refused to use that affirmation to underwrite an autonomous realm of morality separate from Christ's Lordship."[86] For this reason, Hauerwas does not believe in a morality that is based on any norm other than the Christian principle.

Hauerwas is an outspoken Christian pacifist and has promoted nonviolence, having been mentored by Mennonite theologian John Howard Yoder. He is regarded as an opponent of nationalism, particularly American patriotism, arguing that it has no place in the church. He has also been associated with the narrative theology movement.[87]

Hauerwas' theology is Trinitarian. According to him, God is not a concept or principle immediately available for philosophical reflection, but more like a proper name for an agent in a story. "This means that God and God's salvation are not knowable abstracted from history as mediated through the traditions of Israel and the Church. One learns to know God through being part of this embodied narrative."[88] According to Hauerwas, the God at work is the Trinitarian God. He is critical of making "creation" synonymous with "nature."[89] In other words, Hauerwas upholds revelation in opposition to philosophical reflections. For him, religion and salvation are as according to the kingdom of God revealed and actualized by Jesus Christ. He noticeably states. "The kingdom of God is not a human utopian project, but is a reality established by God. The kingdom of God is historically and socially embodied in the community of the Christian Church, even though God's reign is wider than the Church."[90]

---

[84] Hauerwas, *The Hauerwas Reader*, 557.
[85] Hauerwas, *Christian Existence*, 12.
[86] Ibid., 17.
[87] Hauerwas, *The Hauerwas Reader*, 2–10.
[88] Rasmusson, *The Church as Polis*, 179.
[89] Ibid., 181.
[90] Ibid., 186.

As a theologian, Hauerwas critiques the contemporary privatization of faith. His vision of church is "unlimited catholicism."[91] He believes the Christian Church is a real people that exists in definite historical and institutional forms. He stresses that this makes any static, timeless view of the church impossible.[92] "The Church is a historical and, in relation to new social contexts, changing phenomenon."[93] He criticizes the *individualization* of the understanding of salvation. He instead advocates for a church that is communitarian and political. In his work, *Resident Aliens*, Hauerwas states,

> We would like a Church that asserts again that God, not nations, rules the world, that the boundaries of God's kingdom transcends those of Caesar and that the main political task of the Church is the formation of people who clearly see the cost of discipleship and are willing to pay the price.[94]

So fundamental in Hauerwas' writings is his discourse about discipleship. Hauerwas defines discipleship as "a call to be holy people."[95]

> Becoming a Christian," Hauerwas asserts, "is to become part of the Church. By faith we become joined with the body of Christ, which involves our participation and emersion in the daily practices of the Christian Church: prayer, worship, admonition, feeding the hungry, caring for the sick, etc. So we are transformed over time to participate in God's life.[96]

> Therefore, according to Hauerwas, to be a disciple is to be part of the new polis that has the Gospel as its constitution. And Christian life is not something spontaneous, something that comes naturally.[97]

Hauerwas is also critical of the liberal education system in universities and the "democratization" of Christianity. He considers these two to be the most powerful factors contributing to liberalism in as far as they demean

---

[91] Ibid.
[92] Ibid.
[93] Ibid., 190.
[94] Stanley Hauerwas, *Resident Aliens: Life in the Christian Colony* (Nashville, TN: Abingdon Press, 1989), 48.
[95] Rasmusson, *The Church as Polis*, 8.
[96] Ibid., 193.
[97] Ibid., 194.

Christianity. He ascertains that the society has developed convention in the contemporary university that enables the teaching of religion without offense.[98] He states with palpable pain that "most teachers shy away from the responsibility to change our students' lives, and the reason for this is the absence of any sense of legitimacy of authority for that task. Liberals celebrate this, teaching us to call the absence of authority—and the hierarchy on which any account of authority depends—freedom."[99]

Hauerwas appeals to Christians to resist these powers that would subvert the Gospel rather than listening to them and be schemed into compromising their faith. He believes that liberalism emasculated Christianity in the name of societal peace.[100] According to him, it is absurd that it is the Christians themselves policing Christianity in the name of democracy. He thus writes, "The practices of liberal societies have rendered our convictions as Christians puerile. In the name of supporting democracy, Christians police their own convictions to ensure none of those convictions might cause difficulty for making democracy successful."[101]

We find a summary statement of his theological career and contribution in his biography at Duke Divinity School. Below is what is stated therein:

> Professor Hauerwas has sought to recover significance of the virtues for understanding the nature of the Christian life. This search has led him to emphasize the importance of the Church, as well as narrative for understanding Christian existence. His work cuts across disciplinary lines as he is in conversation with systematic theology, philosophical theology and ethics, political theory, as well as the philosophy of social science and medical ethics. He was named "America's Best Theologian" by Time Magazine in 2001.[102]

---

[98] Hauerwas, *Dispatches from the Front*, 15.
[99] Ibid., 15.
[100] Ibid., 17.
[101] Ibid., 105.
[102] Stanley Hauerwas, Faculty/Duke Divinity School, http://www.divinity.duke.edu/portal_memberdata/shauerwas (accessed October 19, 2009).

PART II

Joseph Ratzinger and Stanley Hauerwas against the Culture of Relativism

Chapter One

1.0 Joseph Ratzinger's Diagnosis of the Contemporary Culture of Relativism

1.1 The Culture of Relativism vs. Christian Culture: The Dictatorship of Relativism

The term "relativism" is a relatively new in Christian usage but not as a reality. It can be defined as the supremacy of free will and absolutism of the self, leading man to depend on nothing and no one. It is the rejection of any objectivity and universal values; a rejection of Truth in favor of "truths"; a replacement of Truth (God) with truth (god), and this "truth" is the self. It is an ideology against the possibility of knowing absolute Truth (and absolute truth).

At Mass prior to the conclave, Cardinal Joseph Ratzinger warned of the "dictatorship of relativism"[103] the world is confronted with. In the same homily, Ratzinger noted with concern that the church has experienced many doctrinal winds, many ideological currents, and many styles of thought.[104] He made a critical analysis of the current state of the Christian faith in the following statement:

> The thought of many Christians has often been tossed about by these waves, tossed from one end to the other: from Marxism to liberalism, even to libertinism, from collectivism to radical individualism, from atheism to religious mysticism, from

---

[103] John F. Thornton and Susan B. Varenne, eds., *The Essential Pope Benedict XVI: His Central Writings and Speeches* (New York: HarperCollins Publishers, 2007), 22.
[104] Ibid.

agnosticism to syncretism. To have a clear faith, according to the creed of the Church, is labeled fundamentalism.[105]

He described relativism as "allowing oneself to be led here and there by any wind of doctrine."[106] He also noted that this trend defines our times today—that today "we are witnessing the 'dictatorship of relativism' which does not recognize anything as absolute and leaves as the ultimate measure only the measure of each one and his own desires."[107]

After that homily, and after he was elected pope, the world was alerted afresh to the danger of relativism which appeared as if it was a new phenomenon. However, the homily simply resuscitated a very old phenomenon and which Ratzinger had addressed long before he became pope. Jankunas notes that "the origin of relativism has been traced back to the famous statement of the Greek philosopher Protagoras: 'Man is the measure of all things, of those being that they are, of those not being, that they are not.' It is Pope Benedict XVI's claim that in an unreflected, uncritical, and naïve way, the modern world has been ensnared into relativism."[108]

As a matter of fact, Ratzinger did not initiate the fight against relativism after he was elected pope. Rather, his entire life as a priest, bishop, cardinal, theologian, and as pope, Ratzinger has been up in arms against relativism. Many of his writings reflect this fact. For example, in his address to the presidents of the Doctrinal Commissions of the Bishops' Conferences of Latin America, which took place in Guadalajara, Mexico, May 1996,[109] Ratzinger asserted that relativism is the central problem today. He stressed that thus,

> Relativism has become the central problem for the faith at the present time. No doubt it is not presented only with its aspect of resignation before the immensity of the truth. It is also presented as a position defined positively by the concepts of tolerance and knowledge through dialogue and freedom, concepts that would be limited if the existence of one valid truth for all were affirmed. In turn, relativism appears to be the philosophical foundation of democracy.[110]

---

[105] Thornton and Susan B. Varenne, eds., *The Essential Pope Benedict XVI*, 22.
[106] Ibid.
[107] Ibid.
[108] Gediminas T. Jankunas, *The Dictatorship of Relativism: Pope Benedict XVI's Response* (New York: St. Paul's Press, 2011), 337 (Back cover).
[109] Thornton and Susan B. Varenne, eds., *The Essential Pope Benedict XVI*, 26.
[110] Ibid., 228–229.

From his childhood, Ratzinger was faced with the violation of absolute truth under the Nazi regime. "As its necessary precondition, Nazism depended on the debunking of objective truth and objective morality. Truth had to be derided as irrelevant, and naked will had to be exalted."[111] Ratzinger also experienced Marxism in the 1968 student revolution at Tübingen University. Marxism and Marxists were calling for relativization of all previous notions of ethics and morality and truth—calling them "bourgeois" ideas.[112] They promoted the development of a relativistic conscience in which there would be no absolute truth.

As a bishop, cardinal, theologian, and pope, Ratzinger has continually been concerned about the development of a society that is anti-Christian and antitruth. He has steadfastly held a firm stand against such ideas, as yielding to them would be tantamount to consenting to atheism and rejection of God. He notes that

> in today's liberal democracies, the move to atheism is not, as it was in the 19th century, a move toward the objective world of the scientific rationalistic. That was the "modern" way, and it is now being rejected, in favor of a new "post-modern" way. The new way is not toward objectivity, but toward subjectivism—not toward truth as its criterion, but toward power. Along with that move comes a dictatorial impulse, to treat everyone who has a different view as "intolerant." For instance, those who hold that there are truths worth dying for, and objective goods to be pursued and objective evils to be avoided, are now held to be "intolerant" fundamentalists, and therefore guilty of "discrimination."[113]

In the interview with Zenit on February 23, 2004, Ratzinger—the then prefect of the Congregation of Doctrine of Faith—was asked which problems of the church concerned him the most at present. Cardinal Ratzinger responded,

> I would say simply the present difficulty to believe. There is relativism, which is already spontaneous for the human being of our times. Today it is regarded an act of pride, incompatible with tolerance, to think that we have really received the truth of the Lord. However, it seems that, to be tolerant, all religions

---

[111] Ibid.

[112] Ibid.

[113] http://www.aei.org/print?pub=article&pubId=22328@authors=<a href=scholar/44>Michael (accessed November 1, 2009).

and cultures must be considered equal. In this context, to believe is an act that becomes increasingly difficult. In this way we witness the silent loss of faith, without great protests, in a large part of Christianity. This is the greatest concern. So it is important to ask ourselves how we can reopen the doors to the presence of the Lord, to the revelation that the Church makes of him, in this wave of relativism. Then we will really open a door to tolerance, which is not indifference, but love and respect for the other, reciprocal help on the path of life.[114]

From the above responses, it is patent that the greatest enemy of the Christian faith and Church, according to Ratzinger, is the culture of relativism. For Ratzinger, relativism disintegrates the church since it eradicates the truth. It equates Christianity with other religions. It also erodes the deposit of faith of the truth of revelation. Relativism denies the divinity of Christ and essentially denies God, turning man into a god. It fails to transcend the demonstrable and experiential knowledge, thus falling short of reason, even though it claims Christianity to be unreasonable. Ratzinger asserts that when man reaches this level, he "enters the world, no longer as a gift of the Creator, but as the product of our creativity—and a product that can be selected according to requirements that we ourselves stipulate. In this way, the splendor of the fact that he is the image of God—the source of his dignity—no longer shines upon this man; his only splendor is the power of human capabilities."[115]

Relativism further considers God's existence "improvable and uncertain and, hence, as something belonging to the sphere of subjective choices. In either case, God is irrelevant to public life."[116] Certainly, Ratzinger disagrees with such a reckoning which thrusts God out of the universe which he himself created. Such would be equivalent to denying creation or envisaging God as a watchmaker—who makes watches and never cares to know what happens to them thereafter. According to Ratzinger, God is alive and active in the world, creating and sustaining creation. He holds to the idea of Thomas Aquinas of the Unmoved Mover. The society of man cannot claim to be its own roots. There must be a source outside society from which this society gets its existence. There

---

[114] Part 2 of interview with the prefect of Doctrinal Congregation, "Cardinal Ratzinger on Relativism and Communion for the Remarried (Part 2)," (2/25/2004), *Zenit* http://www.Catholic.org/printer_friendly.php?id=733&section=Featured+Today (accessed November 11, 2009).

[115] Joseph Ratzinger, *Christianity and the Crisis of Cultures* (San Francisco: Ignatius Press, 1995), 26.

[116] Ibid., 30.

is an unmoved mover that moves all things—and "this everyone understands to be God."[117]

Ratzinger critiques the culture of relativism essentially in two perspectives, namely, sociopolitical and religious/moral perspectives. Here below, we shall closely investigate each of these perspectives and how Ratzinger assumes they have been affected by the modern culture of relativism and how they affect the image of God in this world.

1.2 The Sociopolitical Perspective

The nuisance of relativism irritates Ratzinger beyond the face value subjectivity. Indeed relativism aims at turning all forms of objectivity in society into subjectivism. This is adequately dreadful. However, Ratzinger envisages more than a spontaneous subjectivity of society. He believes relativism is a worse phenomenon because, according to him, it is a well-organized philosophy,[118] a systematic movement, which is behind the suppression of particular values of the society while promoting its own tunnel view of reality; hence, the dictatorship of relativism. Ratzinger believes this evil is bound for the destruction of the church and Christianity. According to him, the church is under siege, for "secularism is no longer that element of neutrality which opens up areas of freedom for everyone. It is beginning to turn into an ideology that imposes itself through politics and leaves no public space for the Catholic and Christian vision, which thus risks becoming something purely private and essentially mutilated."[119]

Relativism is thus believed by Ratzinger to be a political movement aiming at, not only replacing Christian authority and influence in society, but worse

---

[117] Robert Barron, *Thomas Aquinas: Spiritual Master* (New York: The Crossroad Publishing Company, 2008), 65.

[118] Ratzinger insists that relativism is the philosophical foundation of democracy. He states, thus, "Democracy, in fact, is supposedly built on the basis that no one can presume to know the true way, and it is enriched by the fact that all roads are mutually recognized as fragments of the effort toward that which is better. Therefore, all roads seek something common in dialogue, and they also compete regarding knowledge that cannot be compatible in one common form. A system of freedom ought to be essentially a system of positions that are connected with one another because they are relative, as well as being dependent on historical situations open to new developments. Therefore, liberal society would be a relativist society: only with that condition could it continue to be free and open to the future," in John F. Thornton and Susan B. Varenne, eds., *The Essential Pope Benedict XVI: His Central Writings and Speeches* (New York: HarperCollins Publishers, 2007), 229.

[119] Sandro Magister, "Clarification" by the Congregation for the Doctrine of the Faith, "on Procured Abortion," (July 10, 2009), *L'Osservatore Romano* http://chiesa.espresso.repubblica.it (accessed December 1, 2009).

still, killing God and replacing his authority with human authority which Ratzinger refers to as "a new coercion and the emergence of a new ruling class."[120] Members of this ruling class, Ratzinger believes, are fostering a new political moralism whose key words are justice, peace, and the conservation of creation.[121] Ratzinger insists that this political moralism does not open the way to regeneration; it actually blocks it.[122]

Hence, the promoters of relativism claim to be acting in the name of freedom and peace. However, in the course of promoting this peace, the very instigators of freedom and peace at the same time deny it to others. They advocate for freedom for some, while restricting it for others. This is selective granting of the so-called freedom. If others should be free, why not let the Christians be free as well? It is therefore clear that there is a well-organized conspiracy to suppress any ideas contrary to what these new rulers christen as freedom and peace.[123] Joseph Ratzinger believes in social and political cohesion and agrees that in the area of politics, the concept of relativism is considerably right, "for there is no one correct political opinion."[124] However, he rejects its application to the religious arena. He maintains that "although a certain right to relativism in the social and political area should not be denied, the problem is raised at the

---

[120] Tracey Rowland, *Ratzinger's Faith: The Theology of Pope Benedict XVI* (Oxford: Oxford University Press, 2008), 114.

[121] Ibid.

[122] Ibid., 114–115.

[123] Meeting with the government members in Benin, Ratzinger had a mention of such conspiracies and their consequences. Here is an excerpt from his speech: "Many conflicts have originated in man's blindness, in his will to power and in political and economic interests which mock the dignity of people and of nature. Human beings aspire to liberty; then to live in dignity; they want good schools and food for their children, dignified hospitals to take care of the sick; they want to be respected; they demand transparent governance which does not confuse private and public interests; and above all they desire peace and justice. At this time, there are too many scandals and injustices, too much corruption and greed, too many errors and lies, too much violence which leads to misery and to death. These ills certainly afflict your continent, but they also afflict the rest of the world. Every people wishes to understand the political and economic choices which are made in its name. They perceive manipulation and their revenge is sometimes violent. They wish to participate in good governance. We know that no political regime is ideal and that no economic choice is neutral. But these must always serve the common good. Hence we are faced with legitimate demands, present in all countries, for greater dignity and above all for greater humanity. Man demands that his humanity be respected and promoted. Political and economic leaders of countries find themselves placed before important decisions and choices which they can no longer avoid," in http://www.vatican.va/holy_father/benedict_xvi/speeches/2011/november/documents/hf_ben-xvi_spe_20111119_corpo-diplom_en.html (accessed on December 7, 2011).

[124] Thornton and Susan B. Varenne, eds., *The Essential Pope Benedict XVI*, 229.

moment of setting its limits. There has also been the desire to apply this method in a totally conscious way in the area of religion and ethics."[125]

The first words of Jesus to his disciples after his resurrection were "Peace be with you" (Jn 20:20). At the great commissioning, he again addressed disciples with words of peace: "Peace I leave with you; my peace I give to you" (Jn 14:27). Jesus concluded his mission with a fulfillment of Isaiah's prophecy of the messiah who would be called "prince of peace" (Is 9:6). At Jesus's birth, the angels proclaimed that peace had downed on people of good will (Lk 2:14). Therefore, Jesus's mission to this world is a mission of peace. Indeed, every human being (and all creation) loves peace. Peace is possibly the most desired element of life. However, the peace that the Lord gives is different from the peace this world gives. When Jesus conferred peace upon his disciples, he also cautioned them: "Peace I leave with you; my peace I give to you. I do not give to you as the world gives" (Jn 14:27). The peace that Jesus gives springs from justice and truth. What he gives is peace and justice in truth. There cannot be peace without justice. Denying some people the opportunity to practice what they believe is denying them justice. Truth naturally precedes justice. Therefore, justice denied is truth denied; it is a rejection of God who is truth.

Ratzinger's arguments against the relativistic sociopolitical atmosphere are along these lines. He argues that "the state must recognize that a basic framework of values within a Christian foundation is the precondition for its own existence and it must learn that there is a truth which is not subject to consensus but which precedes it and makes it possible."[126] The new ruling class, however, tends to suppose that truth depends on human consensus. Their aim seems to be subjecting all things to the vote. This is where they go wrong. When asked by Pilate what truth is, Jesus kept quiet (Jn 18:37–38). He remained silent because he had mentioned earlier, "I am the way, and the truth, and the life" (Jn 14:6). Jesus is the truth, and if he is the truth, it means that truth is God. How can we then subject God to man? Trying to subject truth to our human democratic conditions is trying to raise man above God. Thus, the new ruling class attempts to deny God and turn themselves into gods. Ratzinger refers to this as "the worst howler of man today."[127]

In *Values in a Time of Upheaval*, Ratzinger summarizes a number of insights:

1. The state is not itself the source of truth and morality.
2. The goal of the state cannot consist in a freedom without defined contents.

---

[125] Thornton and Susan B. Varenne, eds., *The Essential Pope Benedict XVI*, 229.

[126] Joseph Ratzinger, *Church, Ecumenism and Politics* (New York: Crossroad, 1988), 219.

[127] Ibid.

3. The state must receive from outside itself the essential measure of knowledge and truth with regard to that which is good.
4. This "outside" cannot be pure reason.
5. Christian faith has proved to be the most universal and rational religious culture
6. The church may not exalt itself to become the state nor work as an organ of power in the state.
7. The church remains outside the state but must assert itself so that in her moral truth may shine forth.[128]

1.3 The Religious/Moral Perspective

Fr. Jankunas wrote in his book, *The Dictatorship of Relativism*, that "the term relativism is laden with ambiguity."[129] Due to its ambiguity, it can therefore have many definitions, each more relevant to a particular perspective. Ratzinger defined it as "an attitude by modern times that does not recognize anything as definitive and whose ultimate goal consists solely of one's ego and desires. It is a letting oneself be tossed here and there, carried about by every wind of doctrine."[130] This definition of Ratzinger fits best the religious or moral perspective. Religious relativism aims at putting all religions, all religious denominations, and all religious orientations at the same level and equal status. The relative in relativism is the democratization of all religious beliefs so that there is no religion that enjoys a better and more privileged position.

However, as mentioned above, Ratzinger thinks there is a deliberate and systematic move targeting particular religious values and particular religious institutions. He roots this in the modern times where he points out three schools behind this trend. The three schools are as below:

1. Modernity represents the severance of the classical-theistic synthesis—free-floating concepts; separated from their roots.
2. Modernity represents a mutation of the classical-theistic—key concepts from Christian roots are given new meanings.
3. Modernity is an entirely new culture—new concepts and values replace the Greek and Christian concepts.[131]

Ratzinger rejects the third school outrightly. He holds that Christian

---

[128] Rowland, *Ratzinger's Faith*, 116–117.
[129] Jankunas, *The Dictatorship of Relativism*, 1.
[130] Thornton and Susan B. Varenne, eds., *The Essential Pope Benedict XVI*, 22.
[131] Rowland, *Ratzinger's Faith*, 107.

revelation is the foundation of a new history which is the end of all history.[132] He believes that it is modernity that is entangled with the Christian heritage however much secular liberal political elites may want to deny this.[133] His basis for making such a conclusion is that the modern culture has a propensity to dismiss faith in creation, and eventually revelation, thus, making all religions being a creation of man. And therefore, since, according to modern culture, all religions are of man's making, they are subsequently equal and can coexist, but the modern culture would actually prefer if they cease to be; for they seem to have outlived their importance.

Maintaining his stance on the primacy of God and Christianity, Ratzinger insists that the Christian Church cannot accept this kind of marginalization.[134] In the collection of essays published in 1988 under the title *The Church, Ecumenism and Politics*, Ratzinger noted with approval that the early Christians would not allow Christ to be included in the pantheon alongside the pagan gods.[135] "Christianity, as a revealed religion, cannot accept to be put under the same basket with other religions of nature. God reveals himself in the Old Testament as the one and the only God, and a jealous God (Ex 3:13–15). In the New Testament, Jesus reveals to us as coming from the Father, and to see him is to see the Father (Jn 14:9)."[136]

Ratzinger's repudiation of an equality of Christianity with other religions has put him at odds with other religious foundations which accuse him of standing in the way of ecumenism. However, Ratzinger strongly believes in ecumenism and even goes beyond ecumenism to embrace interreligious dialogue. His argument is that a revealed faith cannot be contrasted with any other. As head of the Congregation for the Doctrine of the Faith, he and the congregation published *The Lord Jesus* (*Dominus Jesus*)[137] to clarify on this issue. The congregation noted,

> The Church's constant missionary proclamation is endangered today by relativistic theories which seek to justify religious pluralism, superseding certain truths, for example the definitive and complete character of the revelation of Jesus Christ,

---

[132] Joseph Ratzinger, *Principles of Catholic Theology: Building Stones for a Fundamental Theology* (San Francisco: Ignatius Press, 1987), 156.

[133] Rowland, *Ratzinger's Faith*, 108.

[134] Thornton and Susan B. Varenne, eds., *The Essential Pope Benedict XVI*, 23.

[135] Ratzinger, *Church, Ecumenism and Politics*, 213–214.

[136] Ratzinger, *Church, Ecumenism and Politics*, 214.

[137] The Congregation of the Doctrine of the Faith published *Dominus Jesus* on August 6, 2000, in Rome, as a declaration on the Unicity and Salvific Universality of Jesus and the Church.

the nature of Christian faith as compared with that of belief in other religion.[138]

They further stated that belief in other religions is still in search of the absolute truth and still lacking assent to God.[139]

This document precipitated a lot of argument and resentment among other religions, accusing Christianity and the Catholic Church (but particularly Cardinal Ratzinger) of being arrogant and sectarian. To many people in today's society, all religions are and mean one and the same thing.[140] Therefore, there should be no single religion that should consider itself superior to the other. The contemporary world is made to believe that there is a difference of nuance between religions. Belonging to a particular religion seems to be a matter of choice,[141] and those who have the majority decide for the minority.

Therein lies the facet Ratzinger passionately refutes. According to Ratzinger, relativism eliminates truth and replaces it with constantly shifting majority opinions. To him, democracy is placed vis-à-vis the truth. He believes "relativism is the philosophical foundation of democracy."[142] However, he insists that truth must remain. He is worried that any claim to know the truth is widely regarded nowadays as a threat to tolerance and freedom.[143] With regret Ratzinger states,

---

[138] Congregation for the Doctrine of the Faith, *The Lord Jesus: On the Unicity and Salvific Universality of Jesus and the Church* (Nairobi, Kenya: Pauline Publications Africa, 2000), 7.

[139] Ibid., 11.

[140] Ratzinger believes that this could be caused by a renewed sense of nationalism. He thus states, "Today it seems that the Church is being extinguished in souls and is collapsing in communities. The Church is crumbling into nationalistic resentment, in the disparagement of what is foreign, in the glorification of what is one's own." In Joseph Ratzinger: Pope Benedict XVI, *Credo for Today: What Christians Believe*, trans. Michael Miller (San Francisco: Ignatius Press, 2009), 182.

[141] Ratzinger seems to perceive the mushrooming of new churches as a result of this *choosability*, hence, being tossed by every wind of doctrine. According to him, "The churches have becomes our endeavors, and we are either proud or ashamed of them; many little private properties stand side by side, 'our' churches through and through, which we make for ourselves, which belong to us, and which we try to reshape or maintain accordingly. We have lost sight of 'his' Church. Church that is merely ours is a pointless game in a sandbox . . . But [in truth] now as ever, 'his Church' lives behind 'our Church.' I can stand by him only if I stand by and in his Church. . . . it is the Church that, despite all the human foibles of the people in her, gives us Jesus Christ, and only through her can we receive him as a living, authoritative reality that summons and endows me here and now." In Joseph Ratzinger: Pope Benedict XVI, trans. Michael Miller, *Credo for Today: What Christians Believe* (San Francisco: Ignatius Press, 2009), 192–193.

[142] Thornton and Susan B. Varenne, eds., *The Essential Pope Benedict XVI*, 229.

[143] Joseph Ratzinger, *Truth and Tolerance: Christian belief and World Religions* (San Francisco: Ignatius Press, 2003), 114.

In fact, relativism has become the central problem for faith in our time. It defines itself positively on the basis of the concepts of tolerance, dialectic epistemology, and freedom, which would be limited by maintaining one truth as being valid for everyone. A free society is said to be a relativistic society; only on this condition can it remain free and open-ended.[144]

In Ratzinger's thought, this view can be true in politics to a great extent, but he believes that even in politics, one cannot always manage with absolute relativism, for there are things that are wrong and can never become right, and there are things that are right and can never become wrong.[145]

Relativism accuses Christianity of fundamentalism. Ratzinger says that such ideas originate from John Hicks and Immanuel Kant's philosophies.[146] These two taught that we can never know ultimate reality in itself but only its appearance. According to them, there cannot be absolute reality nor an absolute person in himself, but only ideal figures which direct our attention toward the totally other. Jesus was thus consciously relativized, reduced to one religious genius among others.[147]

The belief that there is indeed truth, valid and binding truth, within history itself, in the figure of Jesus Christ and in the faith of the Church, is referred to as fundamentalism. Dialogue has to be an exchange between positions that are fundamentally of equal status and thus mutually relative, with the aim of achieving a maximum of cooperation and integration between various bodies and entities. The relativistic elimination of Christology, and most certainly of ecclesiology, now becomes a central commandment of religion. The belief in the divinity of an individual leads to fanaticism and particularism, to the dissociation of faith from love; and this is the thing that must be overcome.[148]

Relativism, according to Ratzinger, gives religion a new basis along pragmatic lines, with either a more ethical or political coloration.[149] It descends from the truth of revelation to the simple redemption of the self on the socioeconomic

---

[144] Ratzinger, *Truth and Tolerance*, 117.
[145] Ibid., 118.
[146] Ibid., 119.
[147] Ratzinger, *Truth and Tolerance*, 119.
[148] Ibid., 120–121.
[149] Ratzinger, *Truth and Tolerance*, 126.

level. For Ratzinger, this is unbelief that presents itself in form of progress. He thus writes,

> Thus what others necessarily consider unbelief is for some progress, and what was hitherto unthinkable becomes normal: the men who long ago abandoned the Church's Creed can in good conscience regard themselves as the truly progressive Christians. For them, however, the only standard by which to measure the Church is the expediency with which she functions. . . . If there is to be a true theology of the Church now, it seems that it can only consist of taking away her theological attributes and regarding and discussing her as something purely political.[150]

This, according to Ratzinger, is a kind of surrender from the mystery of God and backsliding to the phenomenological world. Ratzinger says that this is the very reason why the gods are returning because they have become more credible than God. "There is renewal of pre-Christian religions and cults."[151] A testimony to this can be found in one of the confessions of an African bishop of the diocese of Masaka in Uganda. Bishop Adrian Ddungu[152] recalls,

> The "Bataka"[153] were a constant headache to us. Shortly after I had left for Rome, the "Bataka" began to have an appeal to their fellow Baganda: All whatever is foreign, or rather whatever is European is bad. The African man has been alienated from nature by religion and money from the Whiteman. Therefore to restore him, religion and money and whatever is from Europe must be destroyed.[154]

Ratzinger makes a similar observation that "today doubts

---

[150] Benedict XVI, trans. Michael Miller, *Credo for Today: What Christians Believe* (San Francisco: Ignatius Press, 2009), 186–188.

[151] Ibid., 128.

[152] Bishop Adrian Kivumbi Ddungu was the second black bishop south of the Sahara in modern times. He succeeded Bishop Joseph Kiwanuka, the first black bishop south of the Sahara in modern times. He was bishop of Masaka Diocese (the diocese of my childhood) from 1962 to 1998.

[153] "Bataka" in this context means those who agitate for traditional values and religious practices. It can also mean people who have been resident in an area for a long time.

[154] John Mary Waliggo et al. *Bishop Adrian K. Ddungu of Masaka Diocese: Vatican Council II Father, Successor of the First Black African Bishop in Modern Times, Preacher and Teacher: His Life, Vocation and Legacy* (Kampala, Uganda: Angel Agencies, 2009), 49.

have arisen about the universality of the Christian faith. The worldwide mission is seen by many as the history of a process of alienation and of dominance by force."[155] He recalls the lamentations of the black South Americans who accused the European Christians of "conquering bodies with the sword and dominating souls with the cross. For the natives and for the enslaved Africans, Christianity appeared as the religion of the enemy who subjugated and killed people."[156] These took the direction of a liberation theology with its shortcomings. We should not divert to liberation theology at this point. We are only pointing out the resentment of the modern cultures toward Christianity and its doctrine, thus rejecting the existence of a universal truth and ushering in a relativism of cultures and religions.

Ratzinger insists that instead of relativizing religion or fighting for the freedom of each culture and religious practice, the fact should be rediscovered that there is a universal truth which cannot be compromised. He says that dialogue of religions and cultures should become more and more a listening to the Logos who is pointing out to us the unity we already share.[157] He further accuses relativism of putting more emphasis on freedom and equality, undermining the underlying truth of the different realities. He insists that "dialogue should always be about truth participating in the underlying Word [Logos]; it is a search for truth, not for mere tolerance."[158] He reminds us not to forget that dialogue is a search for truth, not simply a *modus vivendi*.[159] We should search for the truth, but not ignore the "indispensable elements" of Christian revelation. He notes that, unfortunately, even modern theologians tend to miss this central element and value more the harmony, equality, and the need to take outsiders' views seriously, thus joining the relativistic world.

Conclusively, Ratzinger's concept of the relativistic culture seems to be an all-embracing disease endemic of segments of society, both within and outside of the Christian community.[160] As we shall discuss in later chapters,

---

[155] Ratzinger, *Truth and Tolerance*, 56.
[156] Ratzinger, *Truth and Tolerance*, 56.
[157] Pope Benedict XVI, "On Interreligious Dialogue," (October 26, 2005), *Rain and the Rhinoceros*, http://rainandtherhinoceros.wordpress.com/2005/10/26/pope-benedict-on-inter-religious-di (accessed December 22, 2009).
[158] Ibid.
[159] Ibid.
[160] He is very and more worried about the disease that is eating the church from within when he writes: "The 'death of God' is a very real process, which today reaches deep into

57

Ratzinger's ideas bear a resemblance to Stanley Hauerwas' ideas, who accuses Christians themselves of having learned to police Christian values in the name of democracy.[161] Ratzinger asserts that "secularism or relativism, is no longer that element of neutrality which opens up areas of freedom for everyone, but rather, it is beginning to turn into an ideology that imposes itself through politics and leaves no public space for the Catholic and Christian vision, which thus risks becoming something purely private and essentially mutilated."[162]

Ratzinger's problem with the liberal privatization of religion seems to be that, in the name of tolerance, it favors what is in fact an intolerant suppression of the (ultimately religious) question of this fidelity.[163] He notes that "a society that turns what is specifically human into something purely private and defines itself in terms of a complete secularity—this kind of society will of its nature be sorrowful, a place of despair: it rests on a diminution of human dignity."[164]

1.4 The Significance and Limits of Today's Relativistic Culture

Ratzinger considers the road Europe has taken, by following the Enlightenment culture, not only a wrong way, but a dangerous one as well. He is convinced that these philosophies are characterized by their positivist—and therefore antimetaphysical—character, so that ultimately there is no place for God in them. He thus writes,

> They are based on a self-limitation of the positive reason that is adequate in the technological sphere but entails a mutilation of man if it is generalized. The result is that man no longer accepts any moral authority apart from his own calculations ... It is true that the positivist philosophies contain important elements of truth; but these are based on a self-limitation of reason that is typical of one determined cultural situation, that of the modern West, and as such, certainly cannot be considered

---

the interior of the Church. God is dying in Christendom, so it seems. Resurrection becomes a commissioning event that is perceived in outmoded imagery." In Joseph Ratzinger: Pope Benedict XVI, *Credo for Today: What Christians Believe*, trans. Michael Miller (San Francisco: Ignatius Press, 2009), 186.

[161] Stanley Hauerwas, *Dispatches from the Front: Theological Engagements with the Secular* (Durham, NC: Duke University Press, 1995), 93.

[162] Sandro Magister, "The Church is Under Siege, but Habermas, the Atheist, Is Coming to Its Defense," (November 22, 2004), *L'Osservatore Romano*, http://chiesa.espresso.repubblica.it (accessed December 5, 2009).

[163] Rowland, *Ratzinger's Faith*, 114.

[164] Ibid.

the last word of reason. Although they may seem totally rational, they are not in fact the voice of reason. They too, have their
cultural ties, since they are linked to the situation of the West
today. This is why they are not that philosophy which one day
could enjoy validity throughout the whole world.[165]

He criticizes the relativistic culture as being incomplete, a culture without
roots.[166] He clarifies that this culture "consciously cuts off its own historical
roots, depriving itself of the powerful sources from which it sprang. It detaches
itself from what we might call the basic memory of mankind, without which
man loses his orientation, for now the guiding principle is that man's capability
determines what he does."[167] To illustrate his point, he asserts,

> Man knows how to do many things, and this knowledge in-
> creases all the time. If this knowledge does not find its criterion
> in a moral norm, it becomes a power for destruction, as we can
> already see in the world around us. Man knows how to clone
> human beings, and therefore he does so. Man knows how to
> use human beings as "storerooms" of organs for other men,
> and therefore he does so. He does so because this seems some-
> thing demanded by his own liberty. Man knows how to build
> atom bombs, and therefore he makes them, and he is willing
> in principle to use them, too. Even terrorism is ultimately
> based on this modality of man's "self authorization," not on
> the teachings of the Qur'an.[168]

Endemic to the relativistic culture is self-authorization. Its greatest desire
is total freedom. However, it crosses its limits when it denies freedom to the
other. "Might is right" becomes its rule where the mighty are the legislators
and judges. However, man falls short of own legislation because, above him,
there is a superior reality. God must be the ultimate legislator whose justice is
perfect. Thus, by making himself the ultimate legislator, man turns himself his
own god. In Ratzinger's view, this culture rejects God.

This self-authorization is what Cardinal Ratzinger calls a culture without
roots.[169] Pure rationality without referring to the author of this rationality is

---

[165] Joseph Ratzinger, *Christianity and the Crisis of Cultures* (San Francisco: Ignatius Press,
1995), 40–41.
[166] Ibid., 41.
[167] Ibid.
[168] Ratzinger, *Christianity and the Crisis of Cultures*, 41–42.
[169] Ibid., 41.

self-authorization and therefore getting rid of the roots, which is God. The Enlightenment culture is a culture that gets rid of God and replaces him by man and his freedom and knowledge as the author of all human activity. Ratzinger states that "this philosophy expresses, not a complete reason of man, but one part of it. And this mutilation of reason means that we cannot consider it to be rational at all. Hence, it is incomplete and can recover its health only through re-establishing contact with its roots. A tree without roots dries up."[170]

Ratzinger also accuses the modern culture of "rationalism, of absolutizing a way of thinking and living, that is unlike the historical cultures of humanity, and which imposes itself over all others cultures."[171] It has no tolerance for other thinking and living; it respects no other cultures and accords no privileges to any of them. He thus writes,

> The failure to mention Christian roots is not the expression of a superior tolerance that respects all cultures in the same way and chooses not to accord privileges to any of one of them. Rather, it expresses the absolutization of a way of thinking and living that is radically opposed to all the other historical cultures of humanity. The real antagonism typical of today's world is not that between the diverse religious cultures; rather, it is the antagonism between the radical emancipation of man from God, from roots of life, on the one hand, and the great religious cultures, on the other . . . relativism, which is the starting point of all this whole process, becomes a dogmatism that believes itself in possession of the definitive knowledge of human reason, with the right to consider everything else merely as a stage in human history that is basically obsolete and deserves to be relativized. In reality, this means that we have need of roots if we are to survive and that we must not lose sight of God if we do not want human dignity to disappear.[172]

1.4.1 The Right to Life

The culture of rationality puts itself in charge of life and rules over it, giving reasons that favor some and eliminate the lives of others. The morality of Enlightenment ignored the legislation of God over life, leading to violence against life, thus justifying wars, abortions, euthanasia, cloning, etc. Ratzinger

---

[170] Ibid, 43.
[171] Ibid., 44.
[172] Ibid., 43–44.

calls this a disorder.[173] "The disorder and degeneration that followed the fall of our first parents have left their mark on the creation that God's hands had made absolutely perfect. Violence and unending chain of reciprocal killings have spread through the world, making impossible the pace of a social life ordered in keeping the principles of justice."[174]

He asserts that in Genesis 9:5–6, the Lord said, "Whoever sheds the blood of a human, by a human shall that person's blood be shed; for in his own image God made humankind." By these words, God claims the life of man as his own specific possession: it remains under his direct and immediate protection. It is something sacred. It follows that the recognition of the sacred character of human life and of its inviolability—a principle admitting to exceptions—is not some trivial little problem or a question that may be considered relative, in view of the pluralism of opinions we find in modern society. "There are no 'small murders.' The respect of every human life is an essential condition if a societal life worthy of the name is to be possible. When man's conscience loses respect for life as something sacred, he inevitable ends by losing his own identity."[175]

The right to life is possibly the most violated right today. The violation is largely ardently promoted by the culture of freedom. "Pro-choice" as opposed to "pro-life" is characteristic and indicator of the phenomenon. The Pro-choice group stands on the side of the "free" or "progressive" against the Pro-life group believed to be for the conservative. The Pro-choice people believe they are in charge of their lives and therefore have the right to choose how they live it. They are too much in love for their lives that they prefer to deny life to others, particularly, the least ones—the unborn. Their well-being takes priority to the detriment of other people's lives. For example, a person procuring abortion envisages relief or better health on his/her part, more important than the unborn life. This is a culture that needs to be evangelized according to Ratzinger.

1.4.2 The Law of the Jungle, the Rule of Law

In the culture of rationalism, law is relative; applied selectively. Ratzinger characterized this as a culture of the law of the jungle[176] where the fittest survive. He states,

> In today's pluralistic societies, where various religious, cultural, and ideological orientations coexist, it is becoming ever

---

[173] Ratzinger, *Christianity and the Crisis of Cultures*, 59.
[174] Ibid.
[175] Ibid., 60.
[176] Ibid., 61.

more difficult to guarantee a common basis of ethical values shared by all and capable of providing a sufficient foundation for democracy itself. Very many people are indeed convinced that we cannot do without a minimum of moral values that are recognized and sanctioned in social life; but the substance of such values increasingly evaporates the more we struggle to attain the consensus they must obtain on the level of society. One single value seems not to be the object of discussion, namely, the right of the individual to express himself freely, without any impositions from outside himself, at least so long as his freedom does not infringe the rights of others.[177]

According to Ratzinger, this is how the right to abortion is invoked as a constitutive element in the right to liberty on the part of the woman, the man, and society itself. He accepts that all these rights are real and founded. Nevertheless, it is a fact that this claim to exercise real rights is demanded to the detriment of the life of an innocent human being whose rights are not even taken into consideration. In this way, one becomes blind to the right to life of another, the smallest and weakest person involved, one without a voice. The rights of some individuals are affirmed at the cost of the fundamental rights to life of another individual. This is why every legalization of abortion implies the idea that law is based on power.[178]

Ratzinger makes reference to the Universal Declaration of Human Rights as follows:

> The Universal Declaration of Rights (1948), expresses fully the awareness that human rights—the most fundamental of which, of course, the right to life itself—belong to man by nature; that the state recognizes them but does not in fact confer them; and that they are applicable to all men as such, not because of other secondary characteristics of particular individuals, which others would be entitled to define at their pleasure. It follows that a state that claims the prerogative of defining who is and who is not the subject of the rights, and that consequently accepts that some persons have the right to violate the fundamental right to life of other persons, contradicts the democratic ideal although it continues to appeal to this claim. Such a state imperils the very basis on which it

---

[177] Ratzinger, *Christianity and the Crisis of Cultures*, 61–62.
[178] Ibid., 63.

governs. For when it accepts that the rights of the weakest may be violated, it also accepts that the law of the jungle prevails over the rule of law.[179]

1.4.3 Can Agnosticism Be a Solution?

Spalding defines agnosticism as "the theory of nescience in whatever is not purely phenomenal. It is but a form of skepticism, of the doubt of the possibility of objective knowledge."[180] Agnosticism claims that we cannot know God in himself because our knowledge is limited, and therefore, we cannot act according to something that we cannot know fully. Ratzinger challenges agnosticism by asserting that

> Within the network of human relationships it is impossible for each individual to know everything that is necessary and useful for life and that, therefore, our possibility for action are based on the fact that we ourselves participate by faith in the knowledge of others. When, however, we speak of faith in revelation, we pass beyond the boundaries of that knowledge which is typical of human life. Even if the hypothesis be granted that the existence of God could become an object of knowledge, at least revelation and its contents would remain an object of faith for each one of us, something that surpasses those realities that are accessible to our knowledge. Consequently, in this field there is no one in whom we could put our trust or to whose specialist knowledge we could refer, since no one could have a direct knowledge of such realities on the basis of his own personal studies.[181]

For Ratzinger, of its nature, the question of God cannot forcibly be made an object of scientific research in the strict sense of the term, and this means that the declaration of scientific atheism is an absurd claim—yesterday, today, or tomorrow.[182] However, he notes that this does not mean that by denying submission of God to scientific research, we enter the sphere of the irrational. On the contrary, "what we are looking for is the very foundation of all

---

[179] Ibid., 63–64.
[180] John Lancaster Spalding, *Religion, Agnosticism and Education* (Chicago, IL: A.C. McClure & Co., 1902), 58.
[181] Ratzinger, *Christianity and the Crisis of Cultures*, 84.
[182] Ibid., 86.

rationality; we are inquiring into how its light can be perceived."[183] According to him, there are some fundamental human attitudes that are indispensable methodological presuppositions for the knowledge of God. These include "listening to the message that is brought to us by our own existence and by the world in general; a vigilant attentiveness vis-à-vis the discoveries and the religious experience of humanity; and the decisive and persevering employment of our time and our internal energy on this problem, which concerns each one of us personally."[184]

Agnosticism cannot be a solution. What the modern scientists misconstrue is that God is not part of what can be comprehended by our human knowledge. Science fails to acknowledge its limitations. It fails to realize that God is beyond the phenomena of finite beings. It claims that what cannot be known cannot be believed either. Finite beings cannot comprehend the infinite. However, this does not mean that the infinite does not exist. As a matter of fact, the finite nature of human beings is proof of the existence of the infinite that is the cause of the finite.

Conclusively, Ratzinger classifies relativism in two main categories, namely, the Rationalistic (Enlightenment) culture, and Relativism or Secularism. He perceives these as characterizing the modern societies, not only in Europe and America but also gaining a firm ground in other continents of Asia and Africa. The two cultures, according to Ratzinger, tend to dismiss God from public life and substitute humanity for him. In other words, they turn man into a god; man becomes the ultimate legislator over life and the universe. They dismiss objective values of morality and swap them with the relative and secularized values that affect and promote the well-being of humankind according to human calculations and desires, the end justifying the means.

The present society needs a fundamental theology to preserve the orthodoxy of the faith. This theology is not readily available. Ratzinger's vast knowledge of the above cultures is therefore an appropriate remedy to this crisis of cultures. This is going to be the point of discussion in the next chapter.

---

[183] Ibid., 90.
[184] Ibid., 90–91.

Chapter Two

2.0 The Remedies Ratzinger Offers

Criticizing or dismissing any ideology or system would be tantamount to emptiness without providing possible solutions or remedies to the crisis in question. Ratzinger avoids falling into this trap of empty criticism. He thus suggests wise cautions and remedies to what he conceives as the number one danger to, not only Christianity, but also humanity as a whole. His aim is not to condemn the modern culture, but to correct the wrong trends and elements within that constitute a threat to the culture itself. The remedies he suggests are intended to restore first, and foremost, the place of God in the universe, and second, the place of man as a created being. According to Ratzinger, the culture of relativism makes a grave mistake by interchanging the identity of God and man, abandoning God's will and doing man's will, i.e., removing God from society and replacing him with man.[185] Man, in this case, becomes his own god. Ratzinger suggests a reversal of things.

This chapter will therefore explore the remedies that Joseph Ratzinger suggests to restore the lost identities. The following are the remedies he offers: return to the scriptures; new understanding of Jesus Christ (divine and human); the church as communion; liturgy as a celebration of faith; and a new catechesis.

2.1 Return to the Scriptures

On October 5, 2008, Pope Benedict XVI celebrated Holy Mass in the Basilica of St. Paul Outside the Walls to open the worldwide meeting of bishops

---

[185] Thornton and Susan Varenne, *The Essential Pope Benedict XVI*, 23.

on the relevance of the Bible for contemporary Catholics.[186] In his homily, he noted that the modern culture is thrusting God out of people's lives, resultantly relegating their identity. He expressed his pain that "today, nations once rich in faith and vocations are losing their own identity, under the harmful and destructive influence of a certain modern culture."[187] As it is his usual style, and since the conference was discussing the relevance of the Bible, Ratzinger made recourse to the roots (the word of God) as the ultimate remedy to the destructive modern culture.

At this conference, Ratzinger outpoured his heartfelt love and burning passion for scriptures. He admonished his fellow bishops to evoke the scriptures to their lives and to the lives of the people they lead, because failure to do this becomes contempt for the master. Below is an excerpt from his homily:

> The first reading, taken from the Book of Isaiah, as well as the passage from the Gospel according to Matthew, have presented to our liturgical assembly an evocative allegorical image of Sacred Scripture: the image of the vineyard which we have heard mentioned on the preceding Sundays. The initial passage of the Gospel account refers to the "canticle of the vineyard" which we find in Isaiah. This is a canticle set in the autumnal context of the grape harvest: a miniature masterpiece of Hebrew poetry which must have been very familiar to those listening to Jesus and from which, as from other references by the prophets (cf. Hos 10:1; Jer 2:21; Ez 17:3–10; 19:10–14; Ps 79:9–17), it was easy to understand that the vineyard symbolized Israel. God bestowed the same care upon his vineyard, upon the People he had chosen, that a faithful husband lavishes upon his wife (cf. Ez 16:1–14; Eph 5:25–33). Therefore the image of the vineyard, together with that of the wedding feast, describes the divine project of salvation and is presented as a moving allegory of God's Covenant with his People. In the Gospel, Jesus takes up the canticle of Isaiah but adapts it to his listeners and to the new period in salvation history. The emphasis is not so much on the vineyard as on the workers in it, from whom the landowner's "servants" ask for rent on his behalf. However, the

---

[186] Homily of His Holiness Benedict XVI, "Cappella Papale for the opening of the 12th Ordinary General Assembly of the Synod of Bishops," (October 5, 2008), http://www.vatican.va/holy_father/benedict_xvi/homilies/2008/documents/hf_ben-xvi_hom_20081005_apertura-sinodo_en.html, (accessed February 24, 2010).
[187] Ibid.

servants are abused and even murdered. How is it possible not to think of the vicissitudes of the Chosen People and of the destiny reserved for the prophets sent by God? In the end, the owner of the vineyard makes a final attempt: he sends his own son, convinced that at least they will listen to him. Instead the opposite happens: the labourers in the vineyard murder him precisely because he is the landowner's son, that is, his heir, convinced that this will enable them to take possession of the vineyard more easily. We are therefore witnessing a leap in quality with regard to the accusation of the violation of social justice as it emerges from Isaiah's canticle. Here we clearly see that contempt for the master's order becomes contempt for the master: it is not mere disobedience to a divine precept, it is a true and proper rejection of God: the mystery of the Cross appears.[188]

The emphasis Ratzinger puts on scripture makes it his agenda to restore theology and Christian life to its roots, that is, the Holy Scriptures. He is passionate at rediscovering scripture as the source of the life of the church. He has repeated himself on this almost throughout his career as a theologian and pastor. Recently when he visited Benin in Africa, he told the bishops that "the scriptures must have a central place in the life of the Church and of each Christian. Hence, I encourage you to help people to rediscover scripture as a source of constant renewal, so that it may unify the daily lives of the faithful and be ever more at the heart of every ecclesial activity."[189]

To exhaust Ratzinger's exposition on scripture would require us to write another dissertation. For our purpose in this paper and topic, it suffices to make a categorical statement that in Ratzinger's theological writings, and in all his pastoral messages, the scriptures take the uppermost position. He considers recovering scripture as the number one remedy to the culture of relativism.

---

[188] Homily of His Holiness Benedict XVI, "Cappella Papale for the opening of the 12th Ordinary General Assembly of the Synod of Bishops," (October 5, 2008), http://www.vatican.va/holy_father/benedict_xvi/homilies/2008/documents/hf_ben-xvi_hom_20081005_apertura-sinodo_en.html, (accessed February 24, 2010).

[189] Address of His Holiness Benedict XVI, "Meeting with the Bishops of Benin" (November 19, 2011), http://www.vatican.va/holy_father/benedict_xvi/speeches/2011/november/documents/hf_ben-xvi_spe_20111119_vescovi-benin_en.html (accessed on December 2, 2011).

2.2 Friendship with Jesus: The New Understanding of Jesus Christ

Christology is the foundation for Ratzinger's anthropology. His Christology is a call for a new understanding of Christ. Unique to his Christology is his understanding and recovery of Jesus of Nazareth, with whom he recommends all Christians to have a relationship. Ratzinger subscribes to a personalist Christology.[190] For him, every distance from Christ is a distance from the source of meaning and unity.[191] Thus, Ratzinger calls for a personal relationship with Christ, which he envisions as a journey that takes us from this life to the next. He is challenging modernity to a revision of the suppositions and assumptions Nietzsche instilled in it in such a sustained manner. While Nietzsche claimed that Christianity is the greatest misfortune that had befallen humankind,[192] Benedict XVI responds that Jesus Christ is the greatest fortune imaginable for humankind.[193]

The priority of Logos over ethos, of receiving over making, or being over doing lies at the heart and center of Joseph Ratzinger's theological synthesis. God is the absolute and ultimate source of all being, thus the universal principle of creation. This Logos is at the same time a lover with all the passion of true love. According to Ratzinger, "humanity is God's project. We are first and foremost receivers and not makers; who we are is much more a gift received than a task achieved. He does not deny human freedom and the importance of human action, but rather he stresses that freedom is normed and guided by what we were created as at the start."[194]

For Ratzinger, what is truly important is not makeable but has to be received. What is invisible, spiritual, has priority over the visible, the material. Therefore, "we do not make who we are through what we do but receive who we are from prior creative Love."[195] Ratzinger views the divine-humanity relationship through a distinctively theological lens. Like Augustine, he is conscious of humanity's fallenness and envisages God's dealings with us as being converting and transformative—ultimately paschal; grace purifies and turns nature around. There could not be grace without the cross.[196]

---

[190] de Gaál, *The Theology of Pope Benedict XVI*, 16.

[191] Ibid.

[192] Friedrich Nietzsche, *Basic Writings of Nietzsche*, trans. Walter Kaufmann (New York: Random House, Inc., 1968), 23.

[193] de Gaál, *The Theology of Pope Benedict XVI*, 6.

[194] James Corkery, *Joseph Ratzinger's Theological Ideas: Wise Cautions and Legitimate Hopes* (New York: Paulist Press, 2009), 31–33.

[195] Ibid., 33.

[196] Ibid., 34.

Ratzinger insists that as humans, we have a relationship with the supernatural which is mediated by sacraments. He writes,

> Sacraments are foundational for Christian existence, for they express the vertical dimension of human existence. They point to the call of God, which is the thing that makes human beings human. We are beings of dialogue. What makes us human is that we are called to be partners of God in a dialogue which begins when we are created and this dialogue will never end. In this dialogue we are constituted as relational, other-directed and open. This dialogue becomes human in Christ. This dialogue with God is not an isolated, vertical, or historical affair, but rather it occurs through our dialogue with others. It takes place in history; it occurs in the "we" of our brothers and sisters in Christ with whom we call God Father. Thus humanity has a dialogical character. Each person stands in direct relationship with God. Dialogue is at the center of God's work of creation and salvation. We are made for God. Therefore, programs directed solely to our material well-being will not satisfy our deepest longings.[197]

Ratzinger goes and asserts that man must accept his status as creature, made by a superior reality. According to him, the mentality of "makability" tells us that we must free ourselves from every requirement to receive, from all dependency. We must stand on our own, independent of others and of God. This mentality prevails into society today. Ratzinger responds to this mentality by boldly maintaining that

Relationlessness is not our truth. Cut off from relationships, our truth is denied and with it, our freedom, for freedom and truth go together. God is not the enemy of our freedom, but its ground. When people deny their creatureliness, seeing it as an imposition from outside, they end up replacing God with a capital "G" with a whole host of exploitative small "g" gods, such as commercial forces, greed, public opinion, etc. The tyranny of these is an enslavement far greater (Gen 3:3– the original sin).[198]

Uncoupled from truth, humanity dies, Ratzinger believes.[199] Why? Because as human beings, we receive a dialogical, relational essence and are called to live this in history within an existence that is at once gift and task. "We have

---

[197] Corkery, *Joseph Ratzinger's Theological Ideas*, 38.
[198] Ibid., 40–41.
[199] Ibid., 41.

a responsibility to shape our lives, always in fidelity to what we have received as created beings. We have no freedom of our own. Our freedom is a normed freedom—not blind and directionless, but guided by the light of what is given to us with our creation."[200] But what we experience today is the fact of truth parting company with freedom. And who will restore humanity to its truth? Ratzinger sees no other help than from outside, that is, help from Jesus Christ himself.[201]

Ratzinger articulates Christ as the apex of salvation. He has two Christological emphases. One is the personal character of salvation in Christ. The other is the universal character of Christian salvation. According to him, our deepest human problem is God forgetfulness—lack of faith in God. Our deepest human need is for God's forgiving love. God's son, the second Adam, is sent as the real help "from outside" to do for us what all our human creations could not do: bring us back to the heart of the Father.[202]

Ratzinger says that the main problem today is the modern culture's doubt about Jesus being the Son of God—God himself. He calls it the "real difficulty about Christianity: the profession of faith that the man Jesus, an individual executed in Palestine round about the year 30, is the central and decisive point of all human history."[203] For Ratzinger, this is the core of Christianity. He clearly states, "The historical man Jesus is the Son of God, and the Son of God is the man Jesus. God comes to pass for man through men, nay, even more concretely, through the man in whom the quintessence of humanity appears and who for that very reason is at the same time God himself."[204]

Ratzinger worries about historical science. He insinuates that historical science aims at denying history by dividing faith and history. He notes that the more it does so, the more theology seeks to escape in one way or the other from the dilemma of the simultaneous experience of both. Thus today we meet here and there the attempt to establish Christology securely on the historical plane, to make it visible in spite of everything, by this method of the "accurate" and demonstrable, or the very much simpler enterprise of straightforwardly reducing it to demonstrable.[205]

> He reasons that the historical science restricts investigation
> to the phenomenon (the demonstrable) and thus can no lon-
> ger produce faith. The dilemma of transposing or reducing

---

[200] Ibid., 41.
[201] Corkery, *Joseph Ratzinger's Theological Ideas*, 41–42.
[202] Ibid., 57–58.
[203] Joseph Ratzinger, *Introduction to Christianity* (San Francisco: Ignatius Press, 1968), 193.
[204] Ibid., 194.
[205] Ibid., 196–197.

Christology to history, and that of escaping history completely and abandoning it as irrelevant to faith, can be accurately summarized in the two alternatives in which modern theology is vexed: Jesus or Christ? "Modern theology begins by turning away from Christ and taking refuge in Jesus as a figure who is historically comprehensible, only to make an about-turn at the climax of this movement . . . and flee in the opposite direction back to Christ, a flight, however, that at the present moment is already starting to change back into the new flight from Christ to Jesus."[206]

Ratzinger refers to this as "liberal Christianity,"[207] which reduced the original Creed by a process of "purification." He rejects Harnack's theology[208] as

A fleeing back from the pure kerygma and from the pale ghost of the historical Jesus to the most human beings, whose humanity seems to them in a secularized world like the last shimmer of the divine left after the "death of God." This is what is happening today in the "death of God" theology, which tells us that, although we no longer have God, Jesus remains to us as the symbol of trust that gives us courage to go on in the midst of a world emptied of God, his humanity is to be a sort of proxy for the God who can no longer be discovered.[209]

Ratzinger believes that the attempt to outflank historical Christianity out of the historian's perspective, resorting to construct a pure Jesus by whom one should then be able to live, is intrinsically absurd. He insists that Jesus cannot exist without the Christ, because in reality, Jesus only subsists as the Christ and the Christ only subsists in the shape of Jesus.[210] The Christian faith, Ratzinger asserts, is not a reconstruction or a theory but a present, a living reality.[211]

---

[206] Ibid., 198.

[207] Ratzinger, *Introduction to Christianity*, 198.

[208] Ratzinger worried about Harnack's utterances: "Not the Son but the Father belongs in the Gospel as Jesus preached it . . . Where faith in the Son had divided people—Christians from non-Christians, Christians of different denominations from one another—knowledge of the Father can unite. While the Son only belongs to a few, the Father belongs to all, and all to him. Where faith has parted people, love can bind them together. Jesus versus Christ, and this means 'away from dogma, onward to love.'" In Joseph Cardinal Ratzinger, *Introduction to Christianity* (San Francisco: Ignatius Press, 1968), 199.

[209] Ratzinger, *Introduction to Christianity*, 200.

[210] Ibid., 201.

[211] Ibid.

Ratzinger elucidates that Jesus is the true Messiah—Jesus Christ—a unity that conceals the experience of the identity of existence and mission. The point of departure of faith in Jesus is the cross which frequently confuses the historians. He says that Jesus did not call himself "messiah," but Pilate did in the execution notice in all the international languages of the day, as the executed king = Messiah, *Christus*, of the Jews.[212]

He thus writes,

> This execution notice, the death sentence of history, became with paradoxical unity the "profession of faith," the real starting point and taproot of the Christian faith, which holds Jesus to be the Christ: as the crucified criminal, this Jesus is the Christ, the King. His crucifixion is his coronation; his kingship is his surrender of himself to men, the identification of word, mission, and existence in the yielding up of this very existence. His existence is thus his word. He is word because he is love. From the cross faith understands in increasing measure that this Jesus did not just do and say something; that in him message and person are identical, that he is all along what he says.[213]

Ratzinger has an impeccable belief in Jesus as the Christ. Anyone who recognizes the Christ in Jesus, and who equally recognizes Jesus and the Christ, grasps the total oneness of person and work in the second person of the Blessed Trinity of Christian faith—to him the decisive factor. Their mutual separation is unthinkable. For "to believe in a Christ so understood means simply to make love the content of faith, so that from this angle one can perfectly well say, love is faith."[214]

Ratzinger insists on the true divinity and humanity of Jesus. As we read in John 1:1, "the Word was with God, and the Word was God." This word became flesh and dwelt among us. In other words, Jesus became man—taking on two natures—of God and man. This same Jesus is the one who was condemned to a shameful death and died a failure. But he rose and will return in the future as the Son of Man, Messiah.[215]

Therefore, the method of historians refuting this mystery is invalid according to Ratzinger. He says that the Christology of John and of the church's creed,

---

[212] Ibid., 206.
[213] Ratzinger, *Introduction to Christianity*, 206.
[214] Ibid., 208.
[215] Ibid., 213.

in contrast, goes much farther in its radicalism, inasmuch as it acknowledges being itself as act and states,

> Jesus is his work. Then there is no man behind it all to whom nothing has really happened. His being is pure *actualitas* of "from" and "for." But precisely because this "being" is no longer separable from its *actualitas*, it coincides with God and is at the same time the exemplary man, the man of the future, through whom it becomes evident how very much man is still the coming creature, a being still, so to speak, waiting to be realized; and what a short distance man has even now progressed toward being himself.[216]

Next, Ratzinger turns to the theology of the incarnation and the theology of the Cross. The theology of Incarnation, Ratzinger believes, "is the interlocking of God and man, the redemptive factor, the real future of man, on which all lines must finally converge."[217] On the other hand, "the theology of the Cross is the event, the testimony about the activity of God in the Cross and Resurrection, an activity that conquered death and pointed to Jesus as the Lord and as the hope of humanity."[218] Thus, according to Ratzinger, the theology of the Incarnation must pass over into the theology of the Cross and become one with it. It is the theology of the Cross that gives full meaning to the theology of the Incarnation. Thus, the purpose of the incarnation is fulfilled in the mystery of the Cross—our redemption.[219]

He argues that Jesus Christ is "the last man," the "last Adam," in whom *hominization* has truly reached its goal.[220] He hereby cancels out Hegel's claim that he (Hegel) was "the world spirit—the absolute spirit incarnate."[221] Jesus's existence concerns all mankind Ratzinger claims.

> The New Testament makes this perceptible by calling him an "Adam"; in the Bible this word expresses the unity of the whole creature "man," so that one can speak of the biblical idea of a "corporate personality." So if Jesus is called "Adam," this im-

---

[216] Ibid., 228.
[217] Ibid., 229.
[218] Ibid.
[219] Ratzinger, *Introduction to Christianity*, 229.
[220] Ibid., 235.
[221] Friedrich Hegel, *The Phenomenology of Mind*, trans. George Lichtheim (New York: Harper Torchbooks, 1967), 775.

plies that he is intended to gather the whole creature "Adam" in himself.[222]

He continues to assert that

> faith sees in Jesus the man in whom—on the biological plane— the next two evolutionary leap, as it were, has been accomplished, the man in whom the breakthrough out of the limited scope of humanity, out of its monadic enclosure, has occurred; the man in whom personalization and socialization no longer exclude each other but support each other; the man in whom perfect unity—"the body of Christ," says St. Paul, and even more pointedly "You are all one in Christ Jesus" (Gal 3:28)—and perfect individuality are one; the man in whom humanity comes into contact with its future, because through him it makes contact with God himself, shares in him, and thus realizes its most intrinsic potential. From here onward faith in Christ will see the beginning of a movement in which dismember humanity is gathered together more and more into the being of one single Adam, one single "body"—the man to come.[223]

He believes Johannine theology too points in the same direction. Thus, Jesus's words in John 12:32: "And I, when I am lifted up from the earth, will draw all people to myself," explain the meaning of Jesus's death on the cross. "It thus expresses the direction in which the whole Gospel is intended to point. The event of the crucifixion appears there as a process of opening, in which the scattered man-monads are drawn into the embrace of Jesus Christ, into the wide span of his outstretched arms, in order to arrive, in this union, at their goal, the goal of humanity."[224]

According to Ratzinger, Christian faith is not just a look back at what has happened in the past. Nor is it just an outlook on the eternal; for that would be Platonic and metaphysics. But it is above all things, a looking forward, a reaching out of hope. However, hope would become utopianism if its goal were only a product of man. "It is true hope precisely because it is situated in a three-dimensional coordinate system: the past, that is, the breakthrough that has already taken place; the present of the eternal, which makes divided time like

---

[222] Ratzinger, *Introduction to Christianity*, 236.
[223] Ibid., 239.
[224] Ibid., 239–240.

unity; and he who is to come, in whom God and world will touch each other, and thus, God in world, world in God will truly be the Omega of history."[225]

The awkward position of Christianity lies in the superficiality onto which the religious sentiment seems to have settled down nowadays. Thus, this superficiality must be eliminated so that the Christian faith can be credible, especially to the modern culture. In other words, Christians must live in Christ's exemplary existence, stretching out their arms to others in prayer in imitation of Christ on the cross. Hence, "the principle of love becomes the real point at which the divine manifests itself in the world, brings a further consequence with it."[226]

In conclusion, Ratzinger insists that

> the true Christian is not the denominational party member, but he who through being a Christian has become truly human; not he who slavishly observes a system of norms, but he who has become freed to simple human goodness. He takes the principle of love, if it is to be genuine, to include faith. Only thus, does it remain what it is. For without faith, which we have come to understand as a term expressing man's ultimate need to receive and to the inadequacy of all personal achievement, love becomes an arbitrary need. It cancels itself out and becomes self-righteousness; faith and love condition and demand each other reciprocally. Similarly, in the principle of love there is also present the principle of hope, which looks beyond the moment and its isolation and seeks the whole. Thus our reflections finally lead to their own accord to the words in which Paul named the main supporting pillars of Christianity: "So faith, hope, love abide, these three; but the greatest of these is love" (1 Cor 13:13).[227]

2.3 The Church: Essentially Grounded in the Eucharist (Communion)

Ratzinger stipulates three basic characteristics of the church to which tradition strongly holds. He claims these unmistakably make their appearance: "the Church is apostolic; she is a praying Church, thus tuned toward the Lord—'holy'; and she is one."[228]

---

[225] Ratzinger, *Introduction to Christianity*, 42.

[226] Ibid., 254.

[227] Ibid., 270.

[228] Joseph Ratzinger, *Pilgrim Fellowship of Faith: The Church as Communion* (San Francisco: Ignatius Press, 2002), 61.

The first sign by which the Holy Spirit manifests himself adds a fourth characteristic to these: the presence of the Spirit is displayed in the gift of tongues. In this way it reverses what happened at the tower of Babel. The new community, the new people of God, speaking in all languages, and thus from the first moment of its existence, it is portrayed as "Catholic." The realization of the dynamic contained in this sign obliges the Church to go to the ends of space and time.[229]

According to the description in the Acts of the Apostles, the first Christians persisted in the apostles' teaching and fellowship (communion)—the breaking of bread and the prayers. Ratzinger argues that the Incarnate Son is the "communion" between God and men. Therefore, being a Christian is in reality nothing other than partaking in the mystery of the Incarnation. The church, insofar as she is the church, is the body of Christ.[230]

Ratzinger's use of the term Eucharist as communion points more to the unity that is signified therein. He takes it from St. Paul's usage in his letter to the Romans. Paul mentions the term body of Christ—referring to the church—many times in his letters, but in Romans, he points out a unique element of communion/unity:

Therefore, I urge you, brothers, in view of God's mercy, to offer your bodies as living sacrifices, holy and pleasing to God—this is your spiritual act of worship. Do not conform any longer to the pattern of this world, but be transformed by the renewing of your mind. Then you will be able to test and approve what God's will is—his good, pleasing and perfect will. For by the grace given me I say to every one of you: Do not think of yourself more highly than you ought, but rather think of yourself with sober judgment, in accordance with the measure of faith God has given you. Just as each of us has one body with many members, and these members do not all have the same function, so in Christ we who are many form one body, and each member belongs to all the others. We have different gifts, according to the grace given us. (Rom 12:1–6).

In the First Epistle to the Corinthians, Paul says, "Because there is one bread, we who many are one body, for we all partake of the one bread" (1 Cor 10:17). This unity and oneness seems to be central in Ratzinger's theology of the Eucharist. The culture of relativism is on the other hand, individualistic, and this is the hitch. But the church is a community of believers, living and praying in fellowship. This fellowship and communitarian aspect of the Eucharist is what Ratzinger calls for—to live in communion with Christ and with one another. Ratzinger says that in Matthew 25:31–40, "the Judge does not ask what kind of theory a person has held about God and the world. He is not

---

[229] Ratzinger, *Pilgrim Fellowship of Faith*, 61.
[230] Ibid., 77.

asking about a confession of dogma, but solely about love. That is enough, and it saves a man. Whoever loves is a Christian."[231]

St. Thomas Aquinas stated,

> When Christ was going to leave his disciples in his proper species, he left himself with them under the sacramental species'. Jesus instituted the sacrament so that "there should be at all times among men something to show forth our Lord's Passion," given that "without faith in the Passion there could never be any salvation."[232] "In our pilgrimage, [Christ] does not deprive us of his bodily presence, but unites us with himself in this sacrament through the truth of his Body and Blood,"[233] always seen in their sacrificial condition." "Hence, this sacrament is the sign of supreme charity, and the uplifter of our hope, from such familiar union of Christ with us."[234]

Jesus's decision to stay with his people in the sacrament of the Eucharist is a sign of his great love for mankind. Therefore, the Eucharist is the highest sign of love, a sign of supreme charity as St. Thomas calls it.[235] God is love, Ratzinger emphasizes. *"Ubi caritas et amor, Deus ibi est."* As pope, Benedict XVI is, in an amplified manner, explaining this concept to humanity. His message to humanity is love.[236] His first encyclical letter was under the title *Deus*

---

[231] Benedict XVI, *Credo for Today*, 9.

[232] Thomas Aquinas, *Summa Theologica*, III (New York: Benziger Brothers, Inc.,1948), 73, 5, c.

[233] Ibid., 75, 1, c.

[234] Aquinas, *Summa Theologica*, 75, 1, c.

[235] Ibid., 75, 1, c.

[236] In his book, *Credo for Today*, Ratzinger retells a story about love. He writes, "A story current in late Judaism, in Jesus' time, tells how one day a pagan came to Rabbi Shammai, the famous head of a school, and told him that he would be willing to join the Jewish religion if the Rabbi could tell him about its beliefs in the time someone could stand on one leg. The Rabbi probably though in his mind about the five books of Moses, with all the ideas in them, and everything that Jewish interpretation had added in the meantime and had declared to be equally obligatory, necessary, and essential for salvation. As he went over all this in his mind, he finally had to admit that it would be impossible for him to summarize in a couple of sentences the whole of everything that made up the religion of Israel. The strange petitioner was not a whit discouraged. He went—if we want to put it like that—to the competition: to the other famous head of a school, Rabbi Hillel, and laid the same request before him. In contrast to Rabbi Shammai, Hillel found the suggestion in no way impossible and answered him straight out, 'Whatever is offensive to you yourself, do not do that to your neighbor. That is the whole law. Everything else is interpretation.'" In Ratzinger, *Credo for Today*, 7–8.

Caritas Est, and his second encyclical letter was *Cariats in Veritate.* They are both revolving around love, the true love which can only be experienced in the Eucharist—in communion.

The Eucharist is the greatest gift Jesus bestowed to man. In it, Jesus lives among and within his people, feeding and walking with his people through the desert to the Promised Land. As God bestowed himself to us through his beloved Son Jesus, so are we called to give ourselves to one another. In *Caritas in Veritate,* Pope Benedict illustrates that "the human being is made for gift, which expresses and makes present his transcendent dimension."[237] This means that we are gift; our very lives are gift. We are not our own, but rather God created us out of nothingness, and so, our own existence is gift. Love is the greatest commandment—to love God and neighbor—because everything is gift, and we ought to share our giftness in fraternity.

Ratzinger provides more emphasis:

> Because it is a gift received by everyone, charity in truth is a force that builds community, it brings all people together without imposing barriers or limits. The human community that we build by ourselves can never, purely by its own strength, be a fully fraternal community, nor can it overcome every division and become a truly universal community. The unity of the human race, a fraternal communion transcending every barrier, is called into being by the word of God who is Love. In addressing this key question, we must make it clear on the one hand, that the logic of gift does not exclude justice, nor does it merely sit alongside it as a second element added from without; on the other hand, economic, social and political development, if it is to be authentically human, needs to make a room for the principle of gratuitousness as an expression of fraternity.[238]

Ratzinger puts in the picture that our fraternity is out of gratuitousness. We love because we have been loved. Therefore, our love is in acknowledgment and thankfulness to God for his great gift to us. He thus thinks that even in this progressive and competitive world, there is still room for charity, charity in truth, and not for self-aggrandizement.[239] However, he regrets that, unfortunately, the world economic and political systems are overwhelmed by individualistic and utilitarian motives.

---

[237] Benedict XVI, *Charity in Truth* (Washington DC: Libreria Editrice Vaticana, 2009), 35.
[238] Benedict XVI, *Charity in Truth,* 36.
[239] Ibid.

He further notes that lack of communion or isolation is the real cause of poverty.[240] He acknowledges that all forms of poverty, including the material poverty, are born from isolation, from not being loved or from difficulties in being able to love.[241] Poverty is thus produced by a rejection of God's love by man's basic and tragic tendency to close in on himself, thinking himself to be self-sufficient or merely an insignificant fact, a stranger in the universe. "Today however, humanity appears much more interactive than in the past: this shared sense of being close to one another must be transformed into true communion. The development of peoples depends, above all, on a recognition that the human race is a single family working together in a true communion."[242]

In the conclusion of *Caritas in Veritate*, Benedict makes a statement which qualifies to be a summary for this section:

Without God man neither knows which way to go, nor even understands who he is. Only if we are aware of our calling, as individuals and as a community, to be part of God's family as his sons and daughters, will we be able to generate a new vision and muster new energy in the service of truly integral humanism. The greatest service to development, then, is a Christian humanism that enkindles charity and takes its lead from truth, accepting both as a lasting gift from God.[243]

2.4 Liturgy—Christ's Presence among Us

Next, Joseph Ratzinger presents the liturgy as another remedy. In the *The Feast of Faith*, Ratzinger puts liturgy at the center of Christian life, thus,

> Faced with the political and social crises of the present time
> and the moral challenge they offer to Christians, the problems

---

[240] Ratzinger here seems to suggest and equate lack of communion to selfishness or lack of faith. According him, "There is still an element of selfishness, something of self-satisfaction and looking back at ourselves. . . . It is at this point that faith begins. For what faith basically means is just that this shortfall that we all have in our love is made up by the surplus of Jesus Christ's love, acting on our behalf . . . Ultimately, faith means nothing other than admitting that we have this kind of shortfall; it means opening our hand and accepting a gift. Faith is thus that stage in love which really distinguishes it as love; it consists in overcoming the complacency and self-satisfaction . . . the openness of someone who does not insist on his own capabilities, but is aware of receiving something as a gift and of standing in need of it. Thus, true loving necessarily passes into the gesture of faith, and in that gesture lies a demand for the mystery of Christ . . . to reject it would be to reject both faith and love." in Ratzinger, *Credo for Today*, 12–13.

[241] Benedict XVI, *Charity in Truth*, 60.

[242] Ibid., 36.

[243] Benedict XVI, *Charity in Truth*, 85.

of liturgy and prayer could easily seem to be of second importance. But the question of the moral standards and spiritual resources that we need if we are to acquit ourselves in this situation cannot be separated from the question of worship. Only if man, every man, stands before the face of God and is answerable to him, can man be secure in his dignity as a human being. Concern for the proper form of worship, therefore, is not peripheral but central to our concern for man himself.[244]

Vatican II *Sacrosanctum Concilium*, defines liturgy as "the act in which, especially in the divine sacrifice of the Eucharist, the work of our redemption is accomplished."[245] It continues to elucidate that

It is through the liturgy, especially, that the faithful are enabled to express in their lives and manifest to others the mystery of Christ and the real nature of the true Church the Church is essentially both human and divine, visible but endowed with invisible realities, zealous in action and dedicated to contemplation, present in the world, but as a pilgrim, so constituent that in her the human is directed toward and subordinated to the divine, the visible to the invisible, action to contemplation, and this present world to that city yet to come, the object of our quest."[246] "The liturgical celebration is therefore, an action of Christ the Priest and of his Body, which is the Church, is a sacred action surpassing all others. No other action of the Church can equal its efficacy by the same title and to the same degree.[247]

---

[244] Joseph Ratzinger, *The Feast of Faith: Approaches to a Theology of the Liturgy* (San Francisco, CA: Ignatius Press, 1981), 7.

[245] "Liturgia enim, per quam, maxime in divino Eucharistiae Sacrificio, opus nostrae Redemptionis exercetur," SC 2, DH 4002.

[246] "Summe eo confert ut fideles vivendo exprimant et aliis manifestent mysterium Christi et genuinam verae Ecclesiae naturam, cuius proprium est esse humanam simul ac divinam, visibilem invisibilibus praeditam, actione ferventem et contemplationi vacantem, in mundo praesentem et tamen peregrinam; et ita quidem ut in ea quod humanum est ordinetur ad divinum eique subordinetur, quod visibile ad invisibile, quod actionis ad contemplationem, et quod praesens ad futuram civitatem quam inquirimus," SC 2, DH 4002.

[247] "Proinde omnis liturgica celebratio, utpote opus Christi sacerdotis eiusque Corporis, quod est Ecclesia, est actio sacra praecellenter, cuius efficacitatem eodem titulo eodemque gradu nulla alia actio Ecclesiae adaequat," SC 7, DH 4007.

Ratzinger regrets that "the liturgy is unfortunately manipulated ever more freely, the faithful feel that, in reality, nothing is celebrated, and it is understandable that they desert the liturgy and with it the Church."[248] He suggests that there ought to be no room for such rationalistic and relativistic ideas. All our prayers, the music, body posture, gestures, vestments, and the entire activity of worship should reflect what we believe in; that is, the descent of God among us and not a form of fashion or human drama. "Man himself cannot simply make worship. If God does not reveal himself, man is clutching empty space. When God does not reveal himself, man can, of course, from the sense of God within him, build altars "to the unknown god."

The liturgy is worship of God present in our midst. Ratzinger therefore, cautions that to give proper worship; to stand in the presence of God, man must be worthy in the first place. Like Moses and the burning bush, a person who goes to the presence of God stands on holy ground. To stand on holy ground, one needs to remove his sandals first. Liturgy offers man a chance to stand in the face of God. In liturgy, man speaks with God. Ratzinger states, "The basic reason why man can speak with God arises from the fact that God himself is speech, word. It is a prayer; an act of turning to God, a relationship."[249] Therefore, since there is a relationship with God, there can be a participation in this relationship. Hence, it requires that we relate to God in a way that does not contradict his nature—his nature is Holy.

In the same way, Ratzinger asserts that in liturgy, through the spirit of Christ, we share in the human nature of Jesus Christ. In sharing in his dialogue with God, we share in the dialogue which God is. This is prayer, which becomes a real exchange between God and man.[250] We are then identified with one another in Christ, and this is what we call "church." "We could in fact define 'Church' as the realm of man's discovery of his identity through the identification with Christ as its source."[251] Thus, if it is liturgy that we receive our full identity as a people—a church—then it is necessary that we participate in this feast as regularly as possible. Here, Ratzinger attacks the individualistic tendencies of the culture of relativism which tends to draw people away from liturgy and have private encounter with God. By so doing, this culture robs us of our very identity and our communion with Christ.

Thus, in liturgy, we commune with God and with the saints in giving proper worship to God. Liturgy takes place in the temple—a house for prayer; a house where the Almighty dwells. St. Paul reminds us that we are the temples of the Holy Spirit (1 Cor 6:19–20). If, therefore, the Lord dwells in our hearts, then

---

[248] Thornton and Susan Varenne, *The Essential Pope Benedict XVI*, 144.
[249] Ratzinger, *The Feast of Faith*, 25.
[250] Ibid., 26.
[251] Ibid.

this means that our whole lives must be a continuous worship of God. This is a call for holiness, for proper worship of God must not contradict his nature.

2.5 Catechesis

Ratzinger believes that the worst thing that Christianity has experienced in the twentieth century has not been open antagonism, but indifference toward Christianity.[252] Thus, to address this indifference, faith must once more become the salt that wounds and heals, a summons that challenges us to take a position. Ratzinger states that the last words the risen Lord spoke to his disciples commissioned them to go out into all the world and to be his witnesses (Mt 28:19f). "Therefore, evangelization is an essential part of the Christian faith—this gospel is meant to be handed down. It consists of coming to know a message that concerns everyone, because it is the truth and because man cannot be saved without the truth" (1 Tim 2:4).[253]

He beseeches the church for a renewal of catechesis, whereby faith is translated into love. He says that faith is life; it is a relationship, a knowledge that becomes love and love that comes from knowledge and leads to knowledge. Ratzinger says, "Catechesis aims at coming to know Jesus concretely. It is theoretical and practical initiation into the will of God as revealed by Jesus and lived by the community of the Lord's disciples, the family of God."[254] In other words, catechesis is the instruction of God's people as a response to the Gospel address to reason, integrating man's heart into the mind. It is a tool through which Christians are made familiar with the lifestyle of Christianity.[255]

Ratzinger proposes catechesis as a remedy to the relativistic culture. Because this culture aims at leaving everything to the interpretation of the individual, Ratzinger proposes a formal and centralized way of inculcating and disseminating the deposit of truth to the faithful. He says that in fact, the apostles were the ones to catechize people—educating people about Christ and Christian life. This means Christian life is a tradition that must be learned and passed on from generation to generation. Catechesis is thus didactic.[256] The real problem in today's culture is the attitude which despises the past, but if we are to be true Christians, we need to learn from the past and pass it on; hence, the importance of catechesis. All Christians are agents of the Gospel; that is, a catechist's primary duty is to pass on the faith to the next person.

---

[252] Joseph Ratzinger, *Gospel, Catechesis, Catechism: Sidelights on the Catechism of the Catholic Church*, (San Francisco: Ignatius Press, 1995), 37.
[253] Ibid.
[254] Ratzinger, *Gospel, Catechesis, Catechism*, 56.
[255] Ibid.
[256] Ibid., 57.

2.6 "Relativize Relativisers"

Jankunas states that Ratzinger acknowledges that in the present relativistic climate of the world, there seems to be no formula that would embrace the whole world and unite all persons. Jankunas thus presents two theses: one states that "because of existing pathologies in religion and reason, both must continually allow themselves to be purified and structured by each other, because reason will not be saved without the faith, but faith without reason will not be human."[257] The second thesis states that "although the Christian faith and western secular nationality determine the situation of the world to an extent not matched by another cultural force, nevertheless, it is important that they both learn to listen and to accept a genuine relatedness to other cultures too. Such norms and values would unite the world together once again if accepted universally and cross-culturally."[258]

Relativism adopts Kant's sense of reason, which does not accept any metaphysical knowledge. Ratzinger believes that if metaphysical knowledge is not accepted, and man is forced to remain within the limits of human perception set by Kant, then faith will atrophy. But Ratzinger insists that there exists an infinite God and he addresses us, the finite ones. One will not restore power to faith today by reducing it as much as possible to the indeterminate, but only by seeing it in its entire magnitude. Restoration of the power of faith is what will overcome relativism—relativizing the relativisers.[259]

For Ratzinger, man longs for the infinite, which is only through God, who himself became finite, that the question of being can be addressed. If one denies reason or faith, one denies an important part of a person, specifically, the person's humanness. Reason and religion will have to come together again, without merging into each other. It is not a matter of preserving the interests of all religious bodies.[260]

Ratzinger proposes that faith and reason confront relativism in the following way:

> Faith would allow God's initiative as revealed in the figure of Jesus Christ to invite man into friendship with him, and reason would acknowledge man's ability to respond to the invitation to his longing for truth and the infinite. In this effort to confront and overcome relativism, both faith and reason

---

[257] Jankunas, *The Dictatorship of Relativism*, 209.
[258] Ibid., 209–210.
[259] Ibid., 211.
[260] Ibid., 213.

have to come together, otherwise faith without reason ends in fideism, but reason without faith ends in nihilism.[261]

At the end of *Dominus Jesus*, Ratzinger makes it clear that the equality he sees as being a presupposition of interreligious dialogue refers to the parties who are involved in the dialogue. It does not refer to doctrinal content nor to Jesus Christ in relation to the founders of other religions. Dialogue belongs to the evangelizing mission of the church—proclamation of the truth revealed by God in Christ and entrusted to the church as its mission. Thus, Catholics' primary commitment must be to the proclamation of Christian truth.[262]

Ratzinger insists. "Do not bow to political correctness, for this is what the 'dictatorship of relativism' demands. Instead, get things clear beforehand. Questions of truth must not be sacrificed to the relativistic demands of political correctness."[263]

Hence,

> In an age where objective values are challenged—being made relative to the whims and desires of individuals, Ratzinger emphasizes the idea of createdness as solution to this. Human beings are not just blind products of chance but rather as God's "project," receiving who and what we are from God's creating love. And it is this—this which is received—that norms/guides how we are to live. Hence, there are objective values. Values are discovered not invented.[264]

2.7 Blaise Pascal's Wager, *Veluti etsi Deus Daretur*

Jankunas states that this is about the political moralism of the 1970s[265]—a moralism that took the wrong direction, since it lacked the serenity born of rationality. In this age of the Enlightenment, the attempt was made to understand and define the essential norms of morality by saying that these would be valid *esti Deus non daretur*, even if God did not exist. "We must therefore, reverse the axiom of the Enlightenment and say: even the one who does not succeed in finding the path to accepting the existence of God ought nevertheless to try to live and to direct his life *veluti si Deus daretur*, as if God did indeed exist."[266]

---

[261] Jankunas, *The Dictatorship of Relativism*, 214.
[262] Jankunas, *The Dictatorship of Relativism*, 100–101.
[263] Ibid., 102.
[264] Ibid., 106–107.
[265] Ibid., 217.
[266] Ibid.

Jankunas further says that according to Ratzinger, all who have claimed to know God and to prove his existence without Jesus Christ have done so ineffectively. Apart from him and without scripture, without original sin, without the necessary mediator who was promised and who came, it is impossible to prove absolutely that God exists, or to teach sound doctrine and sound morality.

> Knowledge of God without Christ is incomplete. For it is through Jesus Christ alone that one knows God, and it is only through Jesus Christ that one knows about himself. Knowledge of God as revealed in Jesus Christ also requires faith. If, after all, truth is one, it cannot be equally divided among all religions, nor can the ways in which those religions lead to the truth be equally directed and unequivocal. Therefore, in search for truth, only Christianity is able to satisfy with answers.[267]

2.8 The Power of Witness

At the conclusion of his visit to Britain, in Westminster Hall, Pope Benedict stated,

> I recall the figure of St. Thomas, the great scholar and statesman, who is admired by believers and non-believers alike for the integrity with which he followed his conscience, even at the cost of displeasing the sovereign whose "good servant" he was, because he chose to serve God first. The dilemma which he faced More in those difficult times, the perennial question of the relationship between what is owed to Caesar and what is owed to God, allows me the opportunity to reflect with you briefly on the proper place of religious belief within the political process.[268]

By giving an example of Thomas More, who chose to serve God first and above all, he was appealing to the people of Britain to be witnesses to the faith—putting God first. Through the power of witness that More portrayed, the Catholic faith remained alive amid trials. Even if he was killed, his death

---

[267] Jankunas, *The Dictatorship of Relativism*, 223–224.

[268] Pope Benedict XVI, "Pope's Westminster Hall Speech in Full," (September 17, 2010), BBC News UK, http://www.bbc.co.uk.news/uk-11352704 (accessed October 1, 2010).

did not kill the faith but instead, like Tertullian[269] said, became the seed of Catholicism in Britain. Relativism aims at extorting religion from public life of society. It wants matters of faith to descend into the secrecy of people's hearts for the sake of peaceable living. Relativism is the new main persecutor of Christianity of our time.

The political culture today advocates for democracy and peace for a harmonious living in society. It feels obliged to even rule over matters of faith. It desires to set norms for religion, fashion a morality that is neutral and circumvent mentioning of any "sensitive" issues in public. However, Ratzinger thinks otherwise. For him, neither politics nor religion should dictate norms for the other. Religion is not a problem for legislators to solve, Ratzinger says. And moreover, religion has a part to play in politics. He says,

> The role of religion in political debate is not so much to supply these norms, as if they could not be known by non-believers— still less to propose concrete political solutions, which would lie altogether outside the competence of religion—but rather to help purify and shed light upon the application of reason to the discovery of objective moral principles.[270]

Religion, therefore, forms the conscience and is the light for society, including political organizations. Christians must keep this light burning in their society. Jesus taught, "You are the light of the world. A city built on a hill cannot be hidden. No one after lighting a lamp puts it under the bushel basket, but on the lampstand, and it gives light to all in the house. In the same way, let your light shine before others, so that they may see your good works and give glory to your Father in heaven" (Mt 5:14–16). If Christianity is the light of the world, it must therefore shine, even if this light is not always welcome. Benedict XVI regrets that "there are those who would advocate that the voice of religion be silenced, or at least relegated to the purely private sphere."[271] This often leads to open or secret persecution of believers. It is cause for anxiety for religions and for Christianity in particular.

However, Ratzinger is more worried about the persecution that comes from within—when the Christians, who are supposed to uphold the faith, decide

---

[269] Tertullian stated, "*Sanguis martyrum semen Christianorum*" (The blood of martyrs is the seed of Christians), in Robert D. Sider, *Christian and Pagan in the Roman Empire: The Witness of Tertullian* (Washington, DC: The Catholic University of America Press, 2001), 69.

[270] Pope Benedict XVI, "Pope's Westminster Hall Speech in Full" (September 17, 2010), BBC News UK, http://www.bbc.co.uk.news/uk-11352704 (accessed October 1, 2010).

[271] Ibid.

to compromise their faith. The church has thrived on persecution, and it will continue to subsist until the end of time. However, if those custodians of the faith fear to act it out, then the worst would happen. Ratzinger thinks that in the world of constant change and progressiveness, "there is a tendency to overturn and overhaul everything; get rid of the old and replace them with new. Among those that the world would love to see changed is Christianity itself. The world has no tolerance for Christianity because it posts it in the medieval times."[272] New ideas and systems need to be created instead of clinging to the past, so the world thinks. Those who are inclined to conserving the roots of society are referred to as conservatives; these include those who conserve Christian roots. To conserve is not a bad term, but in this respect, conservatives are so regarded.

Nevertheless, Ratzinger insists,

> Christians could not simply want everything to remain exactly as it was. The book of Revelation, which certainly stands on the periphery of the New Testament with its view of the empire, nevertheless made it clear to everyone that there are things that must not be preserved, things that had to be changed.[273]

Truth is not among the things that need to change. The truth will always remain and will set us free. Ratzinger says that the book of Daniel (2:44) talks of the symbol of a kingdom that the God of heaven and earth will establish and that will never pass away. In this light, Ratzinger seems to say that God's kingdom is eternal. God's Christian empire will never come to an end; and if so, we too are eternal—we have a destiny beyond this world.

2.9 Conclusion

Ratzinger makes recourse to the truth and conscience, as remedy to the relativistic culture. He feels that these two (truth and conscience) cannot be put to a vote. Rather, they are universal concepts from the power above. If these are listened to, then the problem of relativism can be defeated. He thus writes,

> Naturally we tend to think of freedom as the true good of human beings; all other goods seem controversial today. We do not want the state to impose one particular idea of the good on us. The problem becomes even clearer when we employ

---

[272] Joseph Ratzinger, *Values in a Time of Upheaval* (San Francisco: Ignatius Press, 2006), 11.
[273] Ibid., 12.

the concept of truth to clarify the concept of the good, since we think today that respect for the freedom of the individual makes it utterly wrong for the state to decide the question of truth—and this in turn means that we do not think it possible for a community as such to discern truth, and thus truth about what is good. The concept of truth has in fact moved into the zone of antidemocratic intolerance. It is not now a public good, but something private. It may perhaps be the good of specific groups, but it is not the truth of society as a whole. The modern concept of democracy seems indissoluble linked to that of relativism. It is relativism that appears to be the real guarantee of freedom.[274]

According to Ratzinger, "the truth is not a product of politics [the majority] but is antecedent to political activity and sheds light on it. It is not praxis that creates truth but truth that makes praxis possible."[275] Thus, Ratzinger makes it clear that it is truth that is the source of true freedom, just as Jesus said, "The truth will make you free" (Jn 8:32).

[274] Ratzinger, *Values in a Time of Upheaval*, 55.
[275] Ibid., 56.

Chapter Three

3.0 Stanley Hauerwas' Analysis of Modern Society

While Ratzinger visualizes a kind of political conspiracy to relativize the Christian doctrine,[276] Hauerwas envisages a "democratic policing of Christianity."[277] In both ways, the target is the truth of Christianity, being compromised and relativized. Relativizing Christianity breaks down the deposit of truth in the same way democratic policing of Christianity does. Hauerwas describes the letting go of absolute truth, norms, and values and replacing them with subjective/relative ones and systematically ensuring that the objective ones never come back into play. Like Ratzinger, Hauerwas too believes this is a political movement, but stresses more the role of the Christians themselves. According to Hauerwas, "Christians are worse persecutors of Christianity. Most Christians in America are willing to allow fellow Christians to doubt that God is Trinity, but they would excommunicate anyone who does not believe in human rights."[278]

According to Hauerwas, liberalism emasculated Christianity in the name of societal peace. "The 'secular' is not out there in the world, but it is in the souls of most people, including myself, who continue to identify themselves as Christians."[279] Evidently, Hauerwas' greatest pain is that

> Christians have learned to police their convictions in the name
> of sustaining such social orders. They cannot appear in public

---

[276] Thornton and Susan Varenne, eds., *The Essential Pope Benedict*, 229.
[277] Hauerwas, *Dispatches from the Front*, 93.
[278] Ibid., 6.
[279] Ibid., 93.

using explicit Christian language since that would offend other actors in our alleged pluralist polity. But if this is genuinely a pluralist society, why should Christians not be able to express their most cherished convictions in public? If we are in an age of identity-politics, why does the identity of Christians need to be suppressed?[280]

Like Ratzinger, Hauerwas critiques both sociopolitical relativism and religious relativism. He calls for Christians to nonviolently resist relativism. Hauerwas is a pacifist, a moralist, and a systematic theologian with a profound respect for the biblical foundations of Christianity, tradition, and authority of the church.

3.1 The Modern/Contemporary World

While modernity was characterized by rationalism, the contemporary post-modern world is characterized by relativism. Modernism deliberately sought to depart from tradition to new innovative forms of expression, trying to reconcile Christianity with the findings of modern science and philosophy. This meant departing from the Christian roots that constituted the premodern world. It was a period of free expression—unrestricted style of living. Modernism, to a greater extent, led to the imploding of the world systems—sociopolitical, economic, and religious systems. Ihab Hassan defined modernism as:

The disenchantment of our culture with culture itself . . . the bitter line of hostility to civilization that runs through it (modern literature) . . . the idea of losing oneself up to the point of self-destruction, of surrendering oneself to experience without regard to self-interest or conventional morality, of escaping wholly from the societal bond.[281]

Despite the progress which dawned with modernism, there were also dire consequences as well, especially in matters of faith; for religion became a matter of pure rationalism. Man became the center of the universe and God was removed from the world stage. This drift still continues in the postmodern world. Even though Hauerwas does not really recognize the distinction

---

[280] Stanley Hauerwas, *Dispatches from the Front: Theological Engagements with the Secular* (Durham, NC: Duke University Press, 1995), 93.

[281] Ihab Hassan, wrote an article in a book Lawrence Cahoone, ed., *From Modernism to Postmodernism: An Anthology* (Cambridge, MA: Blackwell Publishers Inc., 1996), 391.

between modernity and postmodernity, he realizes that the worst upshot from these two periods was the removal of God from the world. Both the modern and postmodern worlds deny God and turn man into a god.

Hauerwas does not want to refer to the contemporary period as postmodern. He claims,

> I am just postmodern enough not to trust postmodern as a description of our times. The very description "postmodern" cannot help but privilege the practices and intellectual formations of modernity. For example, calling this a postmodern age reproduces the modernist assumption that history must be policed by periods.[282]

The possible danger that Hauerwas envisions in policing history by periods is the fact that this leads to policing Christianity as well, since Christianity is also a historical event. And this is actually what is happening in the contemporary society, where a tendency to situate Christianity in the past is dominant. So postmodernity in one sense would also refer to post-Christianity. Hauerwas states that "modernity was created by a deliberate rejection of the past, but ironically modernity is now our past. Accordingly, post-modernity is still in the line of modernity, as rebellion against rebellion is still rebellion."[283]

Postmodernity can be described as a condition or a state of being associated with changes to institutions and conditions and with social and political results and innovations, globally but especially in the west since the 1960s. It is loosely identified with the Progressive Era.[284] It represents the culmination of the process of constant change in pursuit of progress, where constant change has become the status quo and the notion of progress obsolete.[285] This craze of unwarranted progressiveness worries Hauerwas. What remains of the Christian doctrine in this influx of change? Progress per se is not a bad idea, but what perturbs Hauerwas seems to be the superfluous quest for progress for its own sake without putting into question the foundations of the society. According to Hauerwas, the mere change and progress in the postmodern context impedes the universality or Catholicity and relevance of Christianity today.[286]

---

[282] Stanley Hauerwas, *Sanctify Them in the Truth: Holiness Exemplified* (Nashville, TN: Abingdon Press, 1998), 191.

[283] Ibid.

[284] Michael Murphy, *A Theology of Criticism: Balthasar, Postmodernism, and the Catholic Imagination* (New York, NY: Oxford University Press, 2008), 19.

[285] Murphy, *A Theology of Criticism*, 19.

[286] "In modernity, a mechanistic metaphysic is combined with a sentimental account of God. In this way the pagan assumption that god or the gods are to be judged by how well

Paul Lakeland claims that the semantic implications of postmodernity mislead us.[287] Instead, Paul Lakeland states that the term postmodernity refers to "elements in our contemporary world that manifest a breakdown of what have previously been taken to be 'givens,' fundamental coordinates of experience; and on the other hand, have the sentiments of a continuity of the past, relational to that which it supersedes."[288] Hauerwas tends to understand the postmodern age in the latter sense—that it is a continuation of the modern age, that is, taking the perspectives of the modern age to a higher level. He teaches that "modernity intended to serve the god that mattered for them, that is the human. By so doing, modernity was another form of atheism. 'Postmodernists,' in their quest to be thorough in their atheism, now deny that the human exists."[289]

According to Hauerwas,

> The philosophical developments that gave original impetus to these now widespread political movements intended if possible to defeat or replace Christianity in the name of the human or, failing that, at least to render Christian convictions at best "private" having no role for the public discernment of evil or good.[290]

3.1.1 A Changed World

The strangeness of our times for Christians is perceptible in Hauerwas' statement: "Who do you think you are to tell anyone else how to live? What gives you that right? You must be some kind of fundamentalist or fanatic. I find it odd that in our time many people believe we cannot or should avoid telling one another how to live. That is but a sign of the corruption of our age and why we are in such desperate need of conversion."[291] Hauerwas says that we all live in the same world, we all want the same thing, we all see the same things, conflict is thought to be irrational—a failure to communicate.[292]

---

it or they insure the successful outcome of human purposes is underwritten in the name of Christianity." In Stanley Hauerwas, *Working with Words: On Learning to Speak Christian* (Eugene, Oregon: Cascade Books, 2011), 12, also Cf. *Naming the Silence*, 56–58.

[287] Paul Lakeland, *Postmodernity: Christian Identity in a Fragmented Age* (Minneapolis, MN: Augsburg Fortress, 1997), 1.

[288] Ibid., 1–2.

[289] Hauerwas, *Sanctify Them in the Truth*, 191.

[290] Stanley Hauerwas, *Working with Words: On Learning to Speak Christian* (Eugene, Oregon: Cascade Books, 2011), 31.

[291] Hauerwas, *Dispatches from the Front*, 5–6.

[292] Hauerwas, *Dispatches from the Front*, 6.

Hauerwas believes that the agony of liberal Christians, whose advocates seek to show that Christianity can be made reasonable within the epistemic presuppositions of modernity, is that the very people they are trying to convince could care less. Robbed of any power by the politics of liberalism, what remains for Christianity is to become another "meaning system."[293] "Christian discourse is not a set of beliefs aimed at making our lives more coherent; rather, it is a constitutive set of skills that requires the transformation of the self to rightly see the world."[294]

Hence, for Hauerwas, being Christian is not synonymous with making value free choices. Rather, Hauerwas believes that being Christian means acceptability of being and "creaturedness," because as creatures, there are norms laid out for them by the creator. The argument below illustrates this:

> I have found it hard to know how to enter the debate about abortion since I do not believe the issue for Christians can be framed in "pro-life" or "pro-choice" terms. Such descriptions are attempts to win the political battle on the most minimum set of agreements—that is, that abortion is about the sanctity of life or freedom of women. As a result, abortion is abstracted from those practices through which our lives are ordered that we might as a community be in position to welcome children. The most determinative political loyalty for Christians is the Church. Liberalism produces characters who believe what they do is not who they are, as well as moral theories, deontic and utilitarian alike, that are designed to underwrite the lack of connection between our being and our doing.[295]

Hauerwas also discredits the education systems, particularly in universities. He believes this is one agent of the relativistic notion. He worries that universities have developed the convention in the contemporary university that enables the teaching of religion without offense. For example, Hauerwas points out that "students are offered courses in 'Hebrew Bible' to avoid the Christian designation Old Testament. The problem with such a strategy is that courses in Hebrew Bible usually consist of the reconstruction of the history of the text created by Protestant liberalism."[296]

He notes that the reason most teachers shy away from the responsibility to change their students' lives is the absence of any sense of legitimacy or

---

[293] Ibid., 7.
[294] Ibid., 5–6.
[295] Ibid., 11–12.
[296] Ibid., 15.

authority for that task. "Liberals celebrate this, teaching us to call the absence of authority—and the hierarchy on which any account of authority depends—freedom."[297] He believes that generally, Christians are traditionally and morally discredited for most people in universities. This robs Christian and non-Christian alike of resources for understanding our world. The disciplinary character of the knowledge which dominates the university impedes any serious theological engagement, Hauerwas regrets.[298]

He calls for a Christian resistance to the powers that would subvert the Gospel. He thinks the Roman Catholics are a fascinating example for such a process in America. He feels that instead of confronting a regnant Islam, Christians in the West should instead confront the failings of a dying Christian civilization.

> Our difficulty is that we—the, most secular intellectuals—cannot name that conflict as religious, since most of us have been trained to believe that religion is a thing of the past or a matter of one's private beliefs. Liberalism emasculated Christianity in the name of societal peace. That the Christian traditionally and morally discredited for most people in Universities robs Christian and non Christian alike of resources for understanding our world.[299]

According to Hauerwas, the "secular" is not out there in the world, but it is in the souls of most people, including himself,[300] who continue to identify themselves as Christians.

> I was trained to be a theologian, but one who was capable in the contemporary university. Somehow along the way I have managed to find myself caught in a position that offends most Christians, as well as fitting uneasily into the culture of the

---

[297] Ibid.

[298] Hauerwas, *Dispatches from the Front*, 15.

[299] Ibid., 16–17.

[300] Ironically, relativism seems to be rooted in the hearts of the people who are supposed to uphold it, for instance the present day theologians. Hauerwas says that "some theologians in modernity have tried to split the difference between speech about God and the complexities of human life, with the result that their theology is more about 'us' than about God. When that happens, it is not at all clear that you need the word 'God' at all. If my work has seemed to be in your face, I think it has been so because I have tried to show that 'God' is a necessary word." In Stanley Hauerwas, *Hanna's Child: A Theologians' Memoir* (Grand Rapids, MI: William B. Eerdmans Publishing Company, 2010), 236.

university.[301] I am angry at Christians, including myself, for allowing ourselves to be so compromised that the world can no longer tell what difference it makes to worship the Trinity.[302] Some fear that people will be forced to think what is only politically correct—that is, that they cannot say certain kinds of things about women, blacks, or gay.[303]

It is patent in Hauerwas' teaching that the more dangerous aspect of relativism does not rely in the sociopolitical arrangement, but rather, Christians themselves have learned to police their convictions in the name of sustaining such social orders. He regrets that Christians today fail to appear in public using explicit Christian language since that would offend other actors in our alleged pluralist polity. He then wonders, "But if this is genuinely a pluralist society, why should Christians not be able to express their most cherished convictions in public? If we are in an age of identity-politics, why does the identity of Christians need to be suppressed?"[304]

3.1.2 Religion and Politics in the New World

Hauerwas sees religion and politics as political rivals. In the Middle Ages, there was a separation of state and religion; religion was withdrawing from the world because the world was evil and the church took herself to be holy. Christians were discouraged from getting involved in politics because it was a dirty game. They alienated themselves and "exiled" themselves to the "holy land." This was the case with the monastic movement. However, Hauerwas thinks that withdrawal from the world is no solution. Instead, he seems to think that religion should be as political as possible. He refers to the church as an alternative state—a new polis.[305] For him "Christianity is just a matter of politics as defined by the gospel, to join a countercultural phenomenon, a new polis called Church."[306]

He criticizes the depolitization of the salvation or religion. He believes that the withdrawal of the church from the world in medieval times was a mistake that made the church to develop into a separated sacramental sphere. This in

---

[301] Hauerwas, *Dispatches from the Front*, 19.

[302] Ibid.

[303] Ibid., 86.

[304] Hauerwas, *Dispatches from the Front*, 93.

[305] Stanley Hauerwas, *In Good Company: Church as Polis* (Notre Dame, IN: University of Notre Dame Press, 1995), 184.

[306] Ibid., 184.

turn contributed to the secularization of the world.[307] He therefore suggests an active political Christianity that offers an alternative to the secular politics. Hauerwas re-echoes and re-present Augustine's two cities.[308]

Hauerwas does not concur with the democratic tendencies of Christianity. It is patent in his analysis that these are the cause of the problem. He seems to believe in a more disciplined church under the one authority of God through his word. The word of God is not part of human politics, and it is therefore not subject to majority decisions. Grounded in the word of God, the Christian Church cannot practice an independent democracy, but only in as far as she conforms to the will and authority of her master. Therefore, Hauerwas' feud with democracy stems from the one-sided or tunnel view of reality, that is, the human democratic alone.

> I have provided this background of Christian justifications of democracy because I am obviously extremely critical of them. I regard them as mystifications of the political process in which we find ourselves, and accordingly as failing to provide Christians with the skills of discernment to help us name those powers that rule us. The practices of liberal societies have rendered our convictions as Christians puerile. In the name of supporting democracy, Christians police their own

---

[307] Ibid., 193.

[308] "Accordingly, two cities have been formed by two loves: the earthly by the love of self, even to the contempt of God; the heavenly by the love of God, even to the contempt of self. The former, in a word, glories in itself, the latter in the Lord. For the one seeks glory from men; but the greatest glory of the other is God, the witness of conscience. The one lifts up its head in its own glory; the other says to its God, 'Thou art my glory, and the lifter up of mine head.' In the one, the princes and the nations it subdues are ruled by the love of ruling; in the other, the princes and the subjects serve one another in love, the latter obeying, while the former take thought for all. The one delights in its own strength, represented in the persons of its rulers; the other says to its God, 'I will love Thee, O Lord, my strength.' And therefore the wise men of the one city, living according to man, have sought for profit to their own bodies or souls, or both, and those who have known God 'glorified Him not as God, neither were thankful, but became vain in their imaginations, and their foolish heart was darkened; professing themselves to be wise,—that is, glorying in their own wisdom, and being possessed by pride,—they 'became fools, and changed the glory of the incorruptible God into an image made like to corruptible man, and to birds, and four-footed beasts, and creeping things.' For they were either leaders or followers of the people in adoring images, 'and worshipped and served the creature more than the Creator, who is blessed forever.' But in the other city there is no human wisdom, but only godliness, which offers due worship to the true God, and looks for its reward in the society of the saints, of holy angels as well as holy men, that God may be all in all" in Augustine, *The City of God*, trans. Marcus Dods (New York: Random House, Inc., 1950), 477.

convictions to ensure none of those convictions might cause difficulty for making democracy successful.[309]

Hauerwas further blames Christians' fascination with democracy as "our" form of government. He rules that this has rendered us defenseless when, for example, the state goes to war. "No aspect of democratic ideology has been more destructive to the Church than the assumption that democracy is or should be that form of government in which the people rule."[310]

Conclusively, Hauerwas indicts democracy for robbing the church of virtue. For him, democracy and virtue are enemies; for virtue stems from the fear of God and allowing him to lead man's life, whereas democracy grants total independence to an individual to make decisions that nurture their own destinies. Below, Hauerwas argues,

> The empowerment of the common man has robed the Church internally of those forms of discipline through which people acquire the virtues that ironically may be of service to what people take to be democratic social orders. The problem with American democracy is not the congress, or the president, or the rule of law, or the market, the problem is simply the American people who believe that, at least in the realm of politics, their task is to pursue their own interests.[311]

According to Hauerwas, the church's greatest enemies in the world today are the: "Freedom—institutionalized economically as capitalism and politically as democracy. That story, and the institutions that embody it, is the enemy we must attack through Christian preaching."[312] For Hauerwas, democracy is the root of relativism because it rejects universal values as it identifies them with communism or socialism. Democracy also attacks Christianity for the same reason. But Hauerwas says that

> It would be tempting to put Christians on the side of those who advocate "universal moral values" as a bulwark against "relativism." That strategy, however, fails to see that "relativism" is the creation of the assumption that "universal values" can be

---

[309] Hauerwas, *In Good Company*, 104–105.
[310] Ibid., 105.
[311] Ibid.
[312] Hauerwas, *Sanctify Them in the Truth*, 198.

known apart from formation in a community capable of recog-
nizing the evil it does in the name of those same "values."[313]

3.1.3 Unbelief

Prior to Ratzinger, Balthasar had been perceived as one of the most prominent opponents to modern atheism and disbelief. Hauerwas concurs with him
and joins him in the fight. Balthasar teaches,

> Christianity must be examined primarily in its historical as-
> pect. It cannot be derived from the nature of man; considered
> in the way its historical sources as well as its representatives
> invariably present it, it is a phenomenon that rests wholly on
> the historical fact of the appearance of Christ. This includes
> his life and death, his self-interpretation in word and exis-
> tence, and finally his resurrection from the dead, confirmed
> by trustworthy witnesses. A non-Christian, it is true, may
> afterwards criticize this phenomenon from outside, that is to
> say from the human and scientific point of view. Nevertheless,
> in order to grasp the essence of Christianity, one will first have
> to consider what it says about itself. Its basis is then seen to
> be the existence and self-revelation of Christ as the God-man
> Savior, hence trusting faith in him is the organ that mediates
> the knowledge of this truth.[314]

Like Balthasar, Hauerwas thinks that in order to understand, one needs
to believe first. Hence, faith leads to understanding and understanding breeds
more faith in return. It is Augustine's famous saying, *"Credo ut intelligam"*[315]
reckons well with Hauerwas' belief, or rather, Hauerwas concurs with Augustine.
Christianity however, is facing so many critics and disbelief from people who
base their disbelief on the outside. Most unbelief is based on science and tech-

---

[313] Hauerwas, *Working with*, 31. Hauerwas wonders, "But if we cannot rely on 'universal
values' does that not mean we live in a very dangerous world? The world has been made all
the more dangerous by attempting to save the world from danger by appealing to 'universal
values' that result in justifications to coerce those who do not share what some consider
universal." In Stanley Hauerwas, *Working with Words: On Learning to Speak Christian*
(Eugene, Oregon: Cascade Books, 2011), 32–33.

[314] Hans Urs von Balthasar, *The God Question and Modern Man* (New York: The Seabury
Press, 1967), 1–2.

[315] St. Augustine, *The Fathers of the Church: Writings of St. Augustine*, vol.2 (New York:
Cima Publishing Co., Inc., 1947), 424.

nological attitude. As Balthasar says, instead of man seeing himself as part of the created/nature, "he has become the goal of the upward movement, he sees nature coming towards him."[316]

In this regard, there is no god outside man, but man himself is god which nature serves. Hauerwas, like Balthasar, does not argue on philosophical ground but on the ground of revelation. God's existence and our faith in him do not depend on our competence to prove it; otherwise, if we failed, then he did not exist. In the end, we would be God's creators. So whether we can prove God's existence or not, God exists despite our comprehension of him. Christianity is not rationalistic religion, but rather, a revelation-based faith. For Hauerwas, "We are creatures of a God who has created and redeemed."[317] This is Hauerwas' message to the contemporary atheistic culture.

3.2 Truth and Honor

The truth of Christianity goes concurrently with the honor due to God, the author and origin of the Christian faith. As God's creation, man automatically ought to give a deserving respect and honor to him. This honor due to God goes beyond formal worship. Hauerwas stresses discipleship and witness as central elements in Christianity. He makes recourse to Paul's discussion on the church as the body of Christ. He says that Paul presumes the church is Christ's body, so immortality is not like the body becoming ill or polluted; it is to make the body ill and polluted.[318] Therefore, "questions of man having sexual relations with his stepmother (1 Cor 5), Christian men using prostitutes (1 Cor 6), eating meat sacrificed to idol (1 Cor 8–10), and proper eating of the Lord's supper (1 Cor 11), are all a question of the purity of the body and avoidance of pollution."[319]

Hauerwas thinks that Christians' knowledge of the truth should lead them to act right—giving God the honor he deserves. The honor that God deserves lie in living holy lives, because we are the Body of Christ—sharing in his holiness. Like St. Paul, Hauerwas believes that perfection is not simply a matter of individual will. Instead, "holiness is the result of our being made part of a body that makes it possible for us to be anything other than disciples."[320] He, however, notes that instead of making efforts to keep our bodies uncontaminated; fixing our eyes on the body of Christ, we have rather diverted our attention to

---

[316] Ibid., 24.
[317] Hauerwas, *Working with Words*, 16.
[318] Hauerwas, *Sanctify Them in the Truth*, 82.
[319] Ibid., 82–83.
[320] Ibid., 84.

keeping peace with one another. He feels this is false peace; for without being in peace with God, we cannot claim to live in any peace.[321]

3.2.1 Corruption of the Youth

Stanley thinks that the present trend in university education corrupts the youth. He says that their training is structured in such a way that they are either unbelievers or indifferent to matters of faith.[322] He says that the disciplinary character of the knowledge that so dominates the university impedes any serious theological engagement. He gives his own experience: "I was trained to be a theologian, but one who was capable in the contemporary university. Somehow along the way I have managed to find myself caught in a position that offends most Christians, as well as fitting uneasily into the culture of the university."[323]

He believes that the training of the youth in universities discredits Christian tradition and morality and robs the youth and most people in universities; Christian and non-Christian alike, of resources for understanding our world.[324]

3.2.2 "Resident Aliens"[325]

Hauerwas seems to agree with Peter Berger, not in as far as religious beliefs are void of meaning, but in as far as those who still hold such beliefs are alien to reality in the contemporary world. They are resident aliens.[326] Hauerwas is not insinuating any fundamentalism in terms of forcing everyone to believe. Instead, he believes Christians should in fact remain resident aliens who should not aim at changing the secular society, but rather build a community within

---

[321] Ibid.

[322] He recalls when he turned down an invitation to join a scholars' association. In his words, Hauerwas states, "The National Association of Scholars (NAS) started a chapter in order to oppose what they perceived to be a threat to the university from the postmodernists. I was asked to join but declined the 'honor.' I noted that the modernist epistemological presuppositions that shaped their understanding of 'objectivity' were the grounds that were often used to exclude theology from university curriculums." In Stanly Hauerwas, *Hannah's Child: A Theologian's Memoir* (Grand Rapids, MI: William B. Eerdmans Publishing Company, 2010), 238.

[323] Hauerwas, *Dispatches from the Front*, 19.

[324] Ibid., 17.

[325] Stanley Hauerwas and William Willimon, *Resident Aliens: A Provocative Christian Assessment of Culture and Ministry for People Who Know That Something Is Wrong* (Nashville, TN: Abingdon Press, 1989), 11.

[326] Hauerwas, *Dispatches from the Front*, 18.

the secular society that is unique, living a unique life from the society's. He suggests that Christianity ought to be an alternative society—a society within society whose residents offer and live according to God's will, living Gospel values where people worship God faithfully.[327]

He does not suggest a withdrawal from society so that Christians live in isolation or lead utopian lives. Rather, he suggests that Christians live within the present society as people who make a difference. The image of withdrawal or retreat is all wrong according to him. Hauerwas emphasizes, "The problem is not that Christians, to be faithful, must withdraw. The problem is that Christians have so identified with those orders that they no longer are able to see what difference to be Christian makes. I am not trying to force Christians to withdraw but recognize that they are surrounded."[328]

Thus, Hauerwas suggests that we Christians should learn skills to survive when surrounded by a culture they helped to create but which now threatens to destroy us. Examples of such skills he suggests include fidelity to another person for a lifetime, bringing children into an inhospitable world, praying for reconciliation with enemies, and living lives of truthfulness and honesty.[329]

3.2.3 Flight from *Foundationalism*

The present culture tends to do away with *foundationalism*. There is a current in Christianity that abhors and detaches itself from all traditional foundations and authority. This kind of Christianity wants to be free from all the past and base its teachings on only faith that comes from hearing the word of God. This trend can be referred to as "believers' Church or the free Church tradition—a family of Churches that could be interpreted as standing alongside the Roman Catholic, Orthodox, Lutheran, Reformed and Anglican traditions as a distinct type of tradition. It does not have one recognizable founder. It has no single uniform organization."[330]

This believers' church theology is a very diverse phenomenon. Hauerwas, like Yoder and McClendon, belongs to this stream of Christianity. It has a vision of an "unlimited catholicity." Hauerwas himself describes himself as "a servant to the Church catholic."[331] In another instance, Hauerwas says, "I like to think of myself as a Mennonite camp follower, but as Yoder eloquently argues in *The*

---

[327] Ibid.
[328] Hauerwas, *Dispatches from the Front*, 18.
[329] Hauerwas, *Dispatches from the Front*, 19.
[330] Hauerwas, *In Good Company*, 19.
[331] Ibid., 5.

Priestly Kingdom, he is not a Mennonite theologian, but a theologian of the Church catholic—an ambition I also share."[332]

Hauerwas thinks that *foundationism* or denominational or conventional Christianity was a mistake; that the mainstream underwrites its presumption of superiority.[333] According to him, we can know true belief only when we have struggled to free ourselves from conventional religion.[334] This means that for Hauerwas, there is no need for conventional or organizational religion but to only have faith. His beliefs in this regard re-echo and epitomize Martin Luther's *sola fide, sola gratia,* and *sola scriptura*[335] formulae.

3.2.4 The First Task of the Church (His Understanding of Church)

Hauerwas'd ecclesiology is Pentecostal. Whereas the Catholic Church believes Jesus's resurrection to be the climax of the Christian faith, Hauerwas teaches that Pentecost is the climax of the Christian year.[336] According to him, all is finally summed up through God's new creation of the church. "At Pentecost, God has undone what was done at Babel. The problem at Babel is not human inventiveness; it is when our forebears used their creative gifts to live as if they need not acknowledge that their existence depends on gifts."[337]

Hauerwas elucidates that at the event of Pentecost, the wound of Babel began to be healed. At Babel, God says "let us go down" (Gen 11:7), prefiguring the necessary sacrifice of his Son. The unity of humankind prefigured at Pentecost is not just any unity but that made possible by the apocalyptic work of Jesus of Nazareth. At Pentecost, God created a new language, a language that is more than words—a people whose very differences contribute to their unity.[338]

He further states that the church has a story to tell in which God is the main character. But the church cannot tell that story without becoming part of the tale. "The Church, catholic and apostolic, is not our but God's creation. Moreover, it is not a creation that God did at one point in time and does not need to do again. Rather, it is our belief that what God did at Pentecost he continues to do to renew and to sustain the presence of the Church."[339]

---

[332] Hauerwas, *Dispatches from the Front,* 22.

[333] Ibid.

[334] Ibid.

[335] John Dillenberger, ed., *Martin Luther: Selections from his Writings* (New York: Anchor Books, 1962), 64–65.

[336] Hauerwas, *Christian Existence Today,* 47.

[337] Hauerwas, *Christian Existence Today,* 54.

[338] Ibid., 54.

[339] Ibid.

3.2.5 The Gospel and Cultural Formations

One of the features endemic to the contemporary world—the postmodern society which springs from modern times—is the departure from tradition and another is progressivism which detaches itself from the past cultures. Hauerwas disagrees with people like Reinhold Niebuhr, who wanted to deny Christianity of its cultural roots. He says that Niebuhr assumed that Christ, or at least radical monotheism, was itself not a culture. He believes that such assumptions cannot help but reproduce the assumption of liberal cultures that there is a place to stand free of culture. But he insists that "the very means Niebuhr used to transcendence ironically provided the theological justification for the spiritualization of Christianity—the attempt to make Christianity intelligible without that set of cultural habits called Church."[340]

Christianity is a historical event that started in a cultural environment where Jesus lived and preached using the cultural symbols. It is therefore unintelligible when detached from its cultural roots. Hauerwas strongly believes that congregations cannot sustain a culture able to provide some assistance to the world that threatens to reduce Christianity to mere belief. Christianity, he believes, "is not a set of beliefs, but a state of life."[341] Trying to erase cultural roots of Christianity is equivalent to erasing Christianity itself and God from the world.[342]

Hauerwas says that Christianity is a story about God. "The story of Jesus, which we Christians affirm is nothing less than the story of God's creation on our behalf, is not simply a particular instance of a more universal truth that can be known separately from the story. The story of Jesus is unsubstitutable."[343] He continues to assert that we cannot learn what it means to be a Christian by simply attending to scripture. "Rather, we learn that story by caring for the tombstones of the saints. It is from them that we begin to understand what that story requires and means. For the truth of the story we find in the gospels is finally known only through the kind of lives it produces."[344]

Thus, for Hauerwas, both scripture and tradition are necessary for the full Gospel truth. Tradition gave birth to scripture and in turn scripture enlightens tradition. The two are inseparable; they complement each other. Scripture is made relevant and intelligible in the lives of the people who profess it, and the lives of people who live according to scripture are best explained by the scripture by which they live. Thus, the Gospel and cultural formations are not

---

[340] Hauerwas, *Sanctify Them in the Truth*, 4.
[341] Hauerwas, *Christian Existence Today*, 39.
[342] Ibid., 40.
[343] Hauerwas, *Christian Existence Today*, 39.
[344] Ibid.

incompatible. According to Hauerwas, this is what the modern culture strives to disband.

3.2.6 Christians and the State

Hauerwas believes that Christians are part of the state but at the same time living in an alternative society. He says that Christians have a double citizenship—of both church and state. Thus, "Christians are never just members of the Church but rightly live in the world."[345] He refers to the church as "polis"[346]—an alternative city or state that exists within a state. He continues to state, "The Christian Church is a real people that exists in definite historical and institutional forms—the people that the institutional forms and ministers serve. This makes any static, timeless view of the Church impossible. The Church is a historical and in relation to new social contexts changing phenomenon."[347]

He considers the postmodern society to have a propensity to think that the church is a creation of humanity—a form of system built to control people and turn them into moral beings. All that seems to matter to many people today about religion is morality. States and civil leaders believe that they can create an ethical society without the notion of God. Postmodernism names an interesting set of developments in social orders that are based on the assumption that God does not matter. Hauerwas thinks otherwise. He insists that "for Christians, Israel and the Church are not characters in a larger story called world, but rather world is a character in God's story as known through the story that is the Church."[348]

Therefore, the state should not think that it can take over the jurisdiction of the church, nor must it determine what the church ought to teach. The church has a mandate which originates from Jesus and not from any human authority. Hauerwas prides in his efforts to preserve the church's mandate in a world that is hostile. He thus states,

> My critiques of liberalism, and the challenge I have mounted against the accommodation of the Church to the ethos of modernity is my attempt to help us recover our ability to pray to God, and to imagine what it might mean to be Christian in a world we do not control.[349]

---

[345] Ibid., 6.
[346] Hauerwas, *In Good Company*, 190.
[347] Ibid.
[348] Hauerwas, *Sanctify Them in the Truth*, 192.
[349] Hauerwas, *Hannah's Child*, 237.

3.2.7 "The Killing Compassion"[350]

Most fascinating in the society today is how the modern man understands and desires to live. In this section, Hauerwas exposes the human passion to do away with the "cross." Indeed, every man desires to lead a pain-free life. However, in this exposé, Hauerwas divulges that the modern man instead gets rid of life in the process, other than the cross. In his article, "Eliminating People Who Suffer," he points out the wrong tendencies. He begins with the following meditation:

> A film very much like this was sponsored a few years ago by the American Association of Retarded[351] Citizens. No doubt the film was made with the best of intentions and concern. Surely we ought to prevent retardation. Certainly as many couples as can ought to be encouraged to maintain good pre-natal care. Nevertheless there seems to be something deeply wrong, something disturbing about this film and its message, "Prevent Retardation." Perhaps part of the difficulty involves the dis-analogy between preventing retardation and preventing cancer, polio, or heart diseases, as these latter diseases exist independent of the subjects having the diseases. The disease can be eliminated without eliminating the subject of the disease. But the same is not true of the retarded. To eliminate retardation means to eliminate the subject. To say what is wrong with such a policy involves some of the profoundest questions of human existence, our relationship to God and our assumptions about the nature and necessity of suffering.[352]

Hauerwas admits that it is surely obvious that we should seek to prevent retardation. He teaches that to challenge that assumption would be equivalent to questioning our belief that the world is round or that love is a good thing. "However, like so many of our obvious beliefs, if we ask why they seem so

---

[350] "Compassion can kill. Nowhere do we see this fact more powerfully than in issues raised through the practice of medicine. For modern medicine has had its task changed from care to cure in the name of compassion—a killing compassion." In Stanley Hauerwas, *Dispatches from the Front: Theological Engagements with the Secular*, (Durham, NC: Duke University Press, 1995), 164–165.

[351] This term is "un-suitably" used by Hauerwas. It is retained in this paper for about two reasons. One, because we directly quote Hauerwas, and two, we want to leave his meaning of "retarded" unaltered.

[352] Hauerwas, *The Hauerwas Reader*, 557.

obvious, we often feel unable to supply an answer. It is obvious that we ought to prevent retardation, with the conviction that we ought to prevent suffering."[353]

Hauerwas also notes that no one wills that a child, for example, should endure an illness. No one should will that another person should suffer from hunger. No one should will that a child should be born retarded. Suffering should be avoided. This is a belief as deep as any we have. Yet like many other "obvious" beliefs, the assumption that suffering should always be prevented, when analyzed, becomes increasingly less certain. The reason being it implies eliminating subjects who happen to be retarded. This should at least suggest to us that something is wrong with our straightforward assumption that suffering should always be avoided or, if possible, eliminated.[354]

However, Hauerwas teaches that "to ask why we suffer makes the questioner appear either terribly foolish or extremely arrogant. It seems foolish to ask since in fact we do suffer and no sufficient reason can be given to explain why. Indeed, if it were explained, suffering would be denied some of its power.[355] He insists that the question seems arrogant because it seeks to put us in the position of eating from the tree of good and evil. Only God knows the answer to such questions. He thus says that our task is to learn and not to ask them, but rather to try to make the best of the fact that suffering goes along with being finite and, perhaps, sinful beings.[356]

> Without denying that the question of why we suffer can be foolish and pretentious, I think it is worth asking since it has such an obvious answer: we suffer because we are incomplete beings who depend on one another for our existence. Indeed the matter can be put more strongly since we depend upon others not only for our survival but also for our identity. Suffering is built into our condition because it is literally true that we exist only to the extent that we sustain, or "suffer," the existence of others. This is exactly contrary to cherished assumptions. We believe that our identity derives from our independence, our self-possession.[357]

The irony is, however, that our neediness is also the source of our greatest strength, for our need requires the cooperation and love of others. From that love derives our ability not only to live but to flourish. Our identity, far from deriving

---

[353] Hauerwas, *The Hauerwas Reader*, 557.
[354] Ibid., 558.
[355] Hauerwas, *The Hauerwas Reader*, Stanley Hauerwas, 558.
[356] Ibid.
[357] Ibid., 559.

from our self-possession, or our self-control, comes from being depossessed of those powers that promise only illusory power. Hauerwas maintains that believing otherwise, "fearful of our sense of need, by our attempt to deny our reliance on others, we become all the more subject to those powers."[358] This has particularly significant implications for our relations with the retarded since we "naturally" disdain those who do not or cannot cover up their neediness. Prophets like the retarded only remind us of the insecurity hidden in our false sense of self-possession.[359]

He moves near to the provision of an answer by stating that we suffer because we are inherently creatures of need. He says that our task is to prevent unnecessary suffering. "However, the hard question is to know what constitutes unnecessary suffering. It is even more difficult when the question concerns another as in the case of the retarded."[360]

However, Hauerwas disqualifies the persistence in the notion that the retarded are suffering, and therefore, it would be better for them not to exist than to have to bear such disability. He says that what we assume is not that the retarded suffer from being retarded but rather, because they are retarded, they will suffer from being in a world like ours. He agrees with the fact that these will surely suffer from inadequate housing, inadequate medical care, inadequate schooling, and lack of love and care. They will suffer from discrimination as well as cruel kidding and treatment from unfeeling peers. "All this is certainly true, but it is not an argument for preventing retardation in the name of preventing suffering; rather it is an argument for changing the nature of the world in the interest of preventing such needless suffering we impose on the retarded. Too often the suffering we wish to spare them is the result of our unwillingness to change our lives so that those disabled might have a better life."[361]

In conclusion, Hauerwas' views on the modern culture can be summarized in two of his statements. First, "Liberalism emasculated Christianity in the name of societal peace. The 'secular' is not out there in the world, but it is in the souls of most people, including myself, who continue to identify themselves as Christians."[362] And second, "The strangeness of our times for Christians is apparent in: 'who do you think you are to tell anyone else how to live? What gives you that right? You must be some kind of fundamentalist or fanatic.' I find it odd that in our time many people believe we can or should avoid telling one another how to live. That is but a sign of the corruption of our age and why we are in such desperate need of conversion."[363]

---

[358] Ibid.
[359] Hauerwas, *The Hauerwas Reader*, 560.
[360] Ibid.
[361] Ibid., 561.
[362] Hauerwas, *Dispatches from the Front*, 93.
[363] Ibid., 5–6.

Chapter Four

4.0 Remedies Stanley Hauerwas Proposes

Stanley Hauerwas, like any good writer and theologian, does not only critique the contemporary culture, he also proposes means of rectifying the situation. Despite being regarded as controversial by both theologians and the secular society, he stands firm by his positions. He does not mince his words. He defends what he regards as the truth, supporting his arguments with relevant biblical texts. In this regard, Hauerwas bears a resemblance to Joseph Ratzinger. Both are passionate defenders of the truth, for the truth is the dispenser of true freedom. Jesus said, "The truth will make you free" (Jn 8:32). Comprise, just for its sake, or what Hauerwas christens "persecuting the Christian doctrine or being politically correct,"[364] is not found in the vocabulary for both Hauerwas and Ratzinger.

In this chapter, we shall explore the remedies Hauerwas offers to the contemporary culture which aims at erasing the foundational Christian beliefs.

4.1 "On the Road Again"[365]

Hauerwas' writings convey a message of a crisis of faith: that both the society and the Christians themselves, to a great extent, have strayed from the biblical salvific goals. He believes that the Christian faith has been surrendered or denaturalized in terms of the mere activity of science.[366] He denies that it is meaningful to assign to science qua science such an overriding veridical

---

[364] Hauerwas, *Dispatches from the Front*, 105.
[365] Hauerwas and William Willimon, *Resident Aliens*, 53.
[366] Hauerwas, *Christian Existence Today*, 9.

status.[367] He has refused to use that affirmation to underwrite an autonomous realm of morality separate from Christ's lordship. "Christianity is no world view," Hauerwas says, "not a form of primitive metaphysics, that can be assessed in comparison of alternative world views."[368] His position is rather a defensive one. His purpose is to preserve and sustain the historical identity of the Christian tradition virtually for its own sake.[369]

According to Hauerwas, the church and society need to find their way again, which is the scriptures. For him,

> The Bible is fundamentally a story of a people's journey with God. Scripture is an account of human existence as told by God. In scriptures, we see that God is taking the disconnected elements of our lives and pulling them together into a coherent story that means something. When we lack such a truthful, coherent account, life is likely to be perceived as disconnected, ad hoc. In trying to make sense of life, when we lack a coherent narrative, life is little more than a lurch to the left, a lurch to the right.[370]

4.2 Salvation as Adventure

According to Hauerwas, salvation is an adventure. He is critical of Martin Luther whose understanding of salvation is an incidence that occurs at the profession of faith in God.[371] As in the word, adventure implies and denotes quest, activity, journey, voyage. The *Cambridge Dictionary of American English* defines the term adventure as "an usual, exciting, and possibly dangerous activity, trip or experience."[372] Thus, Hauerwas believes that salvation is a lifelong journey that Christians undertake right from the start of their baptism. His description of salvation is grasped in the following statement: "Salvation is: Jesus saves us from sin and death—a history that requires an alternative history. The social manifestation that makes that history present is Church. Salvation is God's work to restore all creation to the Lordship of Christ, and it is historically and socially mediated."[373] To qualify to be a present history, salvation would require to be procedural; a process, rather than a onetime event.

---

[367] Ibid.
[368] Hauerwas, *Christian Existence Today*, 10.
[369] Ibid., 6.
[370] Hauerwas and William Willimon, *Resident Aliens*, 53.
[371] Dillenberger, ed., *Martin Luther*, 64.
[372] Sidney Landau and Paul Heacock, eds., *Cambridge Dictionary of American English* (New York: Cambridge University Press, 2000), s.v. "Adventure."
[373] Hauerwas, *In Good Company*, 183.

Hauerwas is critical of individualistic and ahistorical accounts of salvation. He stresses the close continuity between Israel, Jesus, and the church. He describes the church as the concrete form of Christ's continuing presence through the spirit.[374] He insists that "we do not know who God is, or what the truly human is, or the concrete content of salvation, separately from the whole history and destiny of Jesus."[375] It is a journey, an adventure, a continuous life-long experience and task.

Hauerwas does not believe that Jesus simply exemplifies a way of life for us to follow. Instead, Hauerwas attaches much importance to the ontological change, and this seems to be his key animosity with his Protestant faith. "Without the ontological change occasioned through Christ's resurrection, there would be no possibility of living as he did. He makes the life and teaching of Jesus, and not only the cross and resurrection, theologically decisive."[376] For Hauerwas, full salvation is when man is transformed, when man undergoes an ontological change. He believes in sanctification as a condition for salvation, unlike his Protestant compatriots whose salvation ends with justification. For, Hauerwas, salvation is eschatological—to be realized fully in the heavenly kingdom. He argues that

> the story of Jesus is the story of the kingdom of God. The kingdom of God is an eschatological concept—a story, a drama with a beginning and an end. This end is revealed and has already begun in the life, death and resurrection of Jesus. The idea that, for example, the Sermon on the Mount is an impossible ideal fails to understand the eschatological context of the teaching of Jesus.[377]

Hence, Hauerwas is not aligned with the relativistic understanding of salvation as an act of faith; and he claims, almost obstinately, that to overcome the relativistic tendencies, we have to walk the long journey of salvation to the end.

4.3 Salvation within the Church

Hauerwas criticizes the depolitization and individualization of the understanding of salvation. For him, salvation and the church are inseparable.

---

[374] Ibid., 184.
[375] Ibid., 185.
[376] Ibid.
[377] Hauerwas, *In Good Company*, 183.

In other words, salvation is possible within the church. His claim is that it is within the church that we get to know who God is. God is not a concept of principle immediately available for philosophical reflection, but more like a proper name of an agent in a story. "God and God's salvation are not knowable abstracted from history as mediated through the traditions of Israel and the Church. One learns to know God through being part of this embodied narrative."[378]

Thus, Hauerwas describes the church as "the concrete form of Christ's continuing presence through the spirit."[379] He says that the Christian Church is real people that exist in definite historical and institutional forms—the people that the institutional forms and ministers serve. This makes any static, timeless view of the church impossible. The church is historical and in relation to new social contexts changing phenomenon.[380] The church is the visible historical and social community that embodies the kingdom of God without which the kingdom of God becomes utopian. The church is the physical kingdom of God even if the kingdom of God is wider than the church.[381]

As the visible kingdom of God, Hauerwas argues that the church is the custodian of salvation. It is within the church that salvation occurs. In other words, salvation belongs to those who belong to this community of believers called church. Hauerwas grasps well Jesus's intention when commissioning his disciples to go and make disciples of all nations (Mt 28:19). By commanding them to baptize people in the name of the Trinity, Jesus willed all people to be united in the Trinity as children of the new and one family. It is to this family/community, which the culture of relativism wishes to break down, that Hauerwas invites Christians to stick to in order to triumph over this culture.

4.4 "People with a Cause"[382]

The real threat of the present culture is its act of jeopardizing matters of faith, reducing them to individual person's interpretations and decisions. Present-day relativism is the extreme individualism that leaves no room, at least in matters of faith, for a common goal. It gives total liberty to each person to discern their cause and consequently pursue their destiny. It leads each individual to follow their own stories—reenacting what happened at the tower of Babel.

On the contrary, Hauerwas insists that God created man for a purpose,

---

[378] Ibid., 179–180.
[379] Ibid., 184.
[380] Ibid., 190.
[381] Ibid., 186.
[382] Hauerwas and William Willimon, *Resident Aliens*, 66.

and as a people of God, we have a common cause. He says that Christians have a common story; "a story not like any other story in the world. The Christian story is a story of God—a story of how God saves."[383] He thus states,

> The story of being a Christian involves claims on our lives which few of us feel able to avow we have fulfilled. Being a Christian involves more than simply believing this or that. The story of Jesus, which we Christians affirm is nothing less than the story of God's creation on our behalf, is not simply a particular instance of a more universal truth that can be known separately from the story. The story of Jesus is as unsubstitutable.[384]

In the similar manner, Hauerwas seems to suggest that the Christian story is a continuous story that has its roots in the scripture but still continues even after the canonical books. The Christian story continues in the life and tradition of the church. "But we can no more learn what it means to be a Christian simply by attending to Scripture. . . . It is from the saints that we begin to understand what that story requires and means. For the truth of the story we find in the gospels is finally known only through the kind of lives it produces."[385]

What is also worth noting is that Hauerwas suggests that the Christian story should not be read only from scripture and the saints, but this story should be read more vividly in the Christians' lives. He explicates that we must learn to live in a world where injustices and scandals cannot be made right. "Our task is not to downplay or deny the evil that we or our forefathers have done, but rather to acknowledge it by learning to live the life of the forgiven. The followers of Jesus can attract others to the way of Jesus by living faithful lives. They must learn to make the story of Jesus their own."[386] Hence, Hauerwas challenges Christians to live by Jesus's words: "You will know them by their fruits" (Mt 7:16).

4.4.1 The Church as God's New Language

In the present age where the world gives the impression that there is need for a new language which puts an end to the Christian language, Hauerwas instead insists that the new world has a new language. Therefore, there is no

---

[383] Hauerwas, *Christian Existence Today*, 26.
[384] Hauerwas, *Christian Existence Today*, 39–40.
[385] Ibid., 40.
[386] Ibid., 41.

need for another. According to him, the church is the new language, created at Pentecost and still continues to the end of time. For Hauerwas, Pentecost is the climax of the Christian year.[387] On Pentecost, according to Hauerwas, all is finally summed up through God's new creation of the church.[388] At Pentecost, Hauerwas states, "God undid what is done at Babel. The problem at Babel was not human inventiveness; it is when our forebears used their creative gifts to live as if they need not acknowledge that their existence depends on gifts."[389]

Hauerwas recognizes the inclination of Tower of Babel still active today. At the Tower of Babel, people wanted to equate themselves with God, so that they could no longer be under his authority but rather live according to their own authority. Hauerwas supposes another Tower of Babel under construction by means of science and technology. He does not, however, condemn technology per se. Rather, he rebuffs the assumption that God's creatures can name themselves,[390] making a name for themselves.

> The problem at Babel is not human inventiveness; it is when our fore-bearers used their creative gifts to live as if they need not acknowledge that their existence depends on gifts. Thus the people said, "Come, let us build ourselves a city, and tower with its top in the heavens, and let us make a name for ourselves, lest we be scattered abroad on the face of the earth." It is not technology that is the problem but the assumption that God's creatures can name themselves—insuring that all who come after will have to acknowledge their existence. They thus erect a tower, an unmistakable edifice, so they will never have to fear being lost in this vast world.[391]

Like Ratzinger, Hauerwas' scrutiny of the present society is that it is attempting, via the "makability" ideology, to do without God. Through advancement of new and modern technology, the present society has turned themselves gods.

At Babel, Hauerwas teaches, God disrupted the old order; Babel became the

---

[387] "At Pentecost we celebrate the birth of the Church by the Holy Spirit. Pentecost is the climax of the Christian year as only now are we able liturgically to tell the whole story of God's redemption of his creation. All is finally summed up through God's new creation of the Church," in Stanley Hauerwas, *Christian Existence Today: Essays on Church, World, and Living in Between* (Durham, NC: Labyrinth Press, 1988), 47.

[388] Hauerwas, *Christian Existence Today*, 47.

[389] Ibid., 48.

[390] Ibid.

[391] Hauerwas, *Christian Existence Today*, 48.

climax of the primeval history.[392] God then started a new plan for a new society with a new language. He started it by calling of Abraham and climaxed it at the Pentecost with such a powerful unity. "The unity of humankind prefigured at Pentecost is not just any unity but that made possible by the apocalyptic work of Jesus of Nazareth. At Pentecost God created a new language, a language that is more than words—a people whose very differences contribute to their unity."[393]

Hauerwas passionately strives to make his readers know that it is factual that "the Church, catholic and apostolic, is not our but God's creation. Moreover, it is not a creation that God did at one point in time and does not need to do again. Rather, it is our belief that what God did at Pentecost he continues to do to renew and to sustain the presence of the Church."[394] He also makes it clear that in this new story, God, and not man, is the main character. He cautions, however, that the creation of such a people is indeed dangerous; for the very strength that comes from our unity has too often led the church to believe that it can build the tower of unity through our own efforts. We try to make God's unity a reality for all people through coercion rather than witness.[395]

4.4.2 God's Existence in a Unity of Persons

Even if Hauerwas does subscribe to a particular denomination, the Methodist Church he advocates for the total unity of the church that Jesus preached and prayed for in John's Gospel, "that they may all be one" (Jn 17:21). He believes that disunity is sin.[396] He preaches a unity and an ecclesiology that is similar to that of the Catholic Church, though he remains Methodist.

According to Hauerwas, unity is what God has given us through Christ's death and resurrection.[397] Disunity is sin. The greatest sin of disunity resides in the Reformation.[398] Even if Hauerwas remains a member of a church that glori-

---

[392] Ibid., 49.
[393] Hauerwas, *Christian Existence Today*, 52–53.
[394] Ibid., 54.
[395] Ibid., 53.
[396] Hauerwas, *Sanctify Them in the Truth*, 241.
[397] Hauerwas' concept of unity is a unity that is in full loyalty. He thus states, "I have a great deal of appreciation for John Paul II, but one of his phrases that I disliked was, 'The family is the domestic church.' I thought, how horrible. The only possible reason we can sustain families is that they are not the church. Families are a threat to the church to the extent that they create loyalties more determinative than our loyalty to the church." In Stanly Hauerwas and Jean Vanier, *Living Gently in Violent World: The Prophetic Witness of Weakness* (Downers Grove, IL: IVP Books, 2008), 57.
[398] Hauerwas, *Sanctify Them in the Truth*, 241.

fies the Reformation as a success, he, on the contrary, believes the Reformation was a failure—a sin. He expresses his dissatisfaction as follows:

> We who remain in the Protestant tradition want to say that reformation was a success, but it only ends up killing us. As Protestants we now take pride in the acknowledgement of our sinfulness in order to distinguish ourselves from Catholics who allegedly believe in works—righteousness (Lk 18:9–14). Unfortunately, the Catholics are right. Christian salvation consists in works. To be saved is to be made holy.[399]

Hauerwas invokes unity of Christians for the successful state of holiness. As long as we remain divided, Hauerwas believes, we are short of holiness and far from God's salvation. He is full of admiration for John Paul II's confession of the Catholic sin of the Reformation, other than perpetuating what divides us. He believes that Protestants think that Christianity is to be identified with sets of beliefs more than with the unity of the spirit occasioned through sacrament. Once Christianity becomes reduced to a matter of belief, we cannot resist questions of whether those beliefs are as true or useful as other beliefs we also entertain. Once more in admiration of the unity that subsists in the Catholic Church, Hauerwas states,

> Catholics understand the Church's unity as grounded in a reality more determinative than our good feelings for one another. We Protestants have not been able to resist nationalistic identification—German Lutherans, American Methodist, Dutch Calvinist, etc. Such disunity distorts the unity of the Gospel found in the Eucharist. Reformation should not be remembered as a celebratory moment, but rather as the sin of the Church.[400]

He elucidates that the unity deserving the Christian Church is that demonstrated in the Eucharist, for the apostle Paul says that as we partake of the one body and the one cup, we ought to become one.[401] His concept of unity is

---

[399] Hauerwas, *Sanctify Them in the Truth*, 241–242.
[400] Hauerwas, *Christian Existence Today*, 244.
[401] "The blessing-cup, which we bless, is it not a sharing in the blood of Christ; and the loaf of the bread which we break, is it not a sharing in the body of Christ? And as there is one loaf, so we, although we are many of us, are one single body, for we all share in the one loaf" (1 Cor 10:16–17).

not simply an ecumenical unity in diversity, but a unity under one ecclesial authority. He agrees with John Paul II's statement,

> Unity is essential to the followers of Christ. It is not just a friendliness or a togetherness, but perfect oneness: "that they may be one even as we are one"—we, Jesus' followers, are to have the oneness of God. In other words, Christians should give themselves completely to each other just as do the Persons of the Trinity, who are themselves complete gift of self. As the Church is the body of Christ (cf. 1 Cor 12:13, Eph 1:23), she should reveal the love and unity of God.[402]

Hence, as a remedy to relativistic culture, Hauerwas suggests that Christians live in the perfect unity of the Trinity. As the English saying goes, "United we stand, divided we fall." The disunity of the Christians is an excellent demonstration for the divisive approach of the relativistic culture.

4.4.3 The Truth and Forgiveness: Peacemaking

Hauerwas' perception of peacemaking is an inimitable one. His peacemaking and nonviolence strategies are more confrontational than an avoidance of conflicts. According to him, we cannot have peace without confronting the evil situations that lead to lack of peace. He bases his argument to the story of the brotherly correction in Matthew 18.[403] In the text, Jesus recommends confrontation of the one who has sinned. Hauerwas does not consider it acceptable to disregard a fault on the presumption that it is better not to disturb the peace. "Rather, you must risk stirring the waters, causing disorder, rather than overlook the sin. Such confrontation is at the heart of what it means to be peacemaker."[404]

Peace is an essential characteristic of the church's nature.[405] It is the essential

---

[402] *The Augustine Club at Columbia University*, "The Need for Full Christian Unity" (March 28, 1996).

[403] "If your brother should commit some wrong against you, go and point out his fault, but keep it between the two of you. If he listens to you, you have won your brother over, if he does not listen, summon another, so that every case may stand on the word of two or three witnesses. If he ignores them, refer it to the Church. If he ignores even the Church, then treat him as you would a Gentile or a tax collector" (Mt 18:15–17).

[404] Hauerwas, *Christian Existence Today*, 90.

[405] According to Hauerwas, the church is built on peace is sent to bring peace to the world, hence, the theme of pacifism. But Hauerwas says that "Pacifism is not a position that you might adopt after getting your Christology straight. Yoder forced me to recognize that that nonviolence is not a recommendation, an ideal, that Jesus suggested we might try to

element of the post-resurrection community. Peace is Jesus's first word to his disciples after his resurrection. And after wishing them peace, Jesus sends them off to take his peace to the world: "Peace be with you. As the Father has sent me, so I send you" (Jn 20:21). He also commands them to forgive sins (Jn 20:22). Hauerwas notes that what is interesting about these two texts (Mt 18:15–17 and Jn 20:21–22), is that they assume the Christian community will always be involved in conflicts and wrongs. Thus,

> The question is not whether such conflicts can be eliminated but rather how we are to deal with the conflict. Conflict is not to be ignored or denied, but rather be forced in the open. The peace that Jesus brings is not a peace of rest but rather a peace of truth. Surely that is why Jesus is so insistent that those who would follow him cannot simply let sins go unchallenged.[406]

He also states that such confrontation is based on the presupposition that forgiveness is also to be offered. Peace is not the name of the absence of conflict, but rather peacemaking is that quality of life and practices engendered by a community that knows it lives as a forgiven people.[407] Such a community cannot afford to overlook one another's sins because they have learned that such sins are threats to being a community of peace.[408] Instead, such sins need confrontation with the intention of forgiveness. We cannot leave time to heal all wounds—waiting for some conflicts to die through the passage of time. We are commanded to engage in a difficult task of confronting those whom we believe have sinned against us so as to bring about reconciliation.

Forgiveness that makes peacemaking possible does not mean that judgment is withheld. Therefore, we do not confront one another from apposition of self-righteousness; "we must come to the other as one who has been forgiven. The point is that we confront one another not as forgivers, not as those who use forgiveness as power, but first and foremost as people who have learned the truth about ourselves—namely, that we are all people who need to be and have been forgiven."[409]

---

live up to. Rather, nonviolence is constitutive of God's refusal to redeem coercively. The crucifixion is 'the politics of Jesus.'" in Hauerwas, *Hannah's Child*, 118.

[406] Hauerwas, *Christian Existence Today*, 92.

[407] "Peace takes time. Put even more strongly, peace crates time by its steadfast refusal to force the other to submit in the name of order." in Stanley Hauerwas and Jean Vanier, *Living in a Violent World: The Prophetic Witness of Weakness* (Downers Grove, IL: IVP Books, 2008), 46.

[408] Hauerwas, *Christian Existence Today*, 91.

[409] Hauerwas, *Christian Existence Today*, 93–94.

Forgiveness, according to Hauerwas, originates from the fact that as a community of believers, we are no longer our own but belong to the community. He teaches that we have been made part of a community in which people no longer regard their lives as their own. We are not permitted to harbor our grievances as ours. "When we think our brother or sister has sinned against us, such an affront is not just against us but against the whole community. A community established as peaceful cannot afford to let us relish our sense of being wronged without exposing that wrong in the hopes of reconciliation."[410] To act like one not in need of forgiveness is to act against the very basis of this community of peacemaking.

"The task of peacemaking," Hauerwas continues, "cannot ignore real wrongs, past or present. No genuine peace can come from simply forgetting past wrongs, but rather must come by encompassing those wrongs in a history of forgiveness."[411] Therefore, Hauerwas believes that it is the task of the church to confront and challenge the false peace of the world, which is too often built on power than truth. The church, Hauerwas believes, cannot help but be a community that confronts the world in uncompromising manner. Compromising our faith values is the real danger for the church today. Hauerwas says that "we Christians now find ourselves most often on the wrong side of the 'progressive' forces of human history. In response, many Christians want to identify with the alleged humanisms. It is a big temptation for the church to say, 'Hey, we're on the side of historical progress, too'!"[412]

4.4.4 Democratic Policy of Christianity

What Hauerwas is more apprehensive about are the "democratic" tendencies of Christianity today. Worth noting, however, is that he does not concern himself with leadership in this matter, but rather with the Christian values—the Christian doctrines. Not only is he concerned about a "cafeteria" Christianity, but also an abridged value of the content of the Christian "recipe." In other words, Hauerwas is concerned that Christians today are Christians "by choice," not "by call." He is worried about Christians who "invite" themselves to be disciples of Jesus and who do not stop at self-invitation, but also choose what to believe.[413] Worse still, even what they choose to believe is chosen on

---

[410] Ibid., 92.

[411] Ibid., 94.

[412] Stanley Hauerwas and Jean Vanier, *Living in a Violent World: The Prophetic Witness of Weakness* (Downers Grove, IL: IVP Books, 2008), 51–52.

[413] "We live in a time when people believe they have no story except the story they chose when they thought they had no story. We believe we should be held responsible only for the things we freely chose when we knew what we were doing . . . The story of freedom is

assumption that it should be of lesser demand on their part—not forever binding for example, and softer as far as their moral demands are concerned.

He suggests a return to the roots. He argues that as creatures that were created and receive our being outside ourselves, we ought to live according to the will of that outside power beyond ourselves. He sees independence or freedom or democracy in matters of faith as the root of sin. He believes it all started at the Tower of Babel. He says that at Babel, "our forefathers used their creative gifts to live as if they need not acknowledge that their existence depends on gifts."[414] Christians today want to get rid of their creaturedness. Thus, for Hauerwas, Babel is the climax of the primeval history.

According to Hauerwas, history repeated itself at the Reformation. In other words, the Reformation was the new Babel; the Reformers reenacted what happened at Babel. Hauerwas believes the Reformation was sin, because with it, the Christian Church sought false freedom. He says,

> The project of modernity was to produce people who believe they should have no story except the story they choose when they had no story. Such a story is called a story of freedom—institutionalized economically as capitalism and politically as democracy. That story, and the institutions that embody it, is the enemy we must attack through Christian preaching.[415]

Modernity and Reformation were the foundation for individual choice of one's own destiny—with complete autonomy. He quotes Robert Casey's[416] decision on abortion: "At the heart of liberty is the right to define one's own concept of existence, of meaning, of the universe, and of the mystery of human life."[417] However, he says that in *Veritatis Splendor,* John Paul II condemns this. According to John Paul II, "in a freedom like that, freedom enjoys a primacy

---

the story we tell ourselves to hide the fact that we are not, indeed, our own creatures . . . We don't get to make our lives up. We get to receive our lives as gifts. The story that says we should have no story except the story we chose when we had not story is a lie. To be human is to learn that we don't get to make our lives because we are creatures." In Hauerwas and Jean Vanier, *Living in a Violent World,* 92–93.

[414] Hauerwas, *Christian Existence Today,* 48.

[415] Hauerwas, *Sanctify Them in the Truth,* 197–198.

[416] Bob Casey was U.S. senator for Pennsylvania. He knew that public service is a privilege and that he was elected to fight for Pennsylvania priorities and Pennsylvania values. He was working to foster financial security for American families, protect our children and invest in their futures, and ensure safety at home and respect abroad. Senator Casey made it his top priority to work to help create and incentivize the creation of family-sustaining jobs and to help workers who lost their jobs through no fault of their own.

[417] Hauerwas, *Sanctify Them in the Truth,* 198.

over truth, to the point that truth itself would be considered a creation of freedom."[418], [419]

Hauerwas thinks that the idea of modern man's context of choice is a bad idea. He says that in the modern or postmodern societies, people believe their lives are the outcome of choices they have made. "No longer is anyone made to be a Christian, but one only becomes a Christian through experience and voluntary commitment."[420] He states that even Luther and Calvin would have been stunned by the suggestion that the church is a collection of individuals in which each person gets to determine their relation to God. He insists, "The truth is that we are not free to choose our own stories inasmuch as we are God's good creation. Freedom lies not in creating our lives, but learning to recognize our lives as gift."[421]

Hauerwas is absolutely right. Freedom does not mean free. True freedom is freedom to do the good and the right. Man's freedom comes from God and returns to him in response to his will. At creation, God gave man freedom to choose between good and evil. When man chose evil, the consequences were sin and death. At the calling of Abraham and at Mount Sinai, God made a covenant with his people—to be their God and they be his people. The choice of Israel is God's initiative and not vice versa. God chose Abraham and determined his destiny—unknown to Abraham. Abraham had to respond by faith. Therefore, our faith and discipleship is a response to the call of God. We do not invite ourselves but only respond. Jesus said, "You did not choose me, I chose you" (Jn 15:16).

God is not part of the choices we make. Choosing our God would imply that there is more than one god and that we prearranged our creation. Today there is common talk, especially among the evangelical Christians, of people confessing having chosen Jesus as their personal savior. This statement reduces Jesus to something below God. It makes him one of many saviors from whom one is at will to choose the best. Hence, the statement itself is relativistic. This annoys Hauerwas. He therefore invites Christians to an obedient faith in God and his teaching. He speaks of his membership to his own church as follows:

> Most of us are there because in some way or another, what we do on Sunday morning pleases us. So I go to Church at Aldersgate because I like the Church which, of course bothers me. In my own ecclesial life I reproduce the kind of Church

---

[418] John Paul II, *Veritatis Splendor: The Splendor of Truth: Regarding Certain Fundamental Questions of the Church's Moral Teaching*, Encyclical Letter (August 6, 1993), 52.

[419] Hauerwas, *Sanctify Them in the Truth*, 198.

[420] Ibid., 79.

[421] Ibid., 198.

shopping I otherwise wish to defeat. The practices that sustain our worship of God at Aldersgate are, as a result, too easily undermined by the alleged voluntary culture that forms our lives separate from worship. We fail to note how we become Christians in spite of ourselves. We lack the means to learn we were chosen before we chose. The so-called voluntary Church nicely underwrites patterns of domination characteristic of capitalist social order with much less basis for critique than was provided by the Catholic Church.[422]

He concludes with words of St. Peter: "But you are a chosen race, a royal priesthood, a holy nation, God's own people" (1 Pt 2:9).[423]

4.4.5 Performing the Faith: Peaceable Rhetoric of God's Church

Hauerwas is a belligerent advocate of the truth. He has zero tolerance to whatever goes against it, and he is uncompromising in his belief. He justifies his rigid position: "How can you live out the radicality of the Christian message without becoming intolerant? I believe Christians in our time cannot avoid being identified as fanatics. I believe there is nothing wrong with intolerance."[424] Despite being criticized on this, Hauerwas has maintained a firm position, stating, "We are either Christians or we are not, and if we are Christians, we must act as Christians—walking our faith—or our faith is in vain."[425]

The contemporary world is characterized by tolerance in the sense of creating an atmosphere of peaceful living—avoiding conflicts. This involves a lot of compromises in one's faith to keep the peace with the other. An example of this is when confession of one's faith in public has an ability to offend another. Is one better off abstaining from it? Hauerwas does not agree with this kind of peace. For him, this is a false peace.

Hauerwas thus recommends that Christians nonviolently resist the negative and relativistic approaches the society takes in the name of peacemaking. According to him, Christian nonviolence is a form of terrorism,[426] for Christians have been sent out into a world of war to challenge the necessity

---

[422] Hauerwas, *Sanctify Them in the Truth*, 163–164.

[423] Ibid., 164.

[424] Ibid., 177.

[425] Hauerwas, *Sanctify Them in the Truth*, 177.

[426] "As a pacifist I obviously think that war and terrorism are not compatible with Christian discipleship. Christian non-violence, therefore, cannot help but appear as fanatical just to the extent it challenges the assumed normality of war and violence. We are not radicals because we assume a radical stance on this or that issue that the world understands as

of war armed only with the weapons of love. Christians are first and foremost called to be witnesses by necessity. Christians must resist such temptations (of violence) not only because violence may not provide true peace, but more so, because the apparent peace provided is not the peace of Christ. "Christians who insist on the politics of Jesus cannot but appear like Islamic fundamentalists—not a bad place to be from my perspective."[427]

What Hauerwas is advocating for is not going to war with one another in the name of faith, but rather, to stop accepting the sidelining of the Christian values by other non-Christian faiths or nonbelievers, and stop compromising our Christian values in the name of making peace—to stop wanting to appear politically right. He is calling upon Christians to perform their Christian values publicly—forming a cluster of witnesses to the public. He shares similar ideas with Joseph Ratzinger who refuses to believe that Christianity is a faith like other faiths. The two men believe that Christianity is a revealed truth equal to no other, and its observance is a command from the Lord. This is Hauerwas' call: "The Church calls you to be an agent of truth in a world of mendacity. Therefore, you must be the most political of people reminding this society of what a politics of truth might look like."[428]

4.4.6 The Lover of God and the Poor

Christianity is built on love. Hauerwas' theology revolves around this ideal too, which is why he strives to conform to the love and the truth ideals (even if he actually falls short of it just like any human being). He is a Christian who loves his God and his truth. For Hauerwas, true love for God is manifested in the love for the poor; for we cannot love God without loving his creation, particularly our neighbor.[429] The biblical neighbor is that person that is in need or troubled or suffering. Hauerwas seems to suggest that it is to these that our

---

radical, but because any stance we assume must be witness to the God of Jesus Christ," in Hauerwas, *Sanctify Them in the Truth*, 178.

[427] Hauerwas, *Sanctify Them in the Truth*, 188.

[428] Hauerwas, *Dispatches from the Front*, 88.

[429] "And who is my neighbor?' Jesus replied, 'A man was going down from Jerusalem to Jericho, and fell into the hands robbers, who stripped him beat him, and went away, leaving him half dead. Now by chance a priest was going down that road; and when he saw him, he passed by on the other side. So likewise a Levite, when he came to the place and saw him, passed by on the other side. But a Samaritan while travelling came near him; and when he saw him, he was moved with pity. He went to him and bandaged his wounds, having poured oil and wine on them. Then he put him on his own animal, brought him to an inn, and took care of him. The next day he took out two denarii, gave them to the innkeeper, and said, "Take care of him; and when I come back, I will repay you whatever more you spend." Which of these three, do you think, was a neighbor to the man who fell into the

love must be directed. He believes that the contemporary man has a propensity toward eliminating them instead of delivering them from their suffering.

To understand what Hauerwas' argument on this, we shall employ his discourse on suffering, which he analyzes via an article about the fate for the retarded. He reprimands the present society which works to eliminate the retarded people instead of the reasons that cause the retardation. He identifies something deeply wrong in the process. According to him, the Christian's response to those who are suffering, like the poor, is the challenge of learning to know, be with, and care for the retarded is nothing less than learning to know, be with, and love God.

> God's face is the face of the retarded, his body is the body of the retarded, his being is that of the retarded. For the God we Christians must learn to worship is not a god of self-suffering power, a god whose self-possession is such that he needs no one; rather he is a God who needs a people, who needs a son. Absoluteness of being or power is not a work of the God we have come to know through the cross of Christ.[430]

Hauerwas continues to stress that in the faces of the retarded, the suffering, and the poor, we are offered an opportunity to see God.[431] For like God, they offer us an opportunity to recognize the character of our neediness. His teachings on the love of the poor and suffering can be summarized in his statement below:

> In truth the retarded in this respect are but an instance of the potential we each have for one another. That the retarded are singled out is only an indication of how they can serve as a prophetic sign of our true nature as creatures destined to need God and, thus, one another. Our learning to share our life with God is no doubt difficult it must be at least as onerous as learning that we can share life with the retarded. But that

---

hands of the robbers?' He said, 'The one who showed him mercy.' Jesus said to him, 'Go and do likewise.'" (Lk 10:29–37)

[430] Hauerwas, *Dispatches from the Front*, 88.

[431] "Modernity gets us caught in some funny contradictions. The presumption that people should not have children if they've been diagnosed with a mental disability—that abortion is the appropriate response. I think that presumption is based on our understanding of compassion; it is humanism gone bad. Christian humanism is determined by the Father's sending of the Son to be one of us. So humanism must always begin with Jesus' humanity" in Hauerwas and Jean Vanier, *Living in a Violent World*, 53.

such a sharing of our sufferings as well as our joys is necessary cannot be doubted. For a world where there is no unpatterned unpurposeful suffering would be devoid of the means to grow out of our selfishness and into love. That is why those who worship such a God are obligated to live confident that we can live well with those whose difference from ourselves we have learned to characterize by the unfortunate label "retarded." For if we did not so learn to live we know we would be decisively retarded: retarded in our ability to turn ourselves to others' needs, regardless of the cost.[432]

4.4.7 The Necessity of Witness: Discipline of Discipleship

The greatest theological teaching of Stanley Hauerwas lies in his discourse on witness and discipleship. For Hauerwas, the whole reason for Christianity is embodied in these two themes. The Gospel and all Christian doctrines would be superfluous without Christians' life of witness; for before his ascension, Jesus said to his disciples: "But you will receive power when the Holy Spirit has come upon you; and you will be my witnesses in Jerusalem, in all Judea and Samaria, and to the ends of the earth" (Acts 1:8). Therefore, disciples are essentially witnesses.

According to Hauerwas, many Christians (liberal Christians) remain relatively indifferent about doctrinal matters, e.g., the Trinity, but assume that one cannot make any compromises when it comes to moral questions, e.g., justice. On the other hand, conservative Christians often claim to care a great deal about doctrine.[433] However, he says that these two trends both lead to the same thing, that is, witness. For "how would a belief in a set of doctrines help form a good disciple if these doctrines are not lived in day to day life? And where else can true moral values come if not the gospel and doctrinal teachings?"[434] Doctrines only become relevant if lived in real life, and moral values are true only when they flow from the Gospel. Hauerwas borrows Cardinal Suhard's words "To be a witness does not consist in engaging in propaganda nor in stirring people up, but in living a living mystery. It means to live in such a way that one's life would not make a sense if God did not exist."[435] Finally, truth is known in the showing. The church must assimilate her groom, Jesus, because she is the body of Christ who is the image of the invisible God. Hence Hauerwas insists,

---

[432] Hauerwas, The Hauerwas Reader, 561–562.
[433] Hauerwas, Sanctify Them in the Truth, 19.
[434] Hauerwas, Sanctify Them in the Truth, 19.
[435] Ibid., 38.

The true character of nature/human nature only comes to light when set within the purview of God's "grace-full" dominion. God's rule or lordship over creation, however, is not exercised externally or "at a distance" but comes close in Jesus Christ. Indeed God's "grace-full" dominion is embodied most preeminently in human form: the fleshly person of Jesus of Nazareth, the prolongation of whose earthly life finds embodiment in the Church.[436]

Hauerwas emphasizes that to reverse the prevailing trend, Jesus needs to incarnate in every individual Christian life, the same way he did long ago into Mary's womb. Word became flesh in Mary, following her "yes" (her faith) and became invisible. Similarly, the word, following our faith, must become incarnate in us and be visible in our daily activities. The apostle James reminds us that "faith without works is barren" (Js 2:20). Therefore, Hauerwas argues that "the loss of the 'self' and the increasing appreciation of the significance of the body's permeability, can help us rediscover holiness not as an individual achievement but as the work of the Holy Spirit building up the body of Christ."[437]

He criticizes the double standards which existed, especially in the Catholic Church. He says that Catholicism, for years, lived a double life where the doctrines had to be enforced among the peasants and the nobles (the clergy), and other Christians of higher social status were not so much obliged to observe the same rules, or they appeared holier. He laments, "Part of the great genius of Catholicism was its ability to sustain Christianity as a way of life for peasants. Christian peasants usually do not think they are called to be holy. It is enough that they pray, obey, and pay—venerating people, sacraments, and relics that are clearly different."[438] As a church, we are all a group of witnesses who must be bound by the same rules regardless of our social status or role in the church.

4.4.8 Truth and Virtue

Stanley Hauerwas is essentially a moral theologian. One may deny that he is a theologian at all, but simply a moralist. However, to be fair, he should best be described as a theologian who combines theological truths and virtue together. For him, Christianity as a set of beliefs or simply put, a system of beliefs, is a futile Christianity. Instead, the truths taught by Christianity must incarnate into the persons that profess them, lest they become not only irrelevant but a disgrace to Christianity. He also believes that true morality originates from

---

[436] Ibid., 45.
[437] Ibid., 78.
[438] Ibid., 38.

God. Therefore, the morality that does not acknowledge God and his precepts are no morality at all.

Holiness is a central teaching in Hauerwas' theology. He proposes that Christians' moral behavior should naturally flow from their beliefs. "If we get our beliefs right, we will then know how to act right."[439] For this one reason, he remains a Methodist because he seems to see the true Christian principles in the theological ideas of John Wesley (1703–1791), a cofounder of the Methodist movement/Church. Wesley was an Anglican clergyman and an evangelist. He broke away from the Church of England because he felt that it was not being holy enough. His concept of Christianity was a personal relationship with Jesus manifested via personal morality.

Hauerwas' approval of Wesley stems from his (Wesley's) concept of Christianity. For Wesley, Christianity was synonymous with holiness or changed lives. Any teaching or doctrine that does not directly serve that purpose held little interest for him. Wesley attacked halfway Christians and lukewarm belief. Hauerwas ascertains that Wesley's attack of such

Was not only an attempt to upgrade the morality of Christians but involved basic questions of the truth and falsity of Christian convictions. His insistence of integrity between what Christians believed and what they did was uncompromising because any temporizing on the part of Christians betrayed the character of their belief. Christians, for Wesley, are a pilgrim people undertaking an arduous but fulfilling journey. It is, therefore, unthinkable that those on that journey would not manifest some predictable and observable empirical change. Wesley's doctrine of perfection rightly denotes that there is an inherent contradiction to claim to be a Christian without that claim making a difference in our lives and how we live.[440]

According to Hauerwas, the peculiar contribution of Wesley and the Methodists to the church universal lies in their struggle to recover the centrality of holiness as integral to the Christian life.[441]

4.4.9 "Put on the Whole Armor of God" (Eph 6:11)

In his letter to the Ephesians,[442] St. Paul urges the Ephesians to put on the full armor of God. By "full armor of God," Paul refers to the truth, justice

---

[439] Hauerwas, *Sanctify Them in the Truth*, 157.

[440] Ibid., 123–124.

[441] Ibid., 124.

[442] "Finally, be strong in the Lord and in the strength of his power. Put on the whole armor of God, so that you may be able to stand against the wiles of the devil. For our struggle is not against enemies of blood and flesh, but against the rulers, against the authorities, against the cosmic powers of this present darkness, against the spiritual forces of evil in

(righteousness), zeal, faith, salvation, and the word of God. These, according to Paul, constitute the full armor of God. But putting on an armor for what? Paul thinks that Christian life is a warfare against the forces of the devil. Christians are at war. Like Paul, Hauerwas believes that Christians are at battle, not against anybody, but against the evil in the society's systems and ideas. For Hauerwas, "Christianity is unintelligible without enemies. To be a Christian is to be made part of an army against enemies."[443]

To win this battle, Hauerwas seems to suggest, one needs a whole armor of God, that is, truth, justice (righteousness), zeal, faith, salvation, and the word of God. Hauerwas is firm in his assertions and belief, of which he is not willing to let go. He believes that this is the only protection for a Christian against the forces of the world.

4.4.10 Prayer

The purpose of Hauerwas' theological writings is to achieve a goal, which is why we believe; that is, attaining eternal life. For him, "Christians are a people who believe that the many narratives that constitute our lives finally have the *telos* of making us God's friends and, in the process, making us friends with one another and even friends with our own life."[444] It is this concept of *telos* that pushes us to devotion to God, "for it is impossible not to take the time [for prayer] if we truly believe we have a destiny beyond this world."[445] His model in prayer life is William Law.[446] In his book *A Serious Call to a Devout and Holy Life*, William claims that "devotion signifies a life given or devoted to God, not just in performance of certain religious duties, but in all the ordinary actions of our life. Indeed the problem is that many Christians are strict as to some times and places of devotion, but when the service of the Church is over, they are but like those who seldom or never come there."[447]

---

the heavenly places. Therefore take up the whole armor of God, so that you may be able to withstand on that evil day, and having done everything, to stand firm. Stand therefore, and fasten the belt of truth around your waist, and put on the breastplate of righteousness. As shoes for your feet put on whatever will make you ready to proclaim the gospel of peace. With all of these, take the shield of faith, with which you will be able to quench all the flaming arrows of the evil one. Take the helmet of salvation and the sword of the Spirit, which is the word of God" (Eph 6:10–17).

[443] Hauerwas, *Sanctify Them in the Truth*, 196.

[444] Ibid., 103.

[445] Ibid., 133.

[446] William Law was an Anglican priest who greatly influenced the eighteenth figures like John Wesley, Hauerwas' model.

[447] William Law, *A Serious Call to a Devout and Holy Life: The Spirit of Love* (New York: Paulist Press, 1978), 47–48.

According to William Law, "it is as absurd to suppose holy prayers without a holiness of life as to suppose a holy life without prayers."[448] Hauerwas likewise agrees that either reason or religion prescribe rules and ends to all the ordinary actions of our life, or they do not, then it is as necessary to govern all our actions by those actions by those rules, as it is necessary to worship God.[449] He believes that "not to pursue perfection is not only irreligious but irrational life, as the Scripture makes it clear, our salvation depends upon the sincerity and perfection of our endeavors to obtain it."[450]

For Hauerwas, the Christian journey is a journey toward perfection, holiness. We are pilgrims, with a destiny beyond this world. Therefore, as pilgrims, we battle against the forces of the devil, and by our powers we cannot emerge victors; for scripture says, "apart from me you can do nothing" (Jn 15:5). It is Hauerwas' conviction that we can try with our whole mighty but devoid of the Lord's grace and strength, we shall try in vain. We have to invoke the power of God to abet our efforts.

In conclusion, this chapter has tried to highlight Hauerwas' remedy to a culture that relativizes matters of faith. His final analysis is that democratic tendency toward faith is the real danger of Christianity today, because it makes faith and Christianity a private matter. On the contrary, he believes that Christianity is instead a gift, a revealed truth we received from God, to which we respond with faith. He is aware of Jesus's command: "go therefore, and make disciples of all nations" (Mt 28:19), but he also realizes that this is not going to be an easy task, and we cannot be victorious by our own powers. He believes like Blessed John Paul II who asserted,

> Therefore, since we have so great a cloud of witnesses surrounding us, let us also lay aside every encumbrance, and the sin which so easily entangles us, and let us with endurance the race that is set before us, fixing our eyes of Jesus, the author and perfecter of faith, who for the joy set before Him endured the cross, despising the shame, and has sat down at the right hand of the throne of God. And if anyone competes as an athlete, he does not win the prize unless he competes according to the rules (c/o Heb 12:1–2, and 2 Tim 2:5).[451]

---

[448] Law, *A Serious Call to a Devout and Holy Life*, 48.

[449] Hauerwas, *Sanctify Them in the Truth*, 130.

[450] Ibid.

[451] John Paul II, "Make Disciples," http://www.theworkofgod.org/JohnPII/pope_life_of_Christ.asp, (accessed October 4, 2010).

PART III

Toward a Christian
Response to Relativism

Chapter Five

5.0 The Common Concerns of Joseph Ratzinger and Stanley Hauerwas

Joseph Ratzinger and Stanley Hauerwas are some of the greatest adversaries of the culture of relativism of our time: Ratzinger on the Catholic side and Hauerwas on the Protestant side. Using different terminologies, and employing different means due to their backgrounds and experiences, they both have the same cause, that is, to confound the relativistic phenomenon and replenish Christianity with its befitting values. In this chapter, we shall closely examine ideas that are common to both. We shall compare and contrast their essential theologies, anthropologies, and ecclesiologies. In an interview with Hauerwas in January 2011, he stated that he and Joseph Ratzinger are on the same planet.[452] It will therefore be in our best interests to discover how true this statement is.

5.1 Contemporary Culture

Both Ratzinger and Hauerwas seem to have one problem with the contemporary world and culture, that is, truthlessness. They view the contemporary culture as one that is void of the truth, which is the result of the relativistic tendencies under which everything has become negotiable. They thus strive to thwart this trend further.

5.1.1 Joseph Ratzinger

In an interview with Peter Seewald, Ratzinger stated,

---

[452] Cf. *Interview with Hauerwas* in the appendix.

It is obvious that the concept of truth has become suspect. Of course it is correct that it has become much abused intolerance and cruelty have occurred in the name of truth. To that extent, people are afraid when someone says, "this is the truth," or even, "I have the truth." We never have it; at best it has us. No one will dispute that one must be careful and cautious in claiming the truth. But to dismiss it as unattainable is really destructive. A large proportion of contemporary philosophies, in fact, consist of saying that man is not capable of the truth. When viewed in that way, man would not be capable of ethical values either. Then he would have no standards.[453]

Therefore, according to Ratzinger, the relativistic contemporary culture wants to get rid of the truth. The truth, whose custodian is the church, is the target of this culture and Ratzinger says that this is the central problem for faith today.[454] The world seems to be aiming at "freeing" itself; toward attaining a self-rule for each individual. However, by distancing itself from the truth, the world enslaves itself further; for the further man is from God, the more he releases that is naked and enslaved. Adam and Eve were the first to experience this (Gen 3), and all humans follow suit. Denial of the truth is the root cause of sin and its consequences.

Ratzinger, who realizes that the world today takes the same route of distancing itself from God and doing away with the truth, comes as a champion of the truth because he believes in Jesus's words, "the truth will make you free" (Jn 8:32).

5.1.2 Stanley Hauerwas

As noted in chapter 3, Stanley Hauerwas and Joseph Ratzinger seem to put on the same pair of glasses in the presence of the contemporary society. According to Hauerwas, democracy is eroding away the truth—breaking it into relativistic or what can be referred to as personal truths. In this regard, truth becomes subjective, but subjective truth is not truth but opinions. Truth is one, objective, eternal, and indivisible. If, as is the case in the contemporary world, truth is democratized, then it ceases to be. Hauerwas envisages the contemporary society as dislodging the truth via policies that are anti-institutionalism and universalism.[455]

---

[453] Benedict XVI, *Light of the World*, trans. Michael J. Miller and Adrian J. Walker (San Francisco: Ignatius Press, 2010), 50.

[454] Thornton and Susan Varenne, eds., *The Essential Pope Benedict XVI*, 227.

[455] Hauerwas, *Christian Existence Today*, 228.

Hauerwas' exertion is toward the restoration of the truth to its rightful position as the guiding principle in private and ethic fabric of society. According to him, there is need for a new Pentecost,[456] a unity that overturns the division brought about by the Tower of Babel. This new Pentecost, he proposes, is to be God's new language by which society lives.

The new Pentecost model is Hauerwas' solution to a relativistic society; he states,

> After Pentecost we can better understand how Jesus' life was from the beginning integral to God's life. For creation itself heralds the presence of this Jesus. From the beginning God's being as Trinity, rather than being a denial of time, is an affirmation of God's timefulness. The unity of humankind prefigured at Pentecost is not just any unity but that made possible by the apocalyptic work of Jesus of Nazareth. At Pentecost God created a new language, a language that is more than words—a people whose very differences contribute to their unity.[457]

According to Hauerwas, the contemporary society has drifted from the truth of the Trinity. Therefore, to go back to this truth is a vocation for every Christian as provided in his teachings to Christian students: "The Church calls you to be agents to truth in a world of mendacity."[458]

5.2 Theological Concerns

Theologically, both Hauerwas and Ratzinger are not only biblical, but also Christo-centered. They write theology that is widely biblical and particularly Christological. Their theological discourses are based on the story of the historical Jesus of Nazareth, retelling this story from Bethlehem to Calvary but making special emphasis on the Paschal Mystery.

5.2.1 Joseph Ratzinger

Ratzinger's main problem is the relativism's rejection of Jesus Christ as Lord and Savior of all. For Ratzinger, the notion that all perspectives are equal is not Christian. While presenting the new book of Pope Benedict XVI, *Jesus*

---

[456] Ibid., 52.
[457] Ibid., 52–53.
[458] Hauerwas, *Dispatches from the Front*, 88.

of Nazareth, to the Vatican press office on Thursday, March 10, 2011, Cardinal Ouellet asserted,

> Given that Christianity is the religion of the Word incarnate in history, it is indispensable for the Church to hold to the real facts and events, precisely because they contain mysteries that theology must reflect on using keys of interpretation that belong to the realm of faith. Understood from this perspective is the Pope's interest in historical-critical exegesis, which he knows well, and of which he draws the best to deepen understanding of the events of the Last Supper, the meaning of the prayer of Gethsemane, the chronology of the Passion and, in particular, the historical traces of the Resurrection.[459]

The entire theological opus of Ratzinger can be referred to as essentially Christological. From the early years of his career as a theologian, Ratzinger's focus has been on the scripture, and particularly on Jesus Christ. He calls for a new understanding of Jesus Christ—his person and ministry. In fact, Ratzinger's theology is an exhortation for Christians to realize that Christianity is an encounter with Jesus Christ. In an interview, Ratzinger was asked if the belief in Jesus being born of a virgin and his rising from the dead is to be considered a child's belief. His response was,

> Simplicity is truth—and truth is simple. Of course, when I myself determine what is allowed to exist and what isn't, when I define the boundaries of possibility, and no one else, then of course phenomena like these have to be excluded. It is an act of intellectual arrogance for us to declare that they are internally contradictory or absurd and, for that reason alone, impossible. The message of Christ and the Church puts credible knowledge about God within our reach. God wanted to enter into this world. God didn't want us to have only a distant inkling of him through physics and mathematics. He wanted to show Himself to us. And so He was able to do what the Gospels recount that He did, just as He was also able to create a new dimension of existence in the resurrection. He was able to go beyond what Teilhard Chardin called the biosphere and the noosphere and

---

[459] Cardinal Marc Ouellet, "Jesus of Nazareth," (March 10, 2011), *Vatican Information Service*, http://www.zenit.org/phprint.php (accessed March 12, 2011).

to institute precisely a new sphere, in which man and the world attain union with God.[460]

It appears to be Ratzinger's ardent aspiration, since his early days as a theologian—to explain the mystery of Jesus and salvation. He always endeavors to make it known that Jesus came into this world to bring God closer to man—that man may have an encounter with God. He concurs with St. Paul who, in his Letter to the Colossians, described Jesus as "the image of the invisible God."[461] St. Paul makes the most emphatic and strongest statement about Jesus. He emphatically demonstrates that Jesus is incomparable. He is above all in heaven and on earth. Likewise, Ratzinger has over the years made the incomparability of Jesus's part of his schema. His theology emphasizes the unrivaled supremacy of Jesus, and he yearns that this supremacy reign over the whole world.

The teaching about the incomparability of Jesus puts Ratzinger and Hauerwas at par; for like Ratzinger, Hauerwas also stresses the uniqueness and supremacy of Jesus. For Hauerwas, Christianity is "a story of Jesus, which we Christians affirm is nothing less than the story of God's creation on our behalf, is not simply a particular instance of a more universal truth that can be known separately from the story. The story of Jesus is as unsubstitutable."[462]

Ratzinger's Christo-centered theology is at the same time Eucharistic because in the Eucharist, man enters into communion with God. Jesus became man so that we may become "gods." This becomes a reality in the Eucharist in which those who receive Jesus are transformed into what they receive. The Eucharist, according to Ratzinger, is the source and summit of Christian life. Like in St. Augustine's theory of illumination,[463] Ratzinger demonstrates that

---

[460] Benedict XVI, *Light of the World*, 167–168.

[461] "He has rescued us from the power of darkness and transferred us into the kingdom of his beloved Son, in whom we have redemption, the forgiveness of sins. He is the image of the invisible God, the firstborn of all creation; for in him all things in heaven and on earth were created, things visible and invisible, whether thrones or dominions or rulers or powers—all things have been created through him and for him. He himself is before all things, and in him all things hold together. He is the head of the body, the church; he is the beginning, the firstborn from the dead, so that he might come to have first place in everything. For in him all the fullness of God was pleased to dwell, and through him God was pleased to reconcile to himself all things, whether on earth or in heaven, by making peace through the blood of his cross" (Col 1:13–20).

[462] Hauerwas, *Christian Existence Today*, 40.

[463] "Just as crimes occur when the mind's motive force, which gives the impetus for action, is corruption and asserts itself in an insolent and disturbed way, and as vicious acts occur if obsession has captured the mind's effective part which is at the root of the impulse to carnal pleasures, so also errors and false opinions contaminate life if the reasoning mind is itself flawed. That was that condition at that time. For I did not know that the soul needs to be enlightened by light from outside itself, so that it can participate in truth, because it

in the Eucharist, God opens man's spiritual eyes, allowing man to clearly see him. In the Eucharist, God is the main actor and not man. In this sacrifice, man is able to realize Jesus—in the same way the disciples on the way to Emmaus recognized him at the breaking of bread (Lk 24:31).

Thus, Ratzinger believes that the Lord, who is in the Eucharist, enlightens the minds of people to know the truth; that it is in the Eucharist that man's eyes are opened, and it is in the Eucharist that man receives his mission to go and tell the good news.

Next, is his "doctrine" of relationality and creatureliness. Ratzinger's theology is a relational theology. It stems from the fact of creation which follows logically that a creature automatically depends and relies on a creator for life and sustainability. He is opposed to the ideology of makability and relationlessness prevailing in the society today. His theology reaffirms that man is a creature of God, and not just a creature, but the *imago Dei*. Therefore, by acting without God, man disassociates himself from his creator and denies that he is a creature. He ceases to be the *imago Dei*. Ratzinger works to reinstate man to his rightful position, that is, as a special creature that is the *imago Dei*. He illustrates,

> The mentality of *"makability"* tells us that we must free ourselves from every requirement to receive, from all dependency. We must stand on our own, independent of others and of God. Ratzinger counters: *relationlessness* is not our own; cut off from relationships, our truth is denied—and, with it, our freedom—for freedom and truth go together. God is not the enemy of our freedom but its ground. When people deny their creatureliness, seeing it as an imposition from outside, they end up replacing God with a capital "G" with a whole host of exploitative small "g" gods, such as commercial forces, greed, public opinion, etc. the tyranny of these is an enslavement far greater (Gen. 3:3—the original sin).[464]

The relationlessness of the contemporary culture is the concrete manifestation of relativism. As a remedy, Ratzinger proposes a rebuilding of the relationship with the Creator—a communion with the Lord. He suggests a reversal of

---

is not itself the nature of truth. You will light my lamp, O Lord. My God you will lighten my darkness (Ps 17:29), and of your fullness we have all received (Jn 1:16). You are the true light who illuminates every man coming into this world (Jn. 1: 9), because in you there is no change nor shadow caused by turning (Jas 1:17)." in John Ryan, *The Confessions of St. Augustine* (New York: Image Books, 1960), 108–109.

[464] Corkery, *Joseph Ratzinger's Theological Ideas*, 40–41.

what happened at the Tower of Babel.[465] What happened at Babel is what the contemporary culture is striving to repeat, living and acting without God. He seems to caution that if the building of this new tower is allowed to continue, it will yield the same dire consequences as at the first tower.

5.2.2 Stanley Hauerwas

Like Ratzinger, Hauerwas' theology is Trinitarian, which can only be described concretely in Jesus of Nazareth. Hence, his theology is also essentially Christological. His theological dialogue seems to be a retelling of the story of Jesus Christ. The story of Jesus, according to Hauerwas, is the story of a Christian and it is the story of God's creation.[466] In this, Hauerwas suggests recourse to creation—man situating himself in the story of creation as one of the creatures. The story of creation is manifested and fulfilled in the story of Christ. Therefore, a Christian is one who situates himself or herself in this story of creation. But this story is not only a story for a Christian but for all humanity, for we are all God's creatures.

The creation theology of Hauerwas makes Hauerwas bear a resemblance to Ratzinger. Hauerwas understands Jesus as the one who came to bond the broken relationship between God and man and bring them once again into a communion. For him, Jesus came to heal the relationship that was broken at the fall and at the Tower of Babel. Like Ratzinger, he also envisages the contemporary culture as repeating the construction of the Tower of Babel by living as if men need not acknowledge that their existence depends on gifts. Technology seems to be the means the modern man uses, though technology is not the problem itself. He points out that "it is not technology that is the problem but the assumption that God's creatures can name themselves; making a name for themselves." [467]

Hauerwas proposes a union in Christ in whom we become one with God our Creator. This union in Christ is fully realized in the Eucharist. In an interview, Hauerwas asserted that the Eucharist is "a rite in which we become part of the body of Christ."[468] Therefore, according to Hauerwas, unity in Christ is key in theology and Christian living. He desires a communion of Christians. "In the Eucharist, Christians learn how to be like Christ; to lead a Christ-centered life."[469]

Finally, Hauerwas rejects natural theology because, according to him, this

---

[465] Joseph Ratzinger, *Pilgrim Fellowship of Faith: The Church as Communion* (San Francisco: Ignatius Press, 2002), 61.
[466] Hauerwas, *Christian Existence Today*, 40.
[467] Ibid., 49.
[468] This was in an *Interview with Hauerwas* on January 28, 2011, at Duke University Divinity School (Cf. appendix).
[469] Cf. *Interview with Hauerwas* in the appendix.

tends to downplay the mystery of revelation, and the greatness of God who cannot be intelligible to finite minds. He states,

> I have little sympathy with natural theology. I had to work against the grain of modern theology's great temptation to make what we believe as Christians intelligible on terms set by the world. On these terms, any claims Christians make about God or the world must be accessible to anyone. In this way theology is natural. For Christians, however, time is apocalyptic, that is, it concerns the otherness and priority of God's cosmic and historical act through Jesus' singular life.[470]

5.3 Anthropologies

The Christian anthropologies of both Joseph Ratzinger and Stanley Hauerwas can be summed up in one word: "witness." John Shelby Spong described anthropology in the following words:

> Anthropology is the name of the academic discipline that studies human nature, human institutions and the interpretive myths of human beings. It seeks to understand the operative definitions by which people live. Christian anthropology would, therefore, be an attempt to state the Christian understanding of human nature which inevitably would constitute the primary building block upon which Christian theology would be built.[471]

The theologies of both Hauerwas and Ratzinger are built on their understanding of human nature. They understand human nature, first and foremost, as a created nature. Creaturedness is central in their anthropology. Thus, as a creation, they suggest that man ought to live as a creature of God; for God had a purpose in creating him, and the same God who created man holds his destiny as well. Their pedestal is the biblical truth of creation.[472] They invite Christians

---

[470] Hauerwas, *Hannah's Child*, 263.

[471] Definition of "anthropology," *Findarticle.com*, http://www.findarticle.com/p/articles/mi, (accessed March 1, 2011).

[472] "In the beginning when God created the heavens and the earth, the earth was a formless void and darkness covered the face of the deep, while a wind from God swept over the face of the waters. Then God said, 'Let there be light'; and there was light. And God saw that the light was good; and God separated the light from the darkness. God called the light Day and the darkness he called Night. And there was evening and there was morning, the first day. And God said, 'Let there be a dome in the midst of the waters, and let it separate the waters

and all people to this basic truth; that man, like any other creature, is a creation of God. They reprimand the modern culture for denying this.

5.3.1 Joseph Ratzinger

Ratzinger insists that man must go back to his roots; that is, to the truth of creation as it is given in the Holy Scriptures and illuminated by the church over

---

from the waters.' So God made the dome and separated the waters from that were under the dome from the waters that were above the dome. And it was so. God called the dome Sky. And there was evening and there was morning, the second day. And God said, 'Let the waters under the sky be gathered into one place, and let the dry land appear.' And it was so. God called the dry land Earth, and the waters that were gathered together he called Seas. And God saw that it was good. Then God said, 'Let the earth put forth vegetation: plants yielding seed, and fruit trees of every kind on earth that bear fruit with the seed in it.' And it was so. The earth brought forth vegetation: plants yielding seed of every kind and trees of every kind bearing fruit with the seed in it. And God saw that it was good. And there was evening and there was morning, the third day. And God said, 'Let there be lights in the dome of the sky to separate the day from the night; and let them be for signs and for seasons and for days and years, and let them be lights in the dome of the sky to give light upon the earth.' And it was so. God made the two great lights—the greater light to rule the day and the lesser light to rule the night—and the stars. God set them in the dome of the sky to give light upon the earth, to rule over the day and over the night, and to separate the light from the darkness. And God saw that it was good. And there was evening and there was morning, the fourth day. And God said, 'Let the waters bring forth swarms of living creatures and let the birds fly above the earth across the dome of the sky.' So God created the great sea monsters and every living creature that moves, of every kind, with which the waters swarm, and every winged bird of every kind. And God saw that it was good. God blessed them saying, "be fruitful and multiply and fill the waters in the seas, and let the birds multiply on the earth.' And there was evening and there was morning, the firth day. And God said, 'Let the earth bring forth living creatures of every kind: cattle and creeping things and wild animals of the earth of every kind.' And it was so. God made the wild animals of the earth of every kind, and the cattle of every kind, and everything that creeps upon the ground of every kind. And God saw that it was good. Then God said, 'Let us make humankind in our image, according to our likeness; and let them have dominion over the fish of the sea, and over the birds of the air, and over the cattle and over all the wild animals of the earth and over every creeping thing that creeps upon the earth.' So God created humankind in his image, in the image of God he created them; male and female he created them. God blessed them, and God said to them, 'Be fruitful and multiply, and fill the earth and subdue it; and have dominion over the fish of the sea and over the birds of the air and over every living thing that moves upon the earth.' God said, 'See, I have given you every plant yielding seed that is upon the face of all the earth, and every tree with seed in its fruit; you shall have them for food. And to every beast of the earth, and to every bird of the air, and to every thing that creeps on the earth, everything that has the breath of life, I have given every green plant for food.' And it was so. God saw everything that he had made, and indeed, it was very good. And there was evening and there was morning, the sixth day" (Gen 1:1–31).

the centuries. He regrets that this basic truth is unfortunately being denied by the prevailing culture. Ratzinger's anthropology is a response to the modern culture's denial of truth. Below is a summation of his opposition:

> It is obvious that the concept of truth has become suspect. Of course it is correct that it has been much abused. Intolerance and cruelty have occurred in the name of truth. To that extent people are afraid when someone says, "This is the truth," or even "I have the truth." We never have it; at best it has us. No one will dispute that one must be careful and cautious in claiming the truth. But simply to dismiss it as unattainable is really destructive. A large proportion of contemporary philosophies, in fact, consist of saying that man is not capable of ethical values, either. Then he would have no standards. Then he would only have to consider how he arranged things reasonable for himself, and then at any rate the opinion of the majority would be the only criterion that counted.[473]

In the above statement, Ratzinger asserts that the prevailing culture is trying to eliminate the truth as the universal standard; hence, making relativity regulate human activity. The first truth of this culture wants to get rid of is the truth of Creation. Ratzinger, as stated earlier, believes that uncoupled from truth, humanity dies. Why? Because,

> As human beings, we receive a dialogical, relational essence and are called to live this in history in an existence that is at once gift and task. We have a responsibility to shape our lives, always in fidelity to what we have received as created beings. We have no freedom of our own. Our freedom is a normed freedom—not blind and directionless, but guided by the light of what is given to us with our creation.[474]

Therefore, the first truth that all theology and religiosity and human activity are based on is the fact that man is a creature of God. When man realizes this, then his relation to the Creator follows automatically.

---

[473] Benedict XVI, *Light of the World*, 50–51.
[474] Corkery, *Joseph Ratzinger's Theological Ideas*, 41–42.

5.3.2 Stanley Hauerwas

Like Ratzinger, Stanley Hauerwas also insists on the truth of creation. He refers to God as a creator and man as part of God's creation; and for him, this is the starting point. He says that God who is at work in creation is the Trinitarian God. Thus, Hauerwas is critical of making "creation" synonymous with "nature."[475] However, this is what the prevailing culture wants to impose on humanity, that the idea of creation is mythological. It denies that there is a force above nature and in which nature finds meaning and fulfillment.

A feasibility study on creation versus evolution stated,

> The popular media often portrays the creation vs. evolution debate as science vs. religion, with creation being religious and evolution being scientific. Unfortunately, if you don't agree with this label, you too are labeled. Regardless of whether you're a creationist or an evolutionist, if you disagree with the stereotype, you're condemned and "exposed" as a religious fanatic who is secretly trying to pass religion off as science or, even worse, trying to disprove science in order to redeem a ridiculous, unscientific, religious worldview.[476]

The above is a good representation of the prevailing relativistic culture regarding ideas of not only creation, but religion as a whole. However, Hauerwas thinks this ideology is inept. He believes in a definitive creator and religion which is not based on science but on revelation.

Hauerwas accuses the contemporary culture of meddling in the world's belief systems and persuading the world to surrender its beliefs to the mere activity of science. According to him, there is no scientific conclusion that would require such revision—particularly those about the ultimate end of the human life or even the world. He is less confident that it is meaningful to assign to science qua science an overriding veridical status. For him, "Christianity is no world view, not a form of primitive metaphysics, that can be assessed in comparison of alternative world views."[477] Hauerwas believes in a God of creation, and he believes this is the God of Christianity. The God of creation is not what human minds perceive scientifically, but rather, he is the God of faith. Unlike in science where man draws from the known to unknown, in faith, we go from the unknown to the known. Science and faith use two different methods. Thus,

---

[475] Hauerwas, *In Good Company*, 181.

[476] "Creation vs. Evolution," *Philosophy All About*, http://www.allaboutphilosophy.org/creation-vs-evolution.htm (accessed March 15, 2011).

[477] Hauerwas, *Christian Existence Today*, 9–10.

Hauerwas teaches that "our being is relational, that is to say, we have a receiver nature which comes from a maker who is God."[478]

This relational nature brings us to another fact of human nature, that is, the fallen nature of man. After God created a perfect universe and perfect man, man misused his freedom against God's order. Man consequently lost his holiness/perfection and original justice. For this reason, man needs redemption, which is also an attribute of the Godhead.

Hauerwas teaches a fallen nature of man, and insists that this is the reason for world order thereafter. He wants the fact of original sin[479] to be retold as a

---

[478] God is the absolute and ultimate source of all being; thus universal principle of creation. Humanity is God's project. We are first and foremost receivers and not makers: who we are is much more a gift received than a task achieved (from Corkery, *Ratzinger's Theological Ideas*, 31–33).

[479] "Now the serpent was more crafty than any other wild animal that the Lord God had made. He said to the woman, 'Did God say, "You shall not eat from any tree in the garden"?' The woman said to the serpent, "We may eat of the fruit of the trees in the garden; but God said, "You shall not eat of the fruit of the tree that is in the middle of the garden, nor shall you touch it, or you shall die.' But the serpent said to the woman, 'You will not die; for God knows that when you eat of it your eyes will be opened, and you will be like God, knowing good and evil.' So when the woman was that the tree was good for food, and that it was a delight to the eyes, and that the tree was to be desired to make one wise, she took of its frit and ate; and she also gave some to her husband, who was with her, and he ate. Then the eyes of both were opened, and they knew that they were naked; and they sewed fig leaves together and made loincloths for themselves. They heard the sound of the Lord God walking in the garden at the time of the evening breeze, and the man and his wife hid themselves from the presence of the Lord God among the trees of the garden. But the Lord God called to the man, and said to him, 'Where are you?' he said, "I heard the sound of you in the garden, and I was afraid, because I was naked; and I hid myself.' Have you eaten from the tree of which I commanded you not to eat?' The man said, 'The woman whom you gave to be with me, she gave me fruit from the tree, and I ate.' Then the Lord God said to the woman, 'What is this that you have done?' The woman said, 'The serpent tricked me, and I ate.' The Lord God said to the serpent, 'Because you have done this, cursed are you among all animals and among all wild creatures; upon your belly you shall go, and dust you shall eat all the days of your life. I will put enmity between you and the woman, and between your offspring and hers; he will strike your head, and you shall strike his heel.' To the woman he said, 'I will greatly increase your pangs in child-bearing; in pain you shall bring forth children, yet your desire shall be for your husband, and he shall rule over you.' And to the man he said, 'Because you have listened to the voice of your wife, and have eaten of the tree about which I commanded you, "You shall not eat of it," cursed is the ground because of you; in toil you shall eat of it all the days of your life; thorns and thistles it shall bring forth for you; and you shall eat the plants of the field. By the sweat of your face you shall eat bread until you return to the ground, for out of it you were taken; you are dust, and to dust you shall return.' The man named his wife Eve, because she was the mother of all who live. And the Lord God made garments of skins for the man and for his wife, and clothed them. Then the Lord God said, 'See, the man has become like one of us, knowing good and evil; and now, he might reach out his hand and

basic truth. He is conscious of humanity's fallenness and envisages God's dealings with us as being converting and transformative, creating a new language.[480] He believes in original sin and its transmission to all humanity. According to him, both original sin and personal sin are a reality that cannot be denied. They are consequences of misuse of freedom by man.[481] Hence, man bears the responsibility of sin. He is opposed to the prevailing culture which downplays the notion of sin and punishment.

5.4 Redemption

Both Ratzinger and Hauerwas, as stated above, believe in a created and fallen humanity that needs redemption. This redemption, according to them, is only possible through the grace of Jesus Christ. They believe in a redemption initiated by God through a call, responded to by faith, efficient through sacraments, and fulfilled in a sanctified/transformed human nature. They understand salvation as a process other than a onetime act. Salvation to them is a journey through life, not attained already in the initial act of faith.

5.4.1 Joseph Ratzinger

According to Joseph Ratzinger, the content of salvation is "Through God's gift of salvation we receive forgiveness for sin and a promise that we shall rise with Christ to eternal life with God."[482] For him, salvation is not something that happens to a person at the point of belief and baptism, but what goes on in him throughout early life to life eternal. For him, salvation is both historical and eschatological. It encompasses all history: past, present, and future.[483] "God conquers man's past—conquers sin—by calling him into the future—into Christ. And in Christ, salvation is present now: Salvation is Person; everywhere

---

take also from the tree of life, and eat, and live for ever'—therefore the Lord God sent him forth from the garden of Eden, to till the ground from which he was taken. He drove out the man; and at the east of the garden of Eden he placed the cherubim, and a sword flaming and turning to guard the way to the tree of life" (Gen 3:1–24).

[480] Hauerwas, *Christian Existence Today*, 53

[481] Ibid., 47–48.

[482] Corkery, *Joseph Ratzinger's Theological Ideas*, 60.

[483] "Only faith can bring love to its proper end. If we think a little further, we also come upon the mystery of hope. For our believing and our loving are still on their way, so long as we remain in this world, and again and again they are in danger of flickering out. No one can say of himself, 'I am completely saved.' In the era of this world, there is no redemption as a past action, already completed; redemption exists only in the mode of hope" in Benedict XVI, *Credo for Today*, 17.

that Christ reigns, there is salvation."[484] Ratzinger believes that salvation is when a person lives and acts as St. Paul taught, "For through the Law I died to the Law, so that I might live to God. I have been crucified with Christ, and it is no longer I who live, but it is Christ lives in me. And the life I now live in the flesh I live by faith in the Son of God, who loved me and gave himself for me" (Gal 2:19-20). He rejects notions of salvation that place salvation either only in history, or only in the present or only in the future.

To both Ratzinger and Hauerwas, salvation is meaningless if it does not lead to conversion or sanctification. It is not what the Reformers embodied only in justification. For them, justification and sanctification go together; salvation is fulfilled in sanctification. Ratzinger continues to insist that the main agent of salvation is God.[485] Sinners have to rely on receiving, on accepting the gift of being turned round, of being converted. Thus, for Ratzinger, "Conversion—*metanoia*—is the fundamental Christian act. Our old existence is taken away and a new one is received. We are drawn beyond the isolation of the 'I' into the 'we' of the believing community—being moved away from egoism and preoccupation with the self into the relational 'we' that is our true character and destiny."[486]

According to Ratzinger, baptism, the beginning of salvation, is a passing from death to new life—death to the old self and birth to new life.[487] He likened baptism to the death story of the wheat grain (Jn 12:24-25). Unless a wheat grain dies, it cannot bear fruit. When it dies, it bears much fruits. A baptized person therefore dies to sin and acts of darkness and lives in the light and acts of the light. Therefore, for Ratzinger, salvation becomes a reality when a redeemed person lives as Jesus told his disciples in the Sermon on the Mount: "You are the light of the world. A city built on a hill cannot be hidden. No one after lighting a lamp puts it under the bushel basket, but on the lampstand, and it gives light to all in the house. In the same way, let your light shine before others, so that they may see your good works and give glory to your Father in heaven" (Mt 5:14-16).

5.4.2 Stanley Hauerwas

Hauerwas does not consider himself a theologian in a strict sense. Rather he calls himself a moralist. This is not to mean that he is not a theologian because he is a moralist. Rather, what he wants to suggest is that he does not write

---

[484] Ibid.
[485] Corkery, *Joseph Ratzinger's Theological Ideas*, 61.
[486] Ibid.
[487] Ibid.

"systematic" theology (in the sense that he does not follow under any denominational tradition), but rather his writings are an ethical guide to the body of Christ. In so doing, he explicates the theological bearings of theology.

Hauerwas' redemption anthropology is summed up in discipleship. His understanding of the notion of salvation is not distinct from discipleship; that is to say, in witnessing to the truth of Christ. His meaning of salvation leans more toward Catholic sanctification than to the Protestant justification. The one saved is one who is transformed into a witness rather than a continuous sinner, whose offenses are not charged against him. Hauerwas' opinion on salvation is the following: "Salvation is: Jesus saves us from sin and death—a history that requires an alternative history. The social manifestation that makes that history present is Church. Salvation is God's work to restore all creation to the Lordship of Christ, and it is historically and socially mediated."[488]

From his description of salvation, the phrase, "restore all creation" is worth noting. It discloses Hauerwas' essential concept of salvation as a restoration, a healing. Hauerwas understands the fact that at the fall, man lost his original justice and holiness which is in need of restoration. Therefore, the redeemed man is a healed man, a restored man, a rehabilitated man. He is not simply acquitted, but his nature is restored to the original. His ideas are in line with the Catholic teaching on sanctification as the infusion of God's love into our hearts, through the Holy Spirit, by which we are regenerated. It is the fullness of justification and forgiveness of sins.[489] He believes in a justification that is a renewal of the inward man, a restoration of the primeval state of humanity. His belief falls in line with the Catholic understanding of justification and salvation. Hauerwas is more Catholic than Protestant.

5.5 Ecclesiology

Both Ratzinger and Hauerwas believe in the salvation that is an exclusive prerogative of the church. The fallen man, according to them, can only be saved within the church. Therefore, the church is necessary for salvation, according to both Ratzinger and Hauerwas. They believe in a church that is a divine institution entrusted to the apostles to continue Jesus's work of salvation. This is in contrast to the common rejection, by the contemporary society, of the church as a divine institution and labeling it a man-made institution.[490]

---

[488] Hauerwas, *In Good Company*, 183.

[489] Johann Adam Möhler, *Symbolism* (New York: The Crossroad Publishing Company, 1997), 104.

[490] "Peter Seewald made very relevant observations about the society today. He said that society's problems have not gotten any better, and this under-scores all the more the urgency of the questions concerning the shape we should give our lives: What are our

5.5.1 Joseph Ratzinger

Ratzinger utterly disagrees with beliefs and accusations that the church is a man-made institution. He observes,

> The modern idea of progress and science has created a mentality that we think will make the "God hypothesis" superfluous. Today man thinks that he himself can do everything that he once awaited from God alone. In light of this would-be scientific intellectual model, matters of faith appear as archaic, as mythical, as belonging to a bygone civilization. Religion, at least the Christian religion, accordingly classified as a relic of the past. As early as the eighteenth century, the Enlightenment was announcing that the Pope, that the Dalai Lama of Europe, was inevitably doomed to disappear one day. The Enlightenment, it was thought, would finally sweep away these mythological holdovers once and for all.[491]

He believes the above described mentalities are realistic. He, on the other hand, affirms that religion and in particular the Christian faith/church is not a phenomenon of the past but a reality that is ever new, for all ages. He notes three basic characteristics of the church: the church is apostolic; she is a praying church, thus tuned toward the Lord—"holy"; and she is one.[492] Second, he notes that the church is always sustained by the Holy Spirit who is present and guiding the church until the end of time. He reiterates the promises Jesus made and

---

values and standards? What are we actually doing with our lives? How do we want to live them in future? We see in our time a world in danger of sliding into the abyss. We see an unrestrained economic system ready to mutate into a predatory capitalism that devours values on a large scale; we see that life in the fast lane is only beyond our means, but it also robs us of our moral compass; we see the growth of a society that plunges ahead restlessly, and with no clear sense of direction, regarding today as wrong what yesterday was still considered right and regarding tomorrow as right what today is still considered wrong. We have illness such as burnout, now a mass phenomenon, and new addiction to things such as video games and pornography. We have the almost unmanageable work-related stress produced by the mania for profit maximization that drives the business world. We have the precarious situation of children who suffer on account of the loss of family relations. We have the dominance of the media, which have developed a culture bent on breaking our taboos, dumbing us down, and blunting our moral sense. We have the offerings of the electronic media, which have the potential to manipulate and destroy the qualities that make us human," in Benedict XVI, *Light of the World*, 133.

[491] Benedict XVI, *Light of the World*, 134.

[492] Ratzinger, *Pilgrim Fellowship of Faith*, 61.

which he believes will be fulfilled: "I tell you, you are Peter and upon this rock I will build my Church and the gates of hell will not overpower it" (Mt 16:18). On another occasion, Jesus told his disciples, "Go therefore and make disciples of all the nations, baptizing them in the name of the Father and the Son and the Holy Spirit, and teaching them to obey everything that I commanded you. And remember, I am with you always, to the end of the age" (Mt 28:19–20). Jesus also told his disciples: "Heaven and earth will pass away, but my words will not pass away" (Mk 13:31). Last but not least, Jesus made this promise:

And I will ask the Father, and he will give you another Advocate, to be with you for ever. This is the Spirit of truth, whom the world cannot receive, because it neither sees him nor knows him. You know him, because he abides with you, and he will be in you. "I will not leave you orphaned; I am coming to you. In a little while the world will no longer see me, but you will see me; because I live, you also will live" (Jn 14:16–19).

Vatican II teaches the same that Ratzinger, the theologian believes and teaches,

The eternal Father, in accordance with the utterly gratuitous and mysterious design of his wisdom and goodness, created the whole universe, and chose to raise up men to share in his own divine life; and when they had fallen in Adam, he did not abandon them, but at all times held out to them the means of salvation, bestowed in consideration of Christ, the Redeemer, "who is the image of the invisible God, the first born of all creature" (Col 1:15). All the elect, before time began, the Father "foreknew and also predestined to become conformed to the image of his Son, that he should be the firstborn among many brethren" (Rom 8:29). He determined to call together in a holy Church those who should believe in Christ. Already present in figure at the beginning of the world, this Church was prepared in marvelous fashion in the history of the people of Israel and in the old Alliance. Established in this last age of the world, and made manifest in the outpouring of the Spirit, it will be brought to glorious completion at the end of time. At that moment, as the Fathers put it, all the just from the time of Adam, "from Abel, the just one, to the last of elect" will be gathered together with the Father in the universal Church.[493]

Ratzinger believes the church instituted by Jesus is not only for all times,

---

[493] LG 2.

but it is also necessary for salvation. Jesus Christ came to redeem the fallen man. He accomplishes this *redemptoris missio* via the church, continually guided by the spirit. The Lord, at the great commissioning, sent out his disciples to go and make disciples of all nations, and teaching them to obey everything he commanded them (Mt 28:19–20). By this very act, the Lord sanctioned his apostles to constitute a community of believers that today we refer to as church. It is this assembly of believers (*Ecclesia*) that will be saved[494] as he affirmed it that "the one who believes and is baptized will be saved" (Mk 16:16). Thus salvation belongs to those who belong to this assembly of faith and vice versa.

However, Ratzinger also knows that salvation is not a human activity but rather an activity of God. It is God who saves, not man, and the spirit of God blows where she will. Therefore, God is at will to include among the saved, even those who may be outside the elect. He talks a different language when it comes to *extra ecclesia nulla salus* dogma. In his homily in 1964, he took the direction of what later the encyclical *Redemptoris Missio*[495] affirmed, that people outside

---

[494] "The first beneficiary of salvation is the Church. Christ won the Church for himself at the price of his own blood and made the Church his co-worker in the salvation of the world. Indeed, Christ dwells within the Church. She is his Bride. It is he who causes her to grow. He carries out his mission through her. The Council makes frequent reference to the Church's role in the salvation of mankind. While acknowledging that God loves all people and grants them the possibility of being saved (cf. 1 Tm 2:4), the Church believes that God has established Christ as the one mediator and that she herself has been established as the universal sacrament of salvation. 'To this catholic unity of the people of God, therefore, . . . all are called, and they belong to it or are ordered to it in various ways, whether they be Catholic faithful or others who believe in Christ or finally all people everywhere who by the grace of God are called to salvation.' It is necessary to keep these two truths together, namely, the real possibility of salvation in Christ for all mankind and the necessity of the Church for salvation. Both these truths help us to understand the *one mystery of salvation*, so that we can come to know God's mercy and our own responsibility. Salvation, which always remains a gift of the Holy Spirit, requires man's cooperation, both to save himself and to save others. This is God's will, and this is why he established the Church and made her a part of his plan of salvation. Referring to 'this messianic people,' the Council says; "It has been set up by Christ as a communion of life, love and truth; by him too it is taken up as the instrument of salvation for all, and sent on a mission to the whole world as the light of the world and the salt of the earth," in John Paul II, *On the Permanent Validity of the Church's Missionary Mandate "Redemptoris Missio"* (Encyclical Letter, December 7, 1990), 17–18.

[495] "The universality of salvation means that it is granted not only to those who explicitly believe in Christ and have entered the Church. Since salvation is offered to all, it must be made concretely available to all. But it is clear that today, as in the past, many people do not have an opportunity to come to know or accept the gospel revelation or to enter the Church. The social and cultural conditions in which they live do not permit this, and frequently they have been brought up in other religious traditions. For such people salvation in Christ is accessible by virtue of a grace which, while having a mysterious relationship to the Church,

the church can also attain salvation. However, he only emphasizes that the church is the sure way to salvation:

> Everything we believe about God, and everything we know about man, prevents us from accepting that beyond the limits of the Church there is no more salvation, that up to the time of Christ all men were subject to the fate of eternal damnation. The question we have to face is not that of whether other people can be saved and how. We are convinced that God is able to do this with or without our theories, with or without our perspicacity, and that we do not need to help him do it with our cogitations. The question that really troubles us is not in the least concerned with whether and how God manages to save *others*. The question that torments us is, much rather, that of why it is still actually necessary for us to carry out the whole ministry of the Christian faith—why, if there are so many other ways to heaven and to salvation, should it still be demanded of us that we bear, day by day, the whole burden of ecclesiastical dogma and ecclesiastical ethics? What is that special thing in Christianity that not only justifies but compels us to be and live as Christians? It became clear enough to us, yesterday, that there is no answer to this that will resolve every contradiction into incontrovertible, unambivalent truth with scientific clarity. Assent to the hiddenness of God is an essential part of the movement of the spirit that we call "faith." And one more preliminary consideration is requisite.[496]

Faith is the requisite of salvation, and scriptures are a guide of how to live our faith. The Lord in his word gives us the way to salvation and gave us the

---

does not make them formally part of the Church but enlightens them in a way which is accommodated to their spiritual and material situation. This grace comes from Christ; it is the result of his Sacrifice and is communicated by the Holy Spirit. It enables each person to attain salvation through his or her free cooperation. For this reason the Council, after affirming the centrality of the Paschal Mystery, went on to declare that "this applies not only to Christians but to all people of good will in whose hearts grace is secretly at work. Since Christ died for everyone, and since the ultimate calling of each of us comes from God and is therefore a universal one, we are obliged to hold that the Holy Spirit offers everyone the possibility of sharing in this Paschal Mystery in a manner known to God," in John Paul II, *On the Permanent Validity of the Church's Missionary Mandate*, 18–19.

[496] Joseph Ratzinger, "Are Non-Christians Saved?" (1964 Sermon), *Beliefnet.com*, http://www.beliefnet.com/Faiths/Catholic/2007/01/Are-Non-Christians-Saved. aspx#ixzz1ICsfuxSJ (accessed March 10, 2011).

church as the channel of this salvation. A deliberate choice not to follow the way of the Lord, by keeping away from his church, is synonymous to protest against salvation itself. The refusal to enter or be part of the new Noah's Ark of salvation is modeled after the first sin of Adam and Eve when they rejected what God had ordained and chose their own way. The consequence of their act was the loss of original justice and divine order. The same therefore would befall those who choose to take a way other than that ordained by God.

The importance Ratzinger accords the church as a channel of salvation is similar to that of Hauerwas. Even if Ratzinger and Hauerwas belong to different denominations, they, on the other hand, concur on the necessity of the church for salvation.

5.5.2 Stanley Hauerwas

Hauerwas is a Methodist Christian with strong Catholic sympathies.[497] His sympathy is manifested in his emphasis on the visibility of church and its character as a disciplined community in contrast to the strong individualism in most of Protestantism, the centrality of sanctification against the strong emphasis on justification by faith, the Bible as read in the Christian community against a simple *sola scriptura* principle, and his strong emphasis on the Eucharist and on the liturgy against spiritualism and rationalism.[498]

According to Hauerwas, we do not know who God is, abstracted from our knowledge of God which is dependent on our living in faithful community with those historic communities we call Israel and the church. "God and God's salvation are not knowable abstracted from history as mediated through the traditions of Israel and the Church. Rather, one learns to know God through being part of this embodied narrative."[499] He closely connects the church with the kingdom of God. He thus asserts,

> The kingdom of God is not a human utopian project, but is a reality established by God. The kingdom of God is historically and socially embodied in the community of the Christian Church, even though God's reign is wider than the Church and even though the Church often has been and is unfaithful. Without the kingdom ideal, the Church loses its identity-

---

[497] Though Hauerwas confesses that in practice he does not belong to any particular denomination, his confession goes, "I have no ecclesial home. Although I have belonged to many congregations [Catholic, Methodist, Lutheran, Episcopalian], I have never had a home in a particular ecclesial tradition" in Hauerwas, *Hannah's Child*, 254.
[498] Hauerwas, *In Good Company*, 26–27.
[499] Ibid., 179.

forming hope; without the Church, the kingdom ideal loses its concrete character.[500]

> To attain the kingdom of God, human beings are better off being members of the church he instituted.

Hauerwas sees the Christian Church as real people that exist in definite historical and institutional forms, the people that the institutional forms and ministers serve.[501] This makes any static, timeless view of the church impossible. According to him, the church is a historical, and in relation to new social contexts, a changing phenomenon.[502] For him, the church is a new and alternative *polis* or *civitas*. Here, he recapitulates the Augustinian City of God.[503] He tends to suggest that the church is the holy city of God as opposed to the earthly city. While those resident in the earthly city are guided by the early precepts, the citizens of the city of God are bound by the rules that govern the city of God. Therefore, belonging to the church also requires a living that befits the holiness of the city.

For Hauerwas, being a Christian means being a disciple of Christ—a witness. He states that

> to learn to know Jesus is not a purely theoretical matter and cannot be separated from being his disciple. We cannot know

---

[500] Ibid., 186.

[501] Hauerwas, *In Good Company*, 186.

[502] Ibid., 190.

[503] "The glorious city of God is my theme in this work, which you, my dearest son Marcellinus, suggested, and which is due to you by my promise. I have undertaken its defence against those who prefer their own gods to the Founder of this city,—a city surpassingly glorious, whether we view it as it still lives by faith in this fleeting course of time, and sojourns as a stranger in the midst of the ungodly, or as it shall dwell in the fixed stability of its eternal seat, which it now with patience waits for, expecting until 'righteousness shall return unto judgment,' and it obtain, by virtue of its excellence, final victory and perfect peace. A great work this, and an arduous; but God is my helper. For I am aware what ability is requisite to persuade the proud how great is the virtue of humility, which raises us, not by a quite human arrogance, but by a divine grace, above all earthly dignities that totter on this shifting scene. For the King and Founder of this city of which we speak, has in Scripture uttered to His people a dictum of the divine law in these words: 'God resisteth the proud, but giveth grace unto the humble.' But this, which is God's prerogative, the inflated ambition of a proud spirit also affects, and dearly loves that this be numbered among its attributes, to 'Show pity to the humbled soul, And crush the sons of pride.' And therefore, as the plan of this work we have undertaken requires, and as occasion offers, we must speak also of the earthly city, which, though it be mistress of the nations, is itself ruled by its lust of rule," in Marcus Dods, ed., *The City of God* (Vol. 1, Edinburgh: T & T Clark), 1.

who Jesus is and what He stands for without learning to be His followers. There is no private discipleship, because salvation is about God's creation of a new polity.[504]

It means that, according to Hauerwas, the church is an institution where those who belong to it are marching toward the heavenly city of God and those to be included in this heavenly city are those who have followed and lived according to guidelines of the city of God here on earth. Hauerwas believes that to be a disciple is to be part of the new *polis* that has the Gospel as constitution. Christian life is not something spontaneous or something that comes naturally.[505] Therefore, our salvation is a journey that begins here on earth and continues through life.

---

[504] Hauerwas, *In Good Company*, 185–186.
[505] Ibid., 194.

Chapter Six

6.0 Fundamental Differences between Ratzinger and Hauerwas

Before we attempt the analysis of Ratzinger and Hauerwas with regard to their differences, we suppose it is important to examine first the doctrinal differences between Catholics and Protestants. These will serve as a conduit to affirming the particularities in their teachings. The differences between Ratzinger and Hauerwas become apparent in the doctrinal symbolisms of both the Catholic and Protestant faiths to which they belong respectively. This is because they are, to a greater extent, influenced by their denominational backgrounds and their thoughts have a leaning toward their particular faiths. This does not rule out that on the other hand, their writings cut across the denominational divide.

However, this paper cannot and is not aimed at an exhaustive contrast between the Catholic and Protestant faiths. This would require a whole independent dissertation. Our interest is to highlight their differences in regard to what our main reference theologians teach and believe. Johann Möhler's *Symbolism* will be our main source in this section.

In particular, we shall examine the basic and essential theological, anthropological, and ecclesiological questions raised by both Ratzinger and Hauerwas. It should also be noted that we shall restrict our analysis to the doctrinal developments that sprouted during the sixteenth-century Reformation. Nevertheless, we shall also briefly direct our gaze toward those who, during the modern times, reiterated the Reformers' teachings (Protestant) and elevated it to higher levels. The reason for integrating these is to help us find the link between the Reformation period and the contemporary period with regard to the divergences from the main church doctrines. The theologians we have chosen to bridge these two periods are Schleiermacher and Kierkegaard.

155

6.1 Doctrinal Differences between Catholicism and Protestantism

Johann Adam Möhler (d. 1838) describes symbolism as the scientific exposition of the doctrinal differences among the various religious parties opposed to each other.[506] However, before he laid down these differences, he made a very significant and very important point, stating, "revolutions are not conducted according to a preconcerted, fully completed system: but, on the contrary, their fundamental principles are wont to be consistently unfolded only in and by practical life, and their heterogeneous parts to be thereby only gradually transformed."[507] Hence, he notes that the Reformation of the sixteenth century did not base its reflections directly on the origin of human nature, but rather, on a very political and therefore subordinate interest. According to Möhler, during the Reformation, "all doctrines were seized and controverted to suit this interest."[508]

He continues to assert that the religious ferment of the sixteenth century, and the ecclesiastical controversies which it produced, are of a totally different nature from the context which divides the Western and Eastern churches. "The controversy, agitated in the west, regards exclusively Christian anthropology. The controversy, on the other hand, agitated in the East, has reference to Christology."[509] The key initiators of these controversies were Luther, Zwingle, and Calvin. Their ideas were mainly a protest to the wrongs in the church at the time. Möhler appropriately asserts, "Protestantism arose partly out of the opposition to much that was undeniably bad and defective in the Church, and therein consists the good it has achieved."[510]

During counter-Reformation, the Catholic Church reorganized herself in what might be referred to as the greatest ecumenical council of all time, the Council of Trent. This council was aimed at correcting, not only the heretical construal of doctrine by the Reformers, but also the mistakes within the church herself. The Council of Trent stands as the document that perfectly articulates the doctrine of the Christian faith. Möhler states that the Council of Trent embraces all the doctrines of the Gospel, and it might be named a confession of the Christian Church in opposition to all non-Christian creeds.[511] Therefore, this council will be a key source of the Catholic teaching in the discussion below.

---

[506] Möhler, *Symbolism*, 1.
[507] Ibid., 23.
[508] Ibid., 2.
[509] Möhler, *Symbolism*, 2.
[510] Ibid., 9.
[511] Ibid., 13–14.

6.2 The Primitive State of Man

6.2.1 The Catholic Teaching

The Catholic Church teaches that the Paradisaic man was endowed with supernatural graces which were greatly weakened at the fall. Adam was originally endowed with holiness and justice as supernatural graces granted to him at creation. This man was also given the opportunity and gift of free will which he abused at the fall.[512] Möhler noted rightly: "On Adam the supernatural gifts were bestowed simultaneously with his natural endowments; that is to say, both were conferred at the moment of his creation."[513] The Reformers denied this as we shall investigate below.

6.2.2 Protestant Teaching

For the purpose of this dissertation, we shall restrict ourselves to the teaching of Martin Luther (Lutheran) and John Calvin (Calvinists) for two reasons: one, because we regard these to be the main Protestant Reformers of the sixteenth century; and two, Hauerwas, who is our main reference in this paper, tends to swing back and forth between the teachings of these two protagonists.

6.2.2.1 Martin Luther (Lutherans)

Johann Möhler believes that Luther brought no new and peculiar views into vogue. He only selected, out of the rich store of theories which the fruitfulness of scholasticism had produced, the one which seemed most favorable to his own opinions. With regard to the original state of man, Luther taught that the original man was endowed with natural and essential grace which he lost at the fall, such that the fallen man remained with nothing supernatural in him to make him rise to his original state.[514] "Against those theologians, who called Adam's acceptableness before God supernatural, Luther asserted it to be 'natural' and in opposition to the schoolmen, who regarded it accidental, he conceived it to be essential to human nature."[515]

---

[512] ND 508, Council of Trent, 5th session, *Decree on Original Sin*, 1546.
[513] Möhler, *Symbolism*, 28.
[514] Dillenberger, ed., *Martin Luther*, 105.
[515] Ibid., 30.

6.3 The Doctrine on Original Sin

6.3.1 The Origin (Whence) of Evil: Free Will

6.3.1.1 The Catholic Teaching

The Catholic Church teaches man was created with the endowment of freedom, in order that the guilt of evil in the world might fall on the head of man.[516] According to the Catholic Church, evil is a result of the disobedience of man—a misuse of man's freedom. At the instigation of the devil, man misused his freedom and disobeyed God. As a result, sin (evil) and death came into this world (Gen 3:1–24). This teaching completely refutes the idea of God being the source of evil. Thus, the existence of evil has something to do with the damaged free will. The Catholic Church rejected the Protestant proposition that God works evil as well as good and that it is not in the power of man to abstain from wickedness.[517]

6.3.1.2 The Protestant Teaching

The main Reformers, Luther, Melancthon, Zwingle, and Beza, denied that man has a free will. Möhler further states that their denial of freedom was calculated to excite an apprehension, that the Catholic doctrine of God's perfect sanctity, to whom sin is an abomination, would be thrown into the shade and that even the most vicious man would be thus sheltered from all responsibility.[518]

6.3.1.2.1 Martin Luther

Luther asserted that man is devoid of freedom; that every (pretended) free action is only apparent; that an irresistible divine necessity rules all things and that every human act is, at bottom, only the act of God.[519] "Free will after the fall is nothing but a word, and as long as it is doing what is within it, it is committing deadly sin. It has the potentiality toward good as an unrealizable capacity only; toward evil, however, always a realizable one."[520] This is servitude of human will, Möhler says.[521]

---

[516] Möhler, *Symbolism*, 37.
[517] ND 510, Council of Trent, 5th session, *Decree on Original Sin*, 1546.
[518] Möhler, *Symbolism*, 37.
[519] Dillenberger, ed., *Martin Luther*, 156–158.
[520] Ibid., 502.
[521] Möhler, *Symbolism*, 32–33.

6.4 The Nature of Original Sin

6.4.1 The Catholic Doctrine on Original Sin

The doctrine of the Catholic Church on original sin might be reduced to the following rephrased propositions.

> Adam, by sin, lost his original justice and holiness, drew down on himself by his disobedience and the displeasure and the judgments of the Almighty, incurred the penalty of death, and thus in all his parts, in his body as well as soul, became strangely deteriorated. His sinful condition is transmitted to all his posterity as descending from him. Man is of himself incapable of acting in a manner agreeable to God, save only by the merits of Jesus Christ. The fallen man's free-will was very much weakened. Not every religious and moral action of man is necessarily sinful; moreover, fallen man still bears the image of God.[522]

Möhler wonders why and how Adam could be subject of such fearful wrath, if he did only what he was obliged to do; if he perpetrated only what he could not avoid. Therefore, Möhler regards the conception of original sin on the part of the Protestants as devoid of sense and reason, because they seem anxious to resuscitate the feeling of sin and the consciousness of guilt.[523] Hence, original sin is put to the responsibility of man—owing to his disobedience by transgressing the condiment of God in paradise, and it injured his posterity, which is acquired by imitation and not propagation.

The Catholic teaching is that "in the fallen and unregenerated man, the transition from original to actual sin is determined by free-will, which possesses the power to resist the carnal propensity in a manner not totally unsuccessful and not merely exterior. Although abandoned to itself, it is unable to accomplish perfect actions, in their inward spirit morally good, and consequently acceptable to God."[524] Sts. Bonaventure's[525] and Thomas Aquinas's[526] explanations of this reality are paramount and worth noting.

---

[522] ND 508, Council of Trent, 5th session, *Decree on Original Sin*, 1546.

[523] Möhler, *Symbolism*, 45.

[524] Möhler, *Symbolism*, 63.

[525] "All who descend from the seed of Adam," says Bonaventure, "have a nature marred not only by punishment, but by guilt. This is manifest in the want of God's intuition, in the ignominy which weighs upon reason, and in the preponderance of evil desire [*concupiscentia*]" in Möhler, *Symbolism*, 48.

[526] St. Thomas Aquinas enlarged on the subject of original sin thus, "As between things opposite, there is an opposite relation, so from original justice its opposite, original sin,

159

6.4.2 Lutherans and Original Sin

In the Augsburg Confession, it is noted, "They [the Protestants] teach, that, after Adam's fall, all men, who are engendered according to nature, are born in sin, - that is to say, without fear of God, without confidence in Him, and with concupiscence."[527] The Catholic theologians at the *Diet of Augsburg*, Eck, Wimpina, and Cochlaeus, remarked that

> the description of original sin, "men were born without fear of God and without confidence in Him," was very unfitting and inadmissible; because the fear of God and confidence in Him consisted in a succession of intellectual acts, which would no more think of demanding of the unconscious child. Original sin exists prior to all self-consciousness.[528]

Luther, however, insisted, "it is the nature of man to sin; sin constitutes the essence of man; the nature of man, since his fall, is become quite changed; original sin that very thing which is born of father and mother. Man as he is born of his father and mother, together with his whole nature and essence, is not only a sinner, but sin itself."[529] The belief that evil is to be propagated by generation through the whole human race constitutes the Lutheran notion of concupiscence. Protestants believe that so long as a man lives here below, original sin is not totally effaced from him even by regeneration or even by the power of God.[530] Lutherans taught that in fallen man, not the slightest good, how paltry soever it may be conceived, has survived; that all so-called actual or personal sins, committed in the self-consciousness of freedom, are only the particular forms and manifestations of original sin.[531]

---

may be explained. The will of man was obedient to God. When the will fell away from God, disorder in all the other faculties of the soul ensued. Thus, in original sin the deprivation of original justice is the formal [causal, determining, and essential] par; but every other disorder in the faculties of the soul is the material part; i.e. the thing determined, the consequence, the manifestation of the essence. The disorder of the other powers of the soul shows itself in the perverted affection to transitory good, wicked desire, '*concupiscentia.*' Thus, in its essence [forma], original sin is the want of original justice; in its manifestation [material] it is evil desire" (Möhler, *Symbolism*, 50).

[527] Eric Lund, ed., "The Augsburg Confession," in *Documents from the History of Lutheranism, 1517–1750* (Minneapolis, MN: Fortress Press, 2002), 60.

[528] Möhler, *Symbolism*, 54–55.

[529] Dillenberger, ed., *Martin Luther*, 203.

[530] Möhler, *Symbolism*, 62.

[531] Ibid., 63.

6.5 The Doctrine on Justification

6.5.1 The Catholic Teaching: Council of Trent

Justification is not a central doctrine in the Catholic faith. It was brainchild of the Reformers, which they found to be the true meaning of salvation. As a response, the Catholic Church addressed the issue in the Counter-Reformation. Therefore, the Catholic teaching on justification is found in the Council of Trent, which states,

> The sinner, alienated from God, is, without being able to show any merit of his own, without being able to put in any claim to grace, or to pardoning mercy, called back to the divine kingdom. This divine call, sent to the sinner for Christ's sake, is expressed not only in an outward invitation, through the preaching of the Gospel, but also in an internal action of the Holy Spirit which rouses the slumbering energies of man. In order to renew the communion with God, if the sinner hearkens to this call, then faith in God's Word is the first effect of divine and human activity, co-operating in the way described. Thus, by the mutual interworking of the Holy Spirit, and of the creature freely co-operating, justification really commences.[532]

Therefore, in the Catholic faith, justification is not only a remission of sins but also the sanctification and renewal of the inner man. Möhler believes that justification in the Catholic sense consists in a total change of the inward man as a whole. By this, we can understand why the Catholic Church should so urgently insist: that faith alone does not justify before God; that it is rather only the first subjective, indispensable condition to be justified, the root from which God's approval must spring—the first title thereon we can establish our claim of divine filiation.[533] He further explains that if faith passes from the understanding, and the feelings, excited through the understanding, to the will; if it pervades, vivifies, and fructifies the will, through the new vital principal imparted to the latter, and engenders the new man created after God; or if love is enkindled out of faith, then only after faith and love doth regeneration or justification ensue.[534]

---

[532] Möhler, *Symbolism*, 82.
[533] Ibid., 121.
[534] Ibid.

6.5.2 The Protestant Form of Justification

According to the Protestant view, the word "justification" signifies, declaring someone just, the acquitting him of sins, and the eternal chastisements of sin, on account of the justice of Christ, which is by God imputed to faith; and it expressly says, "Our justice is not of us. It is a judicial act of God, whereby the believing sinner is delivered from the punishment of sin, but not from sin itself."[535]

6.5.2.1 The Lutheran View

Lutherans taught that Christ is the Lamb of God who takes upon himself the sins of the world in such a way that the sinner grasps at the Redeemer's merits, through faith, which alone justifies.[536] According to Luther, God, on account of Christ's merits, declares the believer just, without his being so in fact, through released from debt and punishment, he is not delivered from sin (original sin).

> God will not lay to our charge the remnant of sin, he will not punish us nor condemn us for it; but will cover it and will freely forgive it, as though it were nothing at all; nor for our sake, neither for our worthiness and works, but for Jesus Christ's sake in whom we believe. Thus, a Christian is both righteous and sinner, holy and profane, an enemy of God and yet a child of God.[537]

Accordingly, in the Lutheran teaching, sanctification is annexed to justification, and faith manifests itself in good works, which are its fruits.[538] According to Lutherans, Möhler says, "the whole work of regeneration is God's doing alone. Man acts a purely passive part therein. The Holy Spirit is exclusively active."[539] For them, justice remains in Christ, not in the inward life of the believer and remains in a purely outward relation to him; by justification, the human will is not healed. Christ casts on the believer his shadow only, under which his continued sinfulness is merely not observed by God.[540]

---

[535] Ibid., 110.
[536] Dillenberger, ed., *Martin Luther*, 55.
[537] Ibid., 130.
[538] Ibid., 72.
[539] Ibid., 8.
[540] "These Maxims have the following consequences: No essential difference, as to moral being, is recognized between the converted and the unconverted. The scriptural antithesis

6.6 Justifying Faith

6.6.1 The Catholic Teaching

The Council of Trent approves that faith is the beginning of all salvation; for without it, it is impossible to please God and to attain his adoption. Faith is the beginning of salvation, but yet not a beginning which can be again abandoned.[541] The Roman Catechism defines faith: "the word faith signifies not so much the act of thinking, or opining, but it has the sense of a firm obligation [contracted in virtue of a free act of submission], whereby the mind decisively and permanently assents to the mysteries revealed by God."[542]

To fathom the notion of justifying faith according to the Catholic teaching, we cannot but refer to what Thomas Aquinas taught. He states,

> Through faith we appropriate to ourselves the sufferings of Christ, so that we become partakers of the fruits of the same (Rom. 3:25). But the faith through which we are cleansed from sin, is not the unloving faith (*fides informis*), which can co-exist with sin, but the faith living through love (*fides formata*). Cardinal Nicholas of Cusa observed: "Faith alone justifies," but then he adds, it must be full-formed faith (*fides formata*) for without works it is dead.[543]

6.6.2 The Lutheran View

Whereas the Catholic doctrine explains the want of a progressive movement of faith, the Protestant view insists on the initial act of faith. The Protestants rejected the notion of the faith which works by charity. In his commentary on the Galatians, Luther asserted that "the faith which should receive its true form and shape from charity is mere idle talk. We are justified by faith only, and not *per fidem formatam charitate*."[544] To Protestants, justifying faith is

---

of the old and the new man and of generation, lose not only their point, but in a great degree their moral significance. The notion of Penance whereby the transition from the one state to the other is brought about is taken as totally mistaken sense; - The impressive language of Holy Writ, respecting the deliverance from sin and the mortification [eradication] of sin in believers, is rendered ridiculous self-delusion," in Möhler, *Symbolism*, 111–112.

[541] John Schroeder, *Canons and Decrees of the Council of Trent* (St. Louis, MO: B. Herder Books Co., 1941), 33.

[542] Möhler, *Symbolism*, 120–121.

[543] Thomas Aquinas, *Summa Theologica*, III (New York: Benzinger Brothers, Inc., 1948), 49.

[544] Dillenberger, ed., *Martin Luther*, 113.

believing and trusting that man has been receiving by God into grace, and that for Christ's sake, who, by his death, has offered up atonements for our sins, he receives forgiveness of the same.

6.7 Good Works

6.7.1 The Catholic Teaching

Möhler says that by "good works," the Catholic Church understands all the moral actions and sufferings of the justified in Christ or fruits of holy feeling and believing love. As in the man truly born again from the spirit, the Catholic Church recognizes a real liberation from sin, a direction of the spirit and the will truly sanctified and acceptable to God, it necessarily follows that she asserts the possibility and reality of truly good works and their consequent meritoriousness.[545] It is therefore only on works consummated in a real vital communion with Christ, the church bestows the predicate "good"; and of a fulfillment of a law, she speaks only insofar as the power of this effect has been given in fellowship with Christ. It is this meritoriousness of good works that Luther reckons presumptuous.

6.7.2 Protestants and Good Works

Luther maintained that no works could possibly be pure and acceptable to God. According to him, every act of man is a mortal sin; even the best work is a venial sin.[546] However, Luther believes in only one correct usage of works. For him, good works are only fruits of the elect rather than contributing to the salvation of man. He teaches thus,

> The Christian who is consecrated by his faith does good works, but the works do not make him holier or more Christian."[547] . . . "We do not, therefore, reject good works; on the contrary, we cherish and teach them as much as possible. We do not condemn then for their own sake but on account of this godless addition to them and the perverse idea that righteousness is to be sought through them.[548]

---

[545] Möhler, *Symbolism*, 157.
[546] Dillenberger, ed., *Martin Luther*, 501.
[547] Ibid., 69.
[548] Ibid., 72.

6.8 Doctrine on Sacraments

6.8.1 Sacraments in General

According to the interpretation of the Council of Trent, justification is, by means of the sacraments either originally infused into us, or subsequently increased, or, when lost, is again restored.[549] In the doctrine of sacraments, we shall consider the differences between Catholics and Protestants in regard to the nature, object of institution, manner in which sacraments communicate grace, and their number.

6.8.1.1 The Catholic Teaching

A sacrament is defined by the catechism of the Council of Trent to be "an outward sign, which, in virtue of the divine ordinance, not only typifies, but works, the supersensual; to wit, holiness and justice."[550] These signs have been instituted by Christ, to serve man as pledges of the forgiveness of sin, of heavenly grace, and of the communion of the Holy Spirit. They are channels (*quasi alvei*) of grace.[551]

Möhler explains that the Catholic Church teaches that the mode in which the sacraments confer sanctifying grace on us is by means of their character, as an institution prepared by Christ for our salvation (*ex opera operato, scilicet a Christo*, in place of *quod operatus est Christus*); that is to say, the sacraments convey a divine power, merited for us by Christ, which cannot be produced by any human disposition, by any spiritual effort of condition; but is absolutely, for Christ's sake, conferred by God through their means. Catholics reckon seven sacraments.[552]

6.8.1.2 The Lutheran View

Möhler believes that Lutherans held a one-sided view of the sacraments, considered as pledges of the truth of the divine promises for the forgiveness of sins. According to the Luther, sacraments were to have no other destination than to make the faithful feel assured that his debt of sins was remitted, and to console and to quiet him. The sacraments are no longer used as channels of grace. Luther explains,

---

[549] Möhler, *Symbolism*, 202.
[550] CCC 1131.
[551] Ibid.
[552] ND 1311, Council of Trent, 7th session, *Canons on the Sacraments in General*, 1547.

In every promise, God presents two things, a word and a sign, in order that we may understand the word to be a testament, and the sign a sacrament. The word of Christ is the testament. Since greater power resides in a word than in a sign, so more power resides in a testament than in a sacrament; for a man may have, and use, a word or testament without a sign or sacrament.[553]

The above teaching essentially rejects the *opus operatum*—the objective character of these means of grace. Möhler states that "the Reformers,[554] whose system everywhere lays too exclusive a stress on the pardon of sins, teach that even the sacraments serve only as instruments for confirming faith in this remission of sins."[555]

---

[553] Dillenberger, ed., *Martin Luther*, 279.

[554] "Melancthon asserts that circumcision is nothing; so is baptism nothing; the communion of the Lord's Supper is nothing; they are rather testimonies and *Spragides* [seals] of the divine will toward thee; mere signs of covenant. The Apology says that a sacrament is a ceremony, or a work instituted by God, wherein that is represented to us, which the grace annexed to the ceremony proffers. The original view of Luther on the sacraments produced very important consequences. As the aforesaid means of salvation, destined only to confirm and consolidate faith in the forgiveness of sins. The number of seven sacraments was reduced to two; and merely the sacraments of baptism and the Lord's Supper retained. Confirmation was only to be a renewal of baptism, and the Lord's Supper considered merely as a pledge for the forgiveness of sins. Zwingle considers the sacraments only as ceremonies whereby a man profess himself a member of the Church, and follower of Christ; throwing aside the belief that the sacraments contribute aught towards justification; since he, whose faith needs such a confirmation, actually possesses none. Reception of the sacraments rather affords the Church an assurance that her followers believe. Calvin's doctrine, with the exception of one point, differs not at all from that of the Lutheran formularies. The point in which he deviates from the Catholics and the Lutheran doctrine, consists especially herein, that he will have the sanctifying grace distinct and separate from the sacraments, as the sensible sign. The former, according to him, is not conjoined with the material element: and hence to every Christian is this element tendered, but no so the divine nourishment. It is only to the elect the divine grace is imparted, and the rest are passed over by God, so grace must by no means be connected with the visible sign. The divine grace works irresistibly. In baptism the non-elect are only outwardly washed. Calvin also admits but two sacraments," in Möhler, *Symbolism*, 207, 208, 209, 216, 217–218.

[555] Möhler, *Symbolism*, 206.

6.9 A Summary of Differences between the Catholic and Protestant Doctrines

No.	Doctrine	Catholic	Protestant
	State of Original Man	The Paradisaic man was endowed with supernatural graces, which were greatly weakened at the fall.	Paradisaic man was devoid of supernatural graces. He was only upheld by natural powers which he lost at the fall.
	Original Sin	A result of the disobedience of Adam and Eve under which they lost the original justice and holiness.	It consists in man's nature. Men are born in sin—that is to say, without fear of God, without confidence in him, and with concupiscence.
	Free Will	Man was created with freedom. Thus, because of his free will, the guilt of evil in the world falls upon his head.	Man has no free will. Any free action is apparent; divine necessity rules all things.
	Justification	Through a divine call, sent through preaching of the Gospel; and by an internal action of the spirit which arouses the energies of man. By cooperation with the spirit, justification in man commences. It is renewal of the inner man.	The declaration of man as just; acquitting him of sins, and the eternal chastisements of sins, on the account of the justice of Christ. It is deliverance from the punishment due to sin.
	Sanctification	The infusion of the love God into our hearts, through the Holy Spirit, by which we are regenerated. It is the fullness of justification and forgiveness of sins.	An annex-of justification in which the will is not healed, but rather, Christ casts on the believer his shadow only, under which his continued sinfulness is merely not observed by God.
	Sanctifying Faith	A free act of submission, whereby the mind decisively and permanently assents to the mysteries revealed by God. Justifying faith is the reunion with God in Christ; it's a faith living through love.	The initial act of faith; the believing and trusting that man has been received by God into grace, and that for Christ's sake, he receives forgiveness of sins.

	Good Works	All the moral actions and sufferings of the justified in Christ, or fruits of holy feeling and believing love. It is cooperation with God's grace, and in as far as such acts are agreeable to God, they are meritorious.	No human works are meritorious because man is essentially sinful. In salvation, only God is active; man plays a passive role.
	Salvation	A process of deliverance from sin and regeneration of a fallen man brought to him by faith through the grace of Christ. It is a journey.	A moment of deliverance from sin through faith by the grace of Christ.
	Sacraments in General	The seven signs that have been instituted by Christ, to serve men as pledges of the forgiveness of sin, of heavenly grace, and of the communion of the Holy Spirit. The sacraments are represented as the channels (*quasi alvei*) of grace.	Pledges of the truth of the divine promises for the forgiveness of sins. The sacraments serve only as instruments for confirming faith in this remission of sins. These are two: Baptism and the Lord's Supper.

In the above depiction of major differences between the Catholic and the Protestant doctrines, the affinity of both Ratzinger and Hauerwas can be distinguished respectively. As we shall further discover below, Hauerwas identifies more with the Lutheran teachings, which are unquestionably inadequate in regard to the whole Christian truth. However, before we embark on their particular affinities, we shall first provide a link between the two epochs, that is, the Reformation period and the contemporary period. By this we mean to point out individuals who kept the Reformers' ideas alive, and who led to their proliferation.

6.10 Major Interlocutors in the Relativistic World

We can state, without hesitation, that the Reformers are responsible for the foundation of the culture of religious relativism via their denial of some Christian doctrines. They started the fire in the sixteenth century that was spread and augmented during the modern times. Some of those that amplified the fire were more philosophers than theologians. High-rated protagonists were Hegel, Kant, Marx, and Nietzsche. It is not our intention to go deeper into their conversations here. This would make this paper more philosophical than theological. For the purpose of this paper, we shall restrict our discussion theological or religious relativistic ideas. We shall scrutinize ideas of two of whom we consider the greatest and most dangerous relativists in the modern times. These were Friedrich Ernst Schleiermacher and SØren Kierkegaard. For our interest, we shall explore their major contributions but will definitely not exhaust all their teachings, since they are not the major point of reference in this paper. However, the inclusion and discussion of their major theological and anthropological ideas will be a great aid to the understating of the trend the contemporary world is taking.

Religious relativism can be specifically spotted in the doctrine of pietism. Pietism, a Protestant movement in the seventeenth and eighteenth centuries, stressed the emotional and personal aspects of religion or faith. It was a protest to the fruitlessness of the Christian lives of the time. It was a movement paved with good intentions, of reviving devotion and practical Christianity. Along the way, however, it lost track and the prevailing relativistic culture appropriately be attributed to it. There were quite a number of proponents of pietism, but one of the greatest we cannot afford skipping is Immanuel Kant. His ideas had great influence on the consequent protestant theologians like Schleiermacher, Kierkegaard (whose main ideas we shall discuss later), and it still has prominent impact in the progressive and Pentecostal churches. Also, to a great extent, pietism and Kant's ideas find their expression in Hauerwas' anthropology.

6.10.1 Immanuel Kant (1724–1804)

Brandt Dixon makes an excellent study and scrutiny of Kant's philosophy. In a special introduction to the *Critique of Pure Reason*, it states,

> The philosophy of Kant marks an epoch in the history of modern thought, since it is the rational outcome of previous speculation, offers a profounder solution of its problems, and forms the basis of a new departure. On the one hand, it sums up the notions formerly held to be essential and necessary, reveals their inadequacy or imperfections, and, on the other hand, opens up a fresh and fruitful field of metaphysical inquiry.[556]

Second, Kant's philosophy and metaphysical discourses stand and link the medieval to the modern world. Dixon notes that in the Middle Ages, as in childhood, opinions were formed subject to external authority; the evidence of perception or of reason had little relative force; judgments and faith needed to conform to the dictations of the masters, the decrees of the church, or the

---

[556] Immanuel Kant, *Critique of Pure Reason* (New York: Willey Book Co., 1943), vii.

words of supernatural revelation. But with a growing trust in reason, the bondage of mere authority was loosened, and a scientific spirit of investigation arose. Men began to acquire a degree of confidence in their ability to discover truth by searching for it, and an assurance that opinions were valid if well attested by reason.[557] Most important is Dixon's observation that "this confidence, however, implies the assumption that the truth, power, or reason of things is within them; and the inquiring mind may appropriate them. . . . The medieval view of the world implied the principle of divine transcendence, but this new view depends upon the principle of divine immanence."[558]

Kant is faulted mostly because of his teaching and assumption of the inertness of the truth within human beings. Kant assumes the self-activity of reason. Dixon once more rightly asserts that "in his philosophy, all objectivity is not explained or assimilated; the thing-in-itself is, as yet, the unintelligible, but it is not, even to Kant, essentially and necessary the unreason."[559] According to Kant, things outside us should not be assumed merely on faith. Rather, metaphysical objects must conform to our cognition. This sparked rationalism on the one hand and relativism on the other.

6.10.2 Friedrich Schleiermacher (1768–1834)

It is unrealistic to discuss relativism (religious) in the modern times without mentioning Schleiermacher. He is arguably one of the major contributors to religious relativism in the modern period. He does not only reduce the deposit of Christian truth, but, as a matter of fact, strips it bear. He stands in the same position like the ancient Arius—he could appropriately be regarded as the Arius of the Modern Age. His contribution to this (relativism) is enormous, but for our purpose, we shall try to highlight only his most treacherous relativistic ideas that became the hinge of all the subsequent relativists.

First and foremost, Schleiermacher starts on the right side of the journey of faith—seeking the truth. He seems to be in agreement with the idea that man is dependent on a superior and exterior being. His starting point is similar to that of Rene Descartes. The nuance between the two is that while Descartes started with a doubt in his famous *"Dubito ergo cogito; cogito ergo sum"* (I doubt there I think; I think therefore I am),[560] Schleiermacher starts in the affirmative. For Schleiermacher, feeling is the beginning of piety or faith. If we could use Descartes's motto, Schleiermacher would assert, *"Tempto ergo cogito, cogito*

---

[557] Ibid.

[558] Ibid., vii–viii.

[559] Kant, *Critique of Pure Reason*, xv.

[560] René Descartes, *Discours de la Methode* (Paris: Librairie Philosophique, 1930), 292.

ergo sum." Both Descartes and Schleiermacher have the same goal and passion, that is, to arrive at the whence of things. Both make a good conclusion at the beginning of their search, that there is a whence of things, which also sustains their quest.

Schleiermacher categorically states, that "the piety which forms the basis of all ecclesiastical communions is, considered purely in itself, neither a Knowing nor a Doing, but a modification of Feeling, or of immediate self-consciousness."[561] He says that feeling and self-consciousness are positioned equivalently side by side. Thus, to him, feeling is not merely understood in the sense of one of the five senses, but rather a self-consciousness as well. This implies passing a kind of judgment over something.[562] Thus, his usage of the term "feeling" or "self-consciousness" forms the basis of all piety or faith or truth according to Schleiermacher. This means that the truth or faith or piety is not some universal objective reality, but rather something as perceived by an individual who "feels" or perceives or is self-conscious of it. To say the least, it is something subjective, something relative.

Schleiermacher takes his principle of faith to life as a whole. He asserted, "Life is to be conceived as an alternation between an abiding-in-self [*Insichbleiben*] and a passing-beyond-self [*Aussichheraustreten*] on the part of the subject. Feeling simply takes place in the subject; it stands alone in antithesis to Knowing and Doing."[563] To him, this feeling or piety is what leads to knowing and doing. It suffices to say that according to Schleiermacher, truth, faith, piety, and even life itself reside in the individual whence they spring beyond the self. His ideas are susceptible to the belief that the individual is the source, the legislator, and judge of the truth. How then can we talk of revelation or God's call as inducing faith in an individual? Thus, Schleiermacher brings faith and truth from the level of revelation to below reason—to the level of mere subjective feeling.

He, like Kant, denied knowledge to give way for faith—that religion cannot be based on metaphysics or science. We would agree with Schleiermacher this far, that religion, and Christianity in particular, is not based on metaphysics or reason. Surely, faith is not subordinate to reason but rather based on revelation. However, Schleiermacher's grave mistake was to give an alternative to metaphysics and science as being something other than revelation. According to him, "religion is based neither on theoretical knowledge nor on morality, it is instead based on an intuition or feeling of the universe. Religion's essence

---

[561] Friedrich Schleiermacher, *The Christian Faith* (Berkeley, CA: Apocryphile Press, 2011), 5.
[562] We used the Latin term "tempto" which means "I test, feel, attempt, or try." This is in line with Schleiermacher's usage of the term "feeling" in his anthropological discourses. It implies passing a judgment over a situation.
[563] Schleiermacher, *The Christian Faith*, 8.

is neither thinking nor acting, but intuition and feeling. It wishes to intuit the universe."[564]

Here is the derivation of Schleiermacher's anthropological error. Intuition, according to Kant, is defined as "that through which a mode of knowledge is in immediate relation to objects."[565] In the first place, according to the definition above, intuition is actually a mode of knowledge. This makes Schleiermacher contradict his own proposition that religion is not based on knowledge. Second, intuition makes this form of knowledge resident in the object itself and not from any outward source. This is not only a denial of revelation but a denial of God himself. It makes religion and Christianity, to which Schleiermacher subscribed, to be not about God but about man. But Christianity does not originate from man but from God.

The term "intuition" did carry implications which Schleiermacher in fact wished to deny. It seems he later realized this and resorted to using the term "feeling" as the basis of religion. According to him, "the piety which forms the basis of all ecclesiastical communions is, considered purely in itself, neither a knowing nor a doing, but a modification of feeling, or of immediate self-consciousness."[566] He showed this change in his work, *The Christian Faith*, where he defined religion more specifically as "a feeling of absolute dependence; the immediate consciousness of 'an immediate existence-relationship.'"[567] Schleiermacher's religious intuition of feeling does not mean religious feeling to be merely noncognitive, but also to incorporate some sort of cognition or belief.[568] This means that according to Schleiermacher, faith or truth is a faculty of the individual object. It is thus subjective and hence relative.

However, the Christian faith does not have a human origin but is a gift from God, and this gift is neither personal nor exclusive. God, through the grace of Jesus Christ, grants it to whomever he wishes, and this gift is given and lived in a community which is the body of Christ—the church. Is this not what Jesus said?

I thank you, Father, Lord of heaven and earth, because you have hidden these things from the wise and the intelligent and have revealed them to infants; yes, Father, for such was your gracious will. All things have been handed over

---

[564] Friedrich Schleiermacher, *On Religion: Speeches to Its Cultured Despisers*, translated by R. Crouter (Cambridge: 1988), 49–50.

[565] Immanuel Kant, *Critique of Pure Reason*, A 19.

[566] Schleiermacher, *The Christian Faith*, 5. He further states, "Our position seems to assume that in addition to knowing, doing, and feeling, there ie no fourth. . . . those other two are placed alongside of feeling" in Schleiermacher, *The Christian Faith*, 7.

[567] Ibid., 12.

[568] Schleiermacher, *The Christian Faith*, 13.

to me by my Father; and no one knows the Father except the Son and anyone to whom the Son chooses to reveal him (Mt 11:26–27).

What else can we then say other than confirming that the culture of religious relativism has a broad foundation in Schleiermacher's theological writings?

Schleiermacher further expounds his worst teaching; that is, he identified Christianity as the highest among the monotheistic or monistic religions. In this teaching, Schleiermacher put Jesus on the same level with other founders of other religions, though of a "higher mediation." This is an outright denial of the divinity of Christ. With this teaching, the Christian creed cannot profess Jesus as Light from Light, True God from True God. Schleiermacher's teaching is contradictory to St. Paul's teaching,

He is the image of the invisible God, the firstborn of all creation; for in him all things in heaven and on earth were created, things visible and invisible, whether thrones or dominions or rules or powers—all things have been created through him and for him. He himself is before all things, and in him all things hold together. He is the head of the body, the church; he is the beginning, the firstborn from the dead, so that he might come to have first place in everything. For in him all the fullness of God was pleased to dwell, and through him God was pleased to reconcile to himself all things, whether on earth or in heaven, by making peace through the blood of his cross (Col 1:15–20).

Hence, Schleiermacher took the relativistic ideas of the Reformers to a higher level. He not only denied the objectivity of truth/faith and revelation, but also denied the divinity and the incomparability of Christ. Thus, he opened doors for many people after him to consider truth as a relative reality, according to how one feels or experiences the grace of faith.

Schleiermacher's anthropology leads to yet another divergent but similar anthropology. Though they have quite different backgrounds, both Schleiermacher and Kierkegaard had a meeting point in their anthropology. Let us now briefly examine Kierkegaard's anthropology.

6.10.3 Søren Aabye Kierkegaard (1813–1855)

Kierkegaard is one of the most prominent defenders of the individual in the nineteenth century. He frantically defended the individual against the church (the state church). His philosophy was against the idealists of his time, e.g., Friedrich Hegel, but also against objective practice of Christianity. He was a true existentialist—rightly fitting to be named "the father of existentialism." In brief, Kierkegaard's intention was a good one, that is, to revitalize the Christian faith. His starting point was a realization of the downplaying of Christianity by the very leaders whose concept of Christianity, Kierkegaard thought was at fault—demanding too little of its adherents.[569] However, along the way, he exaggerated his positions.

Kierkegaard elevated the Lutheran *sola fide* to an exaggerated level. For him, the Christian faith is not a matter of regurgitating church dogma, but rather, a matter of individual subjective passion, which cannot be mediated by the clergy or by human artifacts. It should be noted here that Kierkegaard's subjectivism stems from his Socratic thought project of truth. Like Socrates, Kierkegaard believed that

> a person cannot possibly seek what he knows, and, just as impossible, he cannot seek what he does not know, for what he knows he cannot seek, since he knows it, and what he knows he cannot seek, because, after all, he does not even know what he is supposed to seek. All learning and seeking are but recollecting. Thus the ignorant person merely needs to be reminded in order, by himself, to call to mind what he knows. The truth is not introduced into him but was in him.[570]

This means that the truth is not something from outside of the individual but originates and resides in the individual. According to him, the truth is not given; it is inherent. Faith is not gift but a matter of choice. Kierkegaard believed that the individual is thereby subject to an enormous burden of responsibility, for upon his/her existential choices hangs his/her eternal salvation or damnation. The individual creates through temporal choice a self which will be judged for eternity; on the other side is the exhilaration of freedom in choosing oneself.[571]

With this teaching, can we be erroneous if we put the blame on Kierkegaard for the prevailing religious affiliations or of faith itself? Many Christians today, particularly the Pentecostal and Evangelical Christians, take their faith as a matter of choice. Many Christians claim they chose Jesus as their personal Savior. But what does the Lord say? "You did not choose me but I chose you. And I appointed you to go and bear fruit, fruit that will last" (Jn 15:16). It means

---

[569] He wrote in one of the journals: "I ask: what does it mean when we continue to behave as though all were as it should be, calling ourselves Christians according to the New Testament, when the ideals of the New Testament have gone out of life? The tremendous disproportion which this state of affairs represents has, moreover, been perceived by man. They like to give it this turn: the human race has outgrown Christianity" (Søren Kierkegaard, *Journals*, 446 (19 June 1852).

[570] Søren Kierkegaard, *Philosophical Fragments: Johannes Climacus* (Princeton, NJ: Princeton University Press, 1985), 9.

[571] Kierkegaard, *Philosophical Fragments*, 147–150.

that God who is Truth chose to come to us and dwelt among us, and when he called us and we responded to this call, we were also commissioned to go and bear fruit, meaning to say, to go and spread this gift of faith to other. Therefore, faith is a gift from God and something that is lived communally—obtainable from one individual to the next, and not merely a matter of one's subjective choice.

This commissioning is also proof of mediation, which to Kierkegaard is not necessary. According to him, the self is a relation which relates itself to itself. Therefore, to maintain itself as a relation which relates to its self, the self must constantly renew its faith in the "power which posited it." There is no mediation between the individual self and God by priest or by logical system. There is only the individual's own repetition of faith. In this case, the self is self-determinant, the sole determinant of everything. If it is erroneous, so everything will be erroneous. This teaching rules out of order all authority and dogma because the self is its own teacher—no one should tell it what to do. It is the author of right and wrong, and what is good and bad. But contrary to this, the Lord Jesus sends us to go and teach them "all that I commanded you" (Mt 28:20).

Christians are commissioned to teach truth. This means that, first and foremost, truth is something objective and not subjective; something given and does not originate in man; faith is gift and command at the same time, and not a matter of choice. Jesus's incarnation was meant to save people by granting them the gift of faith so that by walking along its path, they may reach heaven; and so, it is upon every believer to take this gift to the next person. In this regard, we become cosaviors, co-redeemers with Christ. When Kierkegaard denies any mediation and insists that the truth resides in the individual, and so there is no need of a teacher,[572] he renders the Christian mission superfluous. He lays an obstruction to the teaching of the faith—becomes a stumbling block for God's will—for God wants us to go and teach people what he commanded us; so that

---

[572] According to Kierkegaard, there is no need for a teacher, not mediation between a learner and teacher, because the truth resides in the individual. He asserted that "If the teacher is to be the occasion that reminds the learner, he cannot assist him to recollect that he actually does know the truth, for the learner is indeed untruth. That for which the teacher can become the occasion of his recollecting if that he is untruth. But by this calling to mind, the learner is definitely excluded from the truth, even more than when he was ignorant of being untruth. Consequently, in this way, precisely by reminding him, the teacher thrusts the learner away, except by being turned in upon himself in this manner the learner does not discover that he previously knew the truth but discovers his untruth. To this act of consciousness, the Socratic principle applies: the teacher is only an occasion, whoever he may be, even if he is a god, because I can discover my own untruth only by myself, because only when I discover it is discovered, not before, even though the whole world knew it," in Kierkegaard, *Philosophical Fragments*, 14.

his will be done in us, otherwise man's will prevails. If there is no teaching or mediation, then there is no Christian mission at all.

St. Paul would help us answer back to such a teaching. He says,

> Brothers and sisters, my heart's desire and prayer to God for them is that they may be saved. The scripture says, "No one who believes in him will be put to shame." For there is no distinction between Jew and Greek; the same Lord is Lord of all and is generous to all who call on him. For, "Everyone who calls on the name of the Lord shall be saved." But how are they to call on one in whom they have not believed? And how are they to believe in one of whom they have never heard? And how are they to hear without someone to proclaim him? And how are they to proclaim him unless they are sent? As it is written, "How beautiful are the feet of those who bring good news!" but not all have obeyed the good news; for Isaiah says, "Lord, who has believed our message?" So faith comes from what is heard, and what is heard comes through the word of Christ (Rom 10:1; 11–17).

The Christian faith is therefore a mission and every Christian is essentially missionary. This mission would be ridiculous if every individual person gets a direct revelation from God and relates exclusively with God without any need of mediation. There would be no need for preaching or sharing of faith since each individual soul would discern exactly what is required to be saved. Kierkegaard wanted to free individuals from the dominion of the church authorities (perhaps it was quite suppressive in his time), but in so doing, he proliferated a subjectivism and relativism that tempered with the Christian role as missionary and the leadership of the church as Magisterium. From his time, more and more people resented the church's magisterium and its teaching and took whatever they thought was the right Gospel interpretation.

In our time, thousands, perhaps millions, of Christians are treading the same path. In Africa, as we shall observe later (last chapter of this paper), more and more new faith churches and preaching sprout, claiming direct inspiration by the Holy Spirit. There are also many who deny that there is need for a community-based worship, since each individual can commune to God directly. Such people have a "me and my God" kind of attitude. They do not participate in any church assemblies, nor participate in any missionary activity. They tend to believe in the "do not tell me what to do" perspective.

6.11 Particular Differences between Joseph Ratzinger and Stanley Hauerwas

In the previous chapter, we itemized the key subjects (theological, anthropological, and ecclesiological) common to both Ratzinger and Hauerwas. This chapter aims at identifying their diverse propensity stemming from their respective faiths. Above, we highlighted the general ones. Here below, we shall address the particular differences as they are exhibited by both theologians. It should also be noted that these two theologians are both labeled controversial because of their unique way of analyzing and critiquing even their own faiths. Therefore, their ideas may not completely be in agreement with their constituted faiths. Nevertheless, their teachings portray a greater inclination and adherence to their faiths (Catholic and Protestant respectively).

First and foremost, the general differences between Catholic and Protestant doctrines also apply to Ratzinger and Hauerwas as individual theologians. What sums up the differences between Catholic theology and Protestant theology is that Protestantism is relativistic in nature. It draws from the deposit of doctrine and reduces it, breaking it down to a narrower and lesser substance, thus, dividing the truth. Hauerwas acknowledges this in his comments on the Reformation, "Reformation is sin. It is disunity. It is a failure. We who remain in the Protestant tradition want to say that Reformation was a success, but it only ends up killing us. Unity is what God has given us through Christ's death and resurrection. Disunity is a sin."[573]

6.11.1 Theological Differences

Both Ratzinger and Hauerwas developed a Trinitarian and Christo-centric theology. According to them, the godhead is a relation: the Father, and the Son, and the Holy Spirit. This relation was revealed through the word made incarnate. His incarnation meant to bring man (a creature) into communion with the godhead—to share into the divinity of the Trinity. This sharing is brought to life by faith and discipleship. Therefore, our creaturedness, they seem to stress, can best be in communion. Details of their teachings were exposed in earlier chapters. It suffices here to conclude that both Ratzinger and Hauerwas teach a "communion" theology.

Therefore, communion is their bottom line and central theological idea. In other words, we can comfortably assert that both Ratzinger and Hauerwas are "Eucharistic" theologians. They seems to agree with the Catholic teaching

---

[573] Hauerwas, *Sanctify Them in the Truth*, 241–242.

that the Eucharist is the "source and summit"[574] of the Christian life. However, paradoxically, the same central idea in their theology seems to be at the same time their point of departure. Communion (the Eucharist) stands as both the main uniting factor between Ratzinger and Hauerwas' theology and yet their dividing factor. This stems from their understanding of what the Eucharist is.

Ratzinger believes in the real presence of Jesus in the Eucharist in both his divinity and humanity.[575] For him, the Eucharist is the fullness of communion into the divine life. In the Eucharist, heaven and earth meet. It is a *communio*. On the other hand, Hauerwas seems to have a quite different conception of the Eucharist. In an interview, Hauerwas states,

> My understanding is very traditional, normally that this is the rite in which we are made part of the body of Christ; the transformation of this bread into the bread and body of Christ. At the conclusion of our worship [in the book: *Common Prayer*], we [Methodists] pray: "*Eternal God Heavenly Father, you gracious accepted us as living members of your Son Our Savior Jesus Christ and you have fed us with spiritual food in the sacrament of body and blood. Send us now the world and peace. We pray this through Christ our Lord.*" Now that prayer says everything of what happens in the Eucharist. We are sent out to be the body and blood of Christ for the world. And that what happens every time we share in the body and blood of Christ. We are unified with Christ, with one another for the world.[576]

To Hauerwas, therefore, it is not about Jesus's real presence but in those assembled turning into this body of Christ and going out to act as so. Therefore, the theology of the Eucharist stands as the basis for both Ratzinger and Hauerwas' theology, which is also their point of contrast. In Ratzinger's understanding, Jesus acts; while in Hauerwas' understanding, the community acts. This explains why Hauerwas' theology is a call to action on the part of the church—stressing the church's action and not necessarily Jesus's action. His is a theology from below—a theology of makability. On the other hand, Ratzinger's theology is a theology from above—a theology of "receivability"; all is gift, and the church is the vessel containing this gift. We can say that Hauerwas' theological anthropology is less complete.

---

[574] SC 10.
[575] Ratzinger, *Pilgrim Fellowship of Faith*, 102.
[576] Cf. Appendix, *Interview with Hauerwas*.

6.11.2 Anthropological Differences

Joseph Ratzinger believes in the Augustinian power of grace transforming nature. According to the Doctor of Grace, grace is "the help which God gives to men, over and above their natural endowments, to enable them to will and to accomplish actions that may merit eternal salvation."[577] Ratzinger's anthropology seems to be in agreement with St. Augustine's teaching. He envisions a fallen nature in need of redemption but incapable of self-redemption. Therefore, it is only by God's grace that man can be restored to his original justice.

Ratzinger envisages the nature of man as fallen, incapable of ascending to God unless the grace of God aids him. He therefore recalls Christians to sacramental life, because he believes in their power to confer sanctifying grace. For Ratzinger, sacraments are channels (*quasi alvei*) of grace. In sacraments, Ratzinger believes, we meet Christ who grants us his grace to conquer sin. It is therefore no longer us fighting by our own power, but by the power of grace— Jesus who lives in us and fights on our behalf. His anthropology seems to be based on Jesus's words: "I am the vine; you are the branches. Those who abide in me and I in them bear much fruit, because apart from you can do nothing" (Jn 15:5), and in another instance Jesus says, "See, I am sending you out like sheep into the midst of wolves; so be wise as serpents and innocent as doves. When they hand you over, do not worry about how you are to speak or what you are to say; for what you are to say will be given to you at that time; for it is not you who speak, but the Spirit of your Father speaking through you" (Mt 10:16, 19–20).

Worth noting is Ratzinger's minimal attention with regard to the relationship between nature and grace. His anthropology is absolutely non-Thomistic. Thomas Aquinas perceived anthropology via the concept of analogy of being. The *analogia entis* can be described as the teaching that there exists an analogy or correspondence between God and the created order; that reality is divided horizontally into the very different realities of substances and accidents, and vertically into the very different realities of God and creatures. According to Aquinas,

God is whatever he is essentially, and as a result he is existence itself, goodness itself, wisdom itself. Creatures are existent, good, wise, only by sharing in God's existence, goodness, and wisdom, and this sharing has three features. It involves a separation between the creature and what the creature has; it involves a deficient similarity to God; and it is based on a causal relation.[578]

---

[577] Vernon J. Bourke, ed., *The Essential Augustine* (New York: The New American Library of World Literature, Inc., 1964), 176.

[578] Bourke, ed., *The Essential Augustine*. 176.

In brief, Aquinas teaches that God exists in nature in a remote way,[579] and there is a prevenient grace in the fallen man which awakens him to God's call, by which God assists to salvation the free person who seeks it.[580] Ratzinger does not follow this tradition. He exclusively follows an Augustinian-Bonaventurian tradition which tends to emphasize the overpowering encounter with the love and grace (supernatural) of God and which overlooks the relationship between nature and grace on the abstract level.

On the other hand, even though Hauerwas seems to believe in the grace of God, he is nevertheless more inclined to trusting more in the human capacity to conquer the power of evil than in letting the grace of God lead us to victory. An example is his nonviolence resistance doctrine. When asked about the difference between his resistance and that of revolutionalists like Mahatma Gandhi and Nelson Mandela, Hauerwas responded by saying,

> I admire Mandela very much in terms of how he conducted his resistance. There was a lot of violence against him and how he handled comes into question. I take it that it was one of the great achievement of Mandela to have practically overthrown apartheid with non-violence. It is one of the great achievement as John Paul II says in *"Centesimus Annus"* that the soviet domination of Eastern Europe was ended non-violently. I think that was great achievement; I mean, people forget that Martin Luther King was a pacifist. He resisted extraordinarily evil systems of segregation. Those kinds of people, Gandhi, Luther, were extraordinary. That's what Bonheoffer wanted to do. Mine is no different from theirs.[581]

According to Hauerwas, man has power to conquer evil. He believes in the confrontation of the evil in society, and by so doing, it can be defeated once and for all. He references the Gospel of Matthew on brotherly correction.[582]

---

[579] "God is in all things; not, indeed, as part of their essence, nor as an accident; but as an agent is present to that upon which it works." in Aquinas, *Summa Theologica*, III, q.8, a.1.

[580] "In both states [state of integrity and state of corrupt nature] human nature needs the help of God as first Mover, to do or wish any good whatsoever," in Aquinas, *Summa Theologica*, III, q.109, a.2.

[581] This was in an interview with Hauerwas conducted on Friday, January 28, 2011, at Divinity School, Duke University.

[582] "If another member of the church sins against you, go and point out the fault when the two of you are alone. If the member listens to you, you have regained that one. But if you are not listened to, take one or two others along with you, so that every word may be confirmed by the evidence of two or three witnesses. If the member refuses to listen to

He urges that a fault cannot be overlooked on the presumption that it is better not to disturb the peace. "Rather, you must risk stirring the waters, causing disorder, rather than overlook the sin. Such confrontation is at the heart of what it means to be peacemaker."[583] This confrontational attitude is the heart of Hauerwas' anthropology. He believes in the power of man to restore himself to the original state of justice.

Christian anthropology, as part of the larger discipline of anthropology, is concerned essentially with the life and origin of man and his relationship, not only with the world but primarily with God, who is the creator of all things.[584] There are therefore three key players in Christian anthropology, namely, God, man, and the world. These are interconnected in a relational nature. However, the Protestant and Catholic teachings explicate this relation differently, and Ratzinger and Hauerwas follow suit. In the table below, we shall illustrate how these two comprehend this relationship.

6.11.2.1 Their Respective Anthropological Strengths and Weaknesses

Anthropological Themes	Joseph Ratzinger	Stanley Hauerwas
Man: His Life and Origin.	Man is a creation of God and cannot be defined separate from Jesus of Nazareth. The incarnate person of God fulfills humanity. Jesus/Logos is the perfect *imago Dei* in whom this image is fulfilled in humankind. The incarnation is the basis for anthropology. At the center of human life is the Paschal Mystery, which is the full manifestation of God's love.	Man is a creation of God, defined by the community—the church. Humankind is realized and fulfilled in the mystery of Pentecost, in which a new language was created. Human life, according to Hauerwas, is more of a humanism based on social consensus[585] and action other than on the *Logos* who lives and perfects the *imago Dei* in humankind.

---

them, tell it to the church; and if the offender refuses to listen even to the church, let such a one be to you as a Gentile and a tax-collector" (Mt 18:15–17).
583 Hauerwas, *Christian Existence Today*, 90.
584 "This one and only true God, of his own goodness and almighty power, not for the increase of his own happiness, nor for the acquirement of his perfection, but in order to manifest his perfection through the benefits which he bestows on creatures, with absolute freedom of counsel, 'from the beginning of time made at once [*simul*] out of nothing both orders of creatures, the spiritual and the corporeal, that is, the angelic and the earthly, and then [*deinde*] the human creature, who as it were shares in both orders, being composed of spirit and body.'" ND 412, The First Vatican Council, *Dei Filius*.

God, Humankind and the World.	For Ratzinger, man is relational; he cannot live without God and the world. These three are all relational and get their meaning in as far as they live in this relation. His anthropology is essentially one of communion.	While Hauerwas believes in a relational nature of man, he, at the same time, envisages a separateness of living, a resident alienism. In as long as Hauerwas encourages Christians to be resident aliens, living in an "alternative polis," he implicitly encourages and may lead to the medieval Puritanism—fashioning an isolated "holy" society within a larger evil society. This again may lead man to disconnect from one another.[586]
The Fall and Redemption.	Ratzinger believes in the fallenness of man and in his need for redemption. However, this redemption is not achievable without Christ. Fullness of redemption is possible through the sacraments as channels of grace.	For Hauerwas, redemption is in faith in Jesus Christ. But man ascends to it directly without sacramental mediation.

6.11.3 Ecclesiological Differences

In his last prayer, best referred to as the Kingdom Prayer, the Lord prayed, "that they may be one, as we are one" (Jn 17:22). Unity is God's will. This should not be merely institutional, but in truth. As children of the same father, we can only be identified as so in our unity of faith and truth. The division in this faith is a division of the truth, which is one and indivisible. The moment we are divided we are moving toward relativism. In fact, religious schisms are the first signs of religious relativism. Thus, both Ratzinger and Hauerwas present Christian truth (we can dare say), in a way that "relativizes" Christian truth to a third party, meaning they each present the truth according to their faith, even though they both tend to go beyond congregational or institutional sentiments.

In an interview, Hauerwas states,

---

[585] "Hauerwas has a pragmatic criterion of truth, making a community the justification of Christian convictions. Scripture, then, does not have any inherent meaning." In Stephen Webb, "The Very American Stanley Hauerwas," *First Things* (June/July 2002), 14–17.

[586] This, as a result, can lead to separation from God, which puts Hauerwas in the position of a Christian existentialist who can appropriately be christened the Kierkegaard of America.

My view is that the problem is not about relativism but the epistemological conceit that gives you the problem of relativism. Now, once you have left behind the fundamentals of the Christian project, which gives you relativism, because you think that people of different traditions should necessarily know how to defeat the other tradition, and if you can't defeat it, as a matter of fact, you are promoting relativism. I think those foundations or notions are just wrong. What you face is a world of diversity; and you must discover how your tradition might put in question the other tradition, which MacIntyre calls epistemological crisis. Disagreements are possible, and that is a great achievement. Many times we will discover that we don't even know what the other is talking about. And that is why Christianity is ready to listen to the other person. Listening and knowing that disagreements can occur is the beginning of how to defeat relativism.[587]

In the above statement, Hauerwas seems to suggest that the Christian truth goes beyond institutional doctrines. He suggests that Christian truth should go back to the fundamentals of the Christian project. These fundamentals are none other than the scriptures and tradition. However, in reality, we realize that the more the truth is divided, the more it is removed from the fundamentals; hence, leading to relativism. The institutions of the various churches follow a relativistic trend: from the one, holy, Catholic and apostolic church, to the Roman, Anglican, Methodist, and Pentecostal churches. These tear down the deposit of faith and truth.

The major difference between Ratzinger and Hauerwas is that they do theology from a different ecclesiological perspective. For example, Joseph Ratzinger preaches an ecclesiology of seven sacraments while Stanley Hauerwas teaches a possible three sacraments. Ratzinger believes in the one, holy, Catholic, and apostolic church while Hauerwas belongs to the Methodist Church. Ratzinger belongs and believes in the supreme authority of Peter while Hauerwas tends to a decentralized church authority. The problem with a decentralized or democratized authority is that it is not only the authority that is decentralized, but in most cases the truth is also decentralized or relativized.

Hauerwas and Ratzinger agree on different levels. However, there are specific contributions Hauerwas offers on top of what he has in agreement with Ratzinger. As mentioned above, Hauerwas' main theological doctrine is

---

[587] *Interview with Hauerwas* on Friday, January 28, 2011, at Divinity School, Duke University, cf. appendix.

"resident alienism"—insisting on the essential Christian truth (which is also shared by Ratzinger). In addition, however, Hauerwas' uniqueness comes into play in as far as his existential elements are concerned. Specifically, we wish to note here what we consider to be Hauerwas' major anthropological theme, namely, that according to him, humankind is a creation of God defined by the community—the church. Humankind is realized and fulfilled in the mystery of Pentecost, in which a new language was created. Apart from Christianity, human life, according to Hauerwas, is more of a humanism based on social consensus and action other than on the Logos who lives and perfects the *imago Dei* in humankind.

The accusation that Hauerwas is not rooted in any church membership is not to refer to him as a vagabond. On the other hand, this simply helps to describe a man who has deliberately refused to confine his theological ideas to any particular theological school and church community. His membership runs across the religious and denominational divide, and his theology addresses doctrinal issues regardless of institutional attachments and limitations. He is a true "Catholic" theologian.

Chapter Seven

7.0 Ratzinger's and Hauerwas' Contributions to a Recovery of a Christian Formation of Culture

One can say that the pre-modern world spoke the language of God, because the world then was overwhelmed with missionary activity across the globe, with people ready to shed their blood for their faith. During modernity, we can say that the world spoke the language of knowledge or rationalism. The Renaissance was the major driver of the times. Science and technology sprouted to greater heights. Man and reason displaced God and faith on the world stage. In the postmodern period, we can further assert that the world speaks the language of relativism.[588] The individual rights and freedoms have replaced the concern for humanity as it was the case during the modern period. Relativity has taken over from objectivity. Subjective knowledge and truth has overtaken objective knowledge and objective truth. We can conclude that in the contemporary world, futility has conquered rationality.

---

[588] There could be as many definitions of relativism depending on which perspective one considers the term. One good definition is given by Maria Baghramain. She stated, "relativism is the view that cognitive, moral or aesthetic norms and values are dependent on the social or conceptual systems that underpin them and consequently a neutral standpoint for evaluating them is not available to us," in Maria Baghramain, *Relativism* (New York: Routledge, 2004), 1. The best definition we can find is that given by Ratzinger. He defines relativism as "the letting oneself be tossed and swept along by every wind of teaching; an attitude of modern times that does not recognize anything as definitive and whose ultimate goal consists solely of one's ego and desires," in Thornton and Susan Varenne, *The Essential Pope Benedict XVI*, 22. Even if relativism did not begin in the postmodern times, it is more widespread in this age.

While modernism strived to silence voices about God the Creator and replace them with its god—man (humanity)—relativism moves even further to silence the voice of man (humanity) and replace it with yet another voice, the voice of the individual. Ironically, just as Christianity brought God to the stage, modernity brought man, and relativism wishes to bring the individual on stage after eliminating the first two. In other words, relativism wants the individual to rule the world—setting all rules and principles for himself without any outside influence. In its extreme form, relativism wishes to create a world where there is no God, no universal values, no morals, no universal laws, nothing but the "me." The *me* wants to be its own legislator and judge.

Both the God world and the modern world had allies and adversaries. In a similar way, relativism has proponents and challengers as well. On the front line of adversaries, there lie Joseph Ratzinger and Stanley Hauerwas. While the world sings praises for the liberating culture, these two are saying no to what they consider to be a dictatorship and the new form of slavery for humanity. Their resistance to this new world order is their topmost contribution together. Their work is to refuse to be silenced. Instead, they continually raise the voice of God and humanity. All his life and theological career, Ratzinger has been confronting this dictatorship by objecting to its dictates and proving that there is a superior voice—the voice of God. In a similar manner, Stanley Hauerwas also follows in the same direction when he states, "American Christians don't know how to say no. Most of what I do is resistance."[589]

Below; we shall articulate their particular contributions in response to relativism.

7.1 Joseph Ratzinger

7.1.1 Scripture and Tradition

Joseph Ratzinger's theological career and pastoral vocation stems from his background as a boy raised through the midst of an oppressive Nazi regime. The Nazis' regime was not only oppressing and suffocating other political or social ideologies, but it also aimed at undermining the Christian mission. What he experienced in his earlier life made a very significant and indelible mark on him. His mission seems to be to save his people and the world from this oppressive system. Ratzinger therefore set out to look for a higher authority that would offer meaning to life. He found it in the Christian life and particularly in the Bible. As a young seminarian, the scriptures became his source of

---

[589] *Interview with Hauerwas* on Friday, January 28, 2011, at Divinity School, Duke University, cf. appendix.

inspiration. In his memoirs, Ratzinger recalls, "Exegesis has always remained for me the center of my theological work. . . . Sacred Scripture was the 'soul of our theological studies.'"[590]

Therefore, the first contribution of Ratzinger is his "return to the scene" method of doing theology. His use of scriptures in his writings is dominant and extraordinary. He commands a higher understanding of the scriptures and exegesis. Ratzinger engages exegesis as a historical and theological discipline, though he acknowledges that this methodology "is becoming more lively despite a certain resistance to some recent development."[591] Another theologian commenting on his (Ratzinger's) new book said,

> Benedict XVI is really the Pope of the Second Vatican Council when it comes to sacred Scripture. He sees himself exclusively as implementing the directives of Vatican II with regard to how Catholics read the Bible, how we interpret Scripture, both with history, language, culture and literature, but uniting those to tradition, to dogma and to the canon and the sacred Scripture.[592]

Ratzinger yearns for Christianity to return to its roots, that is, scriptures and tradition. The insistence on going back to the roots has been Ratzinger's first and major contribution to Christian scholarship and Christian living today.

7.1.2 Christology: The Person and the Mission of Jesus of Nazareth

Perhaps the better way to describe Joseph Ratzinger is to refer to him as a Christologist. He has not only written extensively about Christological subjects, but his Christology has been of a new and deeper magnitude. His Christology exhibits the depth of his understanding of the person of Jesus and his mission. His greatest teachings on Jesus are presented in his two written volumes titled *Jesus of Nazareth*. In the first volume, Ratzinger says that when he was growing up in the 1930s and 1940s, there were a series of inspiring books about Jesus that portrayed him as a man living on earth, fully human, and at the same time brought God to men—through Jesus, God was made visible. However, he notes that "the situation started to change in the 1950s. The gap between the

---

[590]   Ratzinger, *Milestones*, 52–53.
[591]   Benedict XVI, *Jesus of Nazareth, Part Two* (San Francisco: Ignatius Press, 2011), xiv.
[592]   Anna Maria Basquez, "Pontiff's Book on Christ Marks Many Firsts: Scholars Discuss Novelties of *Jesus of Nazareth*," (March 11, 2011), *Zenit*, http://www.zenit.org/article-31997?I=english (accessed March 12, 2011).

'historical Jesus' and the 'Christ of faith' grew wider and the two visibly fell apart."[593]

Ratzinger therefore took it upon himself to revitalize and bridge the gap between the "historical Jesus" and the Christ of Faith. Ratzinger takes us back to the scene. His Christology is a link between the historical Jesus—the figure of Jesus and the Christ of faith. He does this by means of the historical-critical hermeneutical method and exegesis. His dialogue aims at reconstructing this Jesus by "going behind the traditions of any sources used by Evangelists."[594] The relativistic culture fights to obscure the historicity of Jesus and reducing it to a mere myth. Joseph Ratzinger, on the other hand, attempts to make Jesus's historicity a reality and to ensure an incessant presence of Jesus in the world to the end of time. De Gaál refers to Ratzinger as the anti-Nietzsche.

Ratzinger's passion behind the recovery of the figure of Jesus is the fact that over the years of traditions and reconstructions of Jesus's mission in both scholarly and secular circles, the figure of the historical is becoming increasingly obscured and blurred—becoming more like a photograph of the authors and the ideals they hold. Under such circumstances, it becomes more and more difficult to create a relationship with the person of Jesus which, according to Ratzinger, is most important for a Christian. His goal is to see Christians creating, as he relates, "an intimate friendship with Jesus, on which everything depends, which is in danger of clutching at thin air."[595]

We can, in brief, assert that Christology is the central discipline in Joseph Ratzinger's theology and vocation. Even when he stated that he did not attempt to write Christology,[596] soon after that, he makes a fallback to his rightful theological position when he stated his intention in doing theology. He states, "attempted to develop a way of observing and listening to the Jesus of the Gospels that can indeed lead to personal encounter and that, through collective listening with Jesus' disciples across the age, can indeed attain sure knowledge of the real historical figure of Jesus."[597]

It is crystal clear that Jesus Christ is the center of Ratzinger's theology, and thus, Christology is his core theology. His Christology may be summed up in his statement in the second volume of *Jesus of Nazareth*, when he stated, "The figure of Jesus is the mirror in which we come to know who God is and what he is like."[598] Here, Ratzinger recalls Jesus's very words to his disciples when

---

[593] Benedict XVI, *Jesus of Nazareth*, Part One, xi.
[594] Ibid., xii.
[595] Ibid., xii.
[596] Ibid., xvi.
[597] Ibid., xvii.
[598] Benedict XVI, *Jesus of Nazareth*, Part One, 137.

Phillip asked him to show them the Father. Jesus replied, "Whoever has seen me has seen the Father" (Jn 14:9).

7.1.3 Love: Encounter with God

As pope, Benedict XVI's first two encyclical letters are about the God of love. These are in line with his mission, which is to promote and invite Christians to an intimate friendship with God through Jesus Christ. It is apparent that Pope Benedict is a fervent advocate of love, for *Ubi Caritas et Amor Deus ibi est.* It is evident in the way he begins his first encyclical letter, *Deus Caritas Est.* It begins, "God is love, and those who abide in God, and God abides in them" (1 Jn 4:16).[599] This opening statement constitutes a summary of his teaching and his vision of Christian life and mission. He refers to it as "the heart of the Christian faith: the Christian image of God and the resulting image of mankind and its destiny."[600]

Ratzinger's theology revolves around the theme of love. Having been raised under a hateful Nazi regime, Ratzinger seems to have developed in him a need for a definite plea that would offer man the most fundamental right and fulfillment. He seems to have realized that without love, life has no meaning. Thus, to live a meaningful life, one must live in love. The statement below shades more light:

> In acknowledging the centrality of love, Christian faith has retained the core of Israel's faith, while at the same time giving it new depth and breadth the pious Jew prayed daily the words of the Book of Deuteronomy which expressed the heart of his existence: "Hear, O Israel: the Lord our God is one Lord, and you shall love the Lord our God with all your heart, and with all your soul and with all your might" (Deut 6:4–5). Jesus united into a single precept this commandment of love for God and the commandment of love for neighbor found in the Book of Leviticus: "You shall love your neighbor as yourself" (Lev 19:18 cf. Mk 12:29–31). Since God has first loved us (cf. 1 Jn 4:10), love is now no longer a mere "command"; it is the response to the gift of love with which God draws near to us.[601]

---

[599] Benedict XVI, *God Is Love* Deus Caritas Est (Vatican City: Libreria Editrice Vaticana, 2006), 1.

[600] Ibid., 1.

[601] Benedict XVI, *God Is Love* Deus Caritas Est, 1–2.

In a nutshell, Ratzinger fathoms the church as the new Israel; and so to be that pious people of God and have God draw near to us, there has to be a doorway, and the doorway is love. In the first encyclical letter, *Deus Caritas Est*, Ratzinger seems to address himself to the church, and in the second encyclical letter, *Caritas in Veritate*, he addresses himself to all humanity. He states in *Caritas in Veritate*:

> Development, social well-being, the search for a satisfactory solution to the grave socioeconomic problems besetting humanity, all need this truth. Without truth, without trust and love for what is true, there is no social conscience and responsibility, and social action ends up serving private interests, resulting in social fragmentation.[602]

We cannot but detect Ratzinger's feud with relativism in this statement. What else is relativism interested in, if not breaking down the deposit of truth or social fragmentation?

Ratzinger suggests that a society without love in truth is fragmented, and it serves self-interests. But God's command to humanity is to serve the interests of God and humanity. Fr. Robert Barron makes a good analysis of Benedict's encyclical. He says that this encyclical entails a number of novelties and a new formula: "Love without Truth devolves into sentimentality—something very superficial; Truth without Love is cold and calculative."[603] The culture of relativism tends to be serving the interests of human rights by "freeing" humanity from oppressive forces. It pretends to be in love with humanity. However, it turns around and denies the truth; hence, revealing its true colors and selfish interests. Relativism is not at any one moment, in love with the other, but rather in love with itself.

When asked what truth is, Jesus remained silent. Why? Because he had just stated that he is the truth, the way, and the life. Ultimate truth is God, and God is love. Therefore, devoid of love is devoid of God. Anything that has no relation cannot be referred to as being of love of being love itself. Ratzinger attacks the relativistic organizations which claim to offer charity to humanity without acknowledging the lordship of God, whose agent they are. Such is not love or charity at all.

Ratzinger is a protagonist of replenishing man's life with God. He wants man to encounter God. His goal is to bring God near to man and man near to

---

[602] Benedict XVI, *Charity in Truth* Caritas in Veritate (Vatican City: Libreria Editrice Vaticana, 2009), 4.

[603] Robert Barron, "On Caritas Veritate," Youtube, http://www.mikeadkins.com/article/fr-barron-on-caritas-in-veritate/ (accessed July 21, 2011).

God. He believes this is possible only through love. Ratzinger can appropriately be referred to as the St. Augustine of the twentieth and twenty-first centuries. He has revived Augustinian theology of love and mercy of God to humanity. Like St. Augustine, Ratzinger has let the world know that without the grace and love of God, man is crippled; for Jesus said, "Apart from me you can do nothing" (Jn 15:5).

Since Jesus is the vine and we are the branches,[604] we are his instruments charged with delivering his love, mercy, and compassion to the world. God flies on our wings. Therefore, if the world is to find God and have an intimate encounter and relationship with him, each individual Christian has to play their part. Just as to see Jesus is to have seen the Father (Jn 14:9), so it should be to those who see us. Those who see us should be able to see Jesus in us, and this will be possible through our love. Jesus said, "By this everyone will know that you are my disciples, if you have love for one another" (Jn 13:35). This theme of love runs across all the writings of Joseph Ratzinger.

7.1.4 Liturgy: The Feast of Faith

Stanley Hauerwas states that "Ratzinger is much more Christological centered and has a more profound understanding of Liturgy in particular - the centrality of worship."[605] Ratzinger believes that it is only when man—in fact every man—stands before the face of God and is answerable to him can man be secure in his dignity as a human being; that the question of moral standards and spiritual resources that we need cannot be separated from the question of worship.[606] This shows how central liturgy is in Ratzinger's theology and his life as a pastor.

For Ratzinger, participation in liturgy is allowing God's presence to take over one's life—a surrender to God—so that filled with this power of God, man can go and act according to his command. In other words, for Ratzinger, liturgy is not what happens in church in the various rites, but a continuous living in the presence of God. In so doing, man will avoid living a life unacceptable to God even outside of church. For him, liturgy is governed by the following reflection

---

[604] "I AM the true vine, and my Father is the vine-grower. He removes every branch in me that bears no fruit. Every branch that bears fruit he prunes to make it bear more fruit. You have already been cleansed by the word that I have spoken to you. Abide in me as I abide in you. Just as the branch cannot bear by itself unless it abides in the vine, neither can you unless you abide in me. I am the vine, you are the branches. Those who abide in me and I in them bear much fruit, because apart from you can do nothing" (Jn 15:1–5).

[605] *Interview with Hauerwas* on Friday, January 28, 2011, at Divinity School, Duke University, c/o appendix.

[606] Ratzinger, *The Feast of Faith*, 7.

that he deems fundamental, namely, "how we can pray and join in the Church's praise of God, and how we can see and experience the salvation of man and the glory of God as a single whole."[607]

As stated in chapter 4 above, Ratzinger proposes liturgy as one of the means of confronting the culture of relativism. He believes that relativism's greatest fear is a congregation, a communion, a unity. Its goal is to fashion a disintegrated society via its divide-a-rule strategy. It hates and by all means thwarts unity, especially unity of a religious nature, because it knows the strength of the unity of faith and doctrine.

According to Ratzinger, liturgy is "a community celebration, an act in which the community forms and experiences itself as such."[608] He is a ferocious defender and implementer of the Vatican II liturgical principles, which describes liturgy as a "celebration, an action of Christ the Priest and of his Body, which is the Church."[609] In other words, Ratzinger's comprehends liturgy as a gathering around the Lord who forms us into what he wants us to be.

In liturgy, the Lord forms and transforms us into his body. Therefore, for Ratzinger, every liturgical celebration is a formation session in which we get to know ourselves as a people and move in the same direction following the Master.[610] In other words, liturgy is a uniting factor for God's people, uniting man with man and man with the Lord. The unity therein, it must be noted, is not merely a physical unity but more importantly a spiritual and doctrinal unity.

If there is anything that Ratzinger is dying to achieve, unity is it. He envisions liturgy as an earthly feast foreshadowing the heavenly feast. But according to Ratzinger, this feast is meant for all. Rather, it is meant for those who have been invited and have the wedding garment. The invitation is open to all, but those who make it to the feast are few—"For many are called, but few are chosen" (Mt 22:14). And who are those who are chosen? They are those who walk the journey of faith onto victory; those who run the race to the finish, who keep the faith. Such will be rewarded by the prize of eternal life (2 Tim 4:7). Thus, liturgy is not any regular gathering, but rather an assembly of those with the same destiny. Ratzinger refers to it as The Feast of Faith. In this unity or communion in liturgy, it is not a mere social unity but rather a unity of faith.

Joseph Ratzinger has revived the biblical understanding of liturgy as standing in the presence of God and letting God reveal himself to us. After God reveals himself to us, we then hasten to reveal him to others—a kind of receive and take. He states, "Man himself cannot simply make worship. If God does not reveal himself, man is clutching empty space. When God does not reveal

---

[607] Ibid.
[608] Ratzinger, *The Feast of Faith*, 62.
[609] SC 7.
[610] Ratzinger, *The Feast of Faith*, 25.

himself, man can, of course, from the sense of God within him, build altars 'to the unknown god.'"[611]

Therefore, in Ratzinger's liturgical discourses, we learn that liturgy is not a mere fulfilling of the law of the observance of Sabbath; it is not a moment of only petitioning God with schedules already fixed for him; it is not the time we go to address God, but rather, more importantly, in Ratzinger's perspective, we go to the presence of God to be addressed, to receive him in word and sacrament. After being replenished, we are sent out take him to others.[612] Isn't this what is meant in the final send-off at the close of the Eucharistic celebration by a deacon/priest: *"Ite Missa Est"*?

7.1.5 Historicity of Christianity

Relativists' aspiration is to convince the world that Christianity is a man-made religion based on the biblical myths and on the story of Jesus, himself a myth. They tend to disconcert people from such "mythical" living to "reality." According to them, anything tenet to Christianity is not plausible, and therefore, the truth of Christianity is in jeopardy. A contributor to *Focus on the Family* stated that many religious relativists like to recite a poem, "The Blind Men and the Elephant: A Hindoo Fable," by John Godfrey Saxe. The poem describes how six blind men all approached an elephant from different sides. Each one touched a part of the elephant—its side, its tusk, its trunk, its leg, its ear, and its tail. Then each one described the elephant by what their limited senses told them: a wall, a spear, a snake, a tree, a fan, and a rope. The poem notes, "Though each was partly in the right . . . all were in the wrong."[613] Saxe concludes,

> So, oft in theologic wars
> The disputants, I ween,
> Rail on in utter ignorance
> Of what each other mean
> And prate about an Elephant
> Not one of them has seen![614]

---

[611] Ibid., 25.

[612] The *Catechism of the Catholic Church* states that "the Eucharist commits us to the poor. To receive in truth the Body and Blood of Christ given up for us, we must recognize Christ in the poorest, his brethren." CCC 1397.

[613] Relativism, "Refuting a Common Case on Religious Relativism," *Apologetics Index*, http://www.apologeticsindex.org/r14.html (accessed July 25, 2011).

[614] John Godfrey Saxe, "The Blind Men and the Elephant: A Hindoo Fable," *The Best Loved Poems of the American People* (New York: Doubleday & Co., 1936), 522.

The writer makes a conclusive comment and believes that what relativists fail to realize is that there is one person involved with the story who claims to know the truth: the storyteller. The storyteller claims to truly understand reality, what the elephant (or theological truth) is really like. The story merely reaffirms the need to get our understanding of theology and God right.[615] This writer is in line with Joseph Ratzinger, because all what Ratzinger does is re-stating of the Christian truth as a historical, objective, and universal truth, not subject to reason or human judgment. He attempts to give a detailed account of the historicity of Christianity and continuity of the Christian mission.

The initial words of chapter 1 in *Introduction to Christianity* present a summary of Ratzinger's objective. It reads, "Anyone who tries today to talk about the question Christian faith in the presence of people who are not thoroughly at home with ecclesiastical language and thought soon comes to sense the alien—and alienating—nature of such an enterprise."[616] He gives an example of Kierkegaard's famous story of the clown and the burning village[617] and likens a Christian to this clown who cannot make people to listen to his message.

Ratzinger notices this trend of alienation of the Christian faith in the contemporary society and attempts to correct it. He takes it upon himself to de-alienate the Christian faith by making recourse to its historicity. For him, the central point of Christianity is the word *credo*—the conversion in which man discovers that he is following an illusion if he devotes himself only to the tangible. "Christian belief is much more concerned with God in history, with God as man."[618]

---

[615] Relativism, "Refuting a Common Case for Religious Relativism," *Apologetics Index*, http://www.apologeticsindex.org/r14.html (accessed July 25, 2011).

[616] Joseph Ratzinger, *Introduction to Christianity* (San Francisco: Ignatius Press, 1968), 39.

[617] According to this story, "a traveling circus in Denmark caught fire. The manager thereupon sent the clown, who was already dressed and made up for the performance, into the neighboring village to fetch help, especially as there was a danger that the fire would spread across the fields of dry stubble and engulf the village itself. The clown hurried into the village and requested the inhabitants to come as quickly as possible to the blazing circus and help to put the fire out. But the villagers took the clown's shouts simply for an excellent piece of advertising, meant to attract as many people to the performance; they applauded the clown and laughed till they cried. The clown felt more like weeping than laughing; he tried in vain to get people to be serious, to make it clear to them that this was no stunt, that he was not pretending but was in bitter earnest, that there really was a fire. His applications only increased the laughter; people thought he was playing his part splendidly—until finally the fire did engulf the village; it was too late for help, and both circus and village were burned to the ground," in Joseph Ratzinger, *Introduction to Christianity* (San Francisco: Ignatius Press, 2000), 39–40.

[618] Ratzinger, *Introduction to Christianity*, 54.

7.1.6 Communion

To summarize what we shall consider as Ratzinger's contribution to Christian faith and as his response to relativism, we would like, at the bottom of his contributions, to discuss his teaching about communion; not to make it less important in any way, but rather to make it serve as the seal of his contributions. It should be noted that the culture of relativism hates communion at its very root. Its goal and passion is to break all institutions and ideas of union under any other perspective other than its standpoint. Although there are many different kinds of relativism, they all have two features in common:

1. "They all assert that one thing [e.g., moral values, beauty, knowledge, taste, or meaning] is relative to some particular framework or standpoint [e.g., the individual subject, a culture, an era, a language, or a conceptual scheme].
2. They all deny that any standpoint is uniquely privileged over all others."[619]

This is the trend that Ratzinger so passionately works to reverse. According to him, man lives in a communion that originates from above—from the vertical to the horizontal praxis. Ratzinger believes that humanity subsists in a relationship. Man's being is relational, and this relatedness comes from the ultimate source of all creatures and horizontally stretches to all creatures. Ratzinger's theology is a resonance of Jesus's words to his disciples: "Apart from me you can do nothing" (Jn 15:5). Jesus is the vine and we are the branches, and so, without him, we the branches dry out. Ratzinger stated, "Without God man neither knows which way to go, nor even understands who he is. Only if we are aware of our calling, as individuals and as a community, to be part of God's family as his sons and daughters, will we be able to generate a new vision and muster new energy in the service of truly integral humanism."[620]

Ratzinger's theology is Eucharistic; meaning, it situates the Eucharist as the source and summit of Christian faith. He has played a great role in relating the Eucharist with Christian living. For him, the Eucharistic meal signifies the unity of the church around the heavenly feast. As stated above, Ratzinger describes liturgy as the standing in the presence of God, and the Eucharist is the greatest of liturgy in which God is the main actor. Commenting on Joseph Ratzinger's book, *Called to Communion*, Matthew Lamb said,

---

[619] Relativism, "Different Manifestations of Relativism," *Apologetics Index*, http://www.apologeticsindex.org/r14.html (accessed July 25, 2011).

[620] Benedict XVI, *Charity in Truth* (Washington, DC: Libreria Editrice Vaticana, 2009), 85.

Ratzinger's "Eucharistic ecclesiology" follows the Fathers of Church in uniting the vertical dimension of the risen body and blood, soul and divinity of Christ in the Eucharist with the horizontal dimension of the gathering of the followers of Christ. "The Fathers summed up these two aspects—Eucharist and gathering—in the word 'communio,' which is once more returning to favor today."[621]

7.2 Stanley Hauerwas

Hauerwas is a product of the Yale School which had a great influence on the way he does theology. However, much as he was influenced by the school though, which is largely a liberal theological school, Hauerwas decided to be both an insider and an outsider—meaning that Hauerwas is an insider of the Yale School like a square peg in a round hole. The Yale School can be described as,

> A colloquial name for an influential group of literary critics, theorists, and philosophers of literature that were influenced by Jacques Derrida's philosophy of deconstruction. Many of the theorists were affiliated with Yale University in the late 1970s, although a number of the theorists—including Derrida himself—subsequently moved to or became affiliated with the University of California at Irvine.[622]

Gary Dorrien makes one of the most appropriate summary statement about the trend of liberal theology (which the Yale School is known for). He states,

> . . . The idea of a liberal approach to Christianity—that theology should be based on reason and critically interpreted religious experience, not external authority—has an ironic history in the United States. In the nineteenth century it took root and flowered; in the early twentieth century it became the founding idea of a new theological establishment; in the 1930s it was marginalized by neo-orthodoxy theology; in the 1960s

---

[621] Matthew Lamb, "Joseph Ratzinger's Primer on Ecclesiology," (June 23, 2005), *Zenit*, http://www.ewtn.com/library/Theology/zrtzeccls.HTM (accessed July 25, 2011).
[622] "Yale School," in http://www.wordiq.com/definition/Yale_school_%28deconstruction %29 (accessed on July 5, 2012).

it was rejected by liberation theology; by the 1970s it was often taken for dead.[623]

As a school of thought, the Yale School is more closely allied with the post-structuralist dimensions of deconstruction as opposed to its phenomenological dimensions. Additionally, the Yale School is more similar to the 1970s version of deconstruction that John D. Caputo has described as a "Nietzschean free play of signifiers" and not the 1990s version of deconstruction that was far more concerned with political and ethical questions.[1][2]

In general, the doctrine of deconstruction is embedded in reconstituting the essential Christian truth as Jean Nancy states,

> Christianity presents itself historically and doctrinally as a composition, i.e. a body of narrative and a message. . . . The Christian construction is that of a way of thinking whose center is "the word of God made flesh." The dogma of incarnation, a mystery, . . . addresses itself to the mind of man, asking him to consider what [without his being able to understand it] brings light to that mind and about it.[624]

Such been the contribution of the Yale School to Christian theology, and that is what Hauerwas has lived to deny. His contribution is basically to be a "resident alien." He belongs to the school but stands out and makes a critique of it. We can confidently say that Hauerwas has been the conscience of the Yale School, the light that leads it back to the truth. He yearns to keep the essential Christian truth at the center of not only doing theology, but at Christian living as well.

In an interview, Stanley Hauerwas asserted the following about his legacy:

> I think the most important thing I have done is trying to make graduate students to care about the theological formation of how to think about moral life; and that is better contribution to ongoing formation of the Church. People may say, he is the one started the recovery of virtue, recovery of narratives. I think the centrality of Christ and the Church and Christ in

[623] Gary, Dorrien, "*American Liberal Theology: Crisis, Irony, Decline, Renewal, Ambiguity*," in http://www.crosscurrents.org/dorrien200506.htm (accessed on July 5, 2012).
[624] Jean-Luc Nancy, *Dis-Enclosure: The Deconstruction of Christianity* (New York: NY, Fordham University Press, 2008), 37–38.

the world have been crucial for me. I think that is my lasting contribution.[625]

Hauerwas acknowledges three main elements of his contribution, namely, moral living and recovery of virtue, recovery of narratives, and the centrality of Christ and the church in the world. As a matter of fact, Hauerwas is more of an ethicist than a systematic theologian. His moral theology can be better described as an ecclesiological moral theology. Here below, we are shall analyze his contributions in detail.

7.2.1 Ethics/Recovery of Virtue

In the field of ethics and virtue, it would be unkind and indeed unrealistic if we ignored the praises and remarks made about Hauerwas by various scholars. These comprehensibly illustrate and summarize Hauerwas' contributions and influences to moral theology today. Below are some of the best remarks from *The Hauerwas Reader*. James W. McClendon wrote,

> Stanley Hauerwas is the theological ethicist of our times. Those who disagree with him need to know why they do and those who agree, as do I, need his splendid case made clear. This reader, the best of his work, is the way for either sort to come to terms with this American master.[626]

Francis Cardinal George commented about him in the following words:

> Covering a range of ethical concerns from healthcare to warfare, these essays show again how Stanley Hauerwas brings together Evangelical and Catholic foundations for an ethics based on faith. The articles ring true, which is to say they speak first of Christ and only then of life in Him.[627]

His namesake, Stanley Fish, stated, "or decades now Stanley Hauerwas has been the most eloquent voice proclaiming the morality of particularity of

---

[625] *Interview with Hauerwas* on Friday, January 28, 2011, at Divinity School, Duke University, cf. appendix.
[626] John Berman and Michael Carwright, eds., *The Hauerwas Reader* (Durham, NC: Duke University Press, 2001), back cover.
[627] Ibid., Advance praise for *The Hauerwas Reader*, inside front cover.

universalism. In a liberal culture that voice is heard as both alien and unreasonable, accusations Hauerwas no doubt cherishes."[628]

The above comments are fascinating, especially because they are made by highly rated scholars. They could perhaps suffice, but the two comments below are so tempting, almost unresistible. Jeffrey Stout wrote the following: "Stanley Hauerwas is the most prolific and provocative theological ethicist writing in the United States. Hauerwas is too important to be ignored."[629] And last but not least, Duncan Forrester of the University of Edinburgh remarked as follows: "For many years Stanley Hauerwas has been lobbing peaceable bombs into the moral theologians' playground, awakening them from their undogmatic slumbers to the importance of truthful action. Hauerwas is always challenging, provocative, illuminating, exasperating, disturbing, and fresh."[630]

There is no need for more explanations of Hauerwas' contribution in this area. The highlighted remarks say it all. These comments were made by theologians from different Christian denominations. Drawing attention and recognition from various denominations makes Hauerwas' writings a teaching that cuts across denominational dogmatics. However, this should not be taken to mean that they are ambiguous, populist, or syncretistic in nature. Rather, their unistic nature stems from their radical nature. Hauerwas has the art of bringing the biblical message alive in almost all ethical circumstances without fear or favor. Hauerwas' major contribution in this area is his insistence on the idea of God in moral matters. All he is doing is attempting to reinstate God into ethics, against the relativists whose ethics does not acknowledge or even mention God. According to Hauerwas, such a moral ethic is a contradiction; not an ethic at all, because it diverges from the Lawgiver.

In his own words, Hauerwas states, "I have been critical of the moral limits of liberalism. Insofar as the Church can reclaim its integrity as a community of virtue, it can be of great service in liberal societies. I have refused to use that affirmation to underwrite an autonomous realm of morality separate from Christ's Lordship."[631] This has been and still is Hauerwas' advocacy in the moral theology circles. In otherwise, for Hauerwas, moral law flows from God's divine law, otherwise it is no law. For him, God created man with a purpose, and only when man lives according to this purpose can he claim to live morally right. God is the supreme law onto which all other laws must conform.

---

[628] Berman and Michael Carwright, eds., *The Hauerwas Reader*, Advance praise for *The Hauerwas Reader*, inside front cover.

[629] Berman and Michael Carwright, eds., *The Hauerwas Reader*, inside front cover.

[630] Ibid.

[631] Hauerwas, *Christian Existence Today*, 17.

7.2.2 The Recovery of Narratives

Stanley Hauerwas has also been very instrumental in recovering the narratives or story theology. His springboard was the prevailing relativistic flaunt of story theology, where story has simply become a new word for myth, making all stories count equally.[632] The problem with this is that it puts the Christian story at the same level with other religious stories. Hauerwas does not consent to this. According to him, the Christian story is a unique one, not one among many, not a great, greater, or greatest of many stories. It is a story of its own right. It is a story of the Supreme God, told and revealed through his Son, Jesus Christ, in whom all things were created,[633] *Lumen de lumine, Deum verum de Deo vero*—Light from Light, true God from true God.[634]

Hauerwas' narrative theology wishes to tell a story of Christianity as a story of Jesus who, as St. Paul says,

> Is the image of the invisible God, the first-born of all creation, for in him were created things in heaven and on earth: everything visible and everything invisible. All things were created through him and for him he exists before all things, and in him all things hold together. He is the Head of the Body, the Church. He is the beginning, the first-born from the dead, so that he should be supreme in every way. (Col 1:15–18).

This is perhaps the greatest and most emphatic statement regarding the nature of Jesus in the whole Bible. It affirms the divinity and supremacy of Jesus. As we profess in the creed, he is "Light from Light, true God from true God." In other words, Jesus is God.

Hauerwas is on the forefront in presenting this true image of Jesus to the world, and as a result, affirming the correct position of Christianity in the world. He lets Christians know that the story of being a Christian has claims on their lives; it involves more than simply believing this or that. Hauerwas states,

> The story of Jesus, which we Christians affirm is nothing less than the story of God's creation on our behalf, is not simply a particular instance of a more universal truth that can be known separately from the story. The story of Jesus is as

---

[632] Ibid., 25.
[633] "Through Him, all things were made, without Him nothing exists" (Jn 1:3).
[634] DH 150.

unsubstitutable. But we can no more learn what it means to be a Christian simply by attending to Scripture. Rather, we learn that story by caring for the tombstones of the saints. It is from them that we begin to understand what that story requires and means. For the truth of the story we find in the gospels is finally known only through the kind of lives it produces.[635]

In brief, Hauerwas' theology retells the Christian story as a unique story, a story from, of and by God to humanity. For Hauerwas, this story is not one that one can read and either like or dislike, believe or reject. Rather, he wants the world to know that this is a story brought to humanity—an invitation to humanity by God to live this story in their lives. The Christian story, according to Hauerwas, becomes meaningful insofar as man lives by it. This has been one of Hauerwas' contributions to the story theology, which leads to his other great contribution, namely, discipleship.

7.2.3 Discipleship

It may be appropriate to describe Hauerwas as the Dietrich Bonheoffer (1906–1945) of America, because he brings to life and develops Bonheoffer's teaching of discipleship and assimilates his nonviolent resistance. All Hauerwas' theology is an account of discipleship. His goal is to make his readers become "followers," in the sense of imitators of the Lord. Ironically put, Hauerwas' theology attempts to bring God into a society that has been invaded by a culture that strives to remove God from people's lives and existence. Hauerwas cautions his readers to remain courageous disciples of Christ, consistently taking the cross all the way to Calvary onto victory. For Hauerwas, a disciple of Christ is one who is ready to carry his cross every day and follow Christ;[636] one who dares the challenges of the world but does not submit to them; for Jesus said, "If any want to become my followers, let them deny themselves and take up their cross and follow me. For those who want to save their life will lose it, and those who lose their life for my sake will find it" (Mt 16:24–25).

Second, discipleship according to Hauerwas is a call to be holy. This is very central in Hauerwas' writings. A disciple is a witness. Hauerwas teaches that

---

[635] Hauerwas, *Christian Existence Today*, 40.
[636] For Hauerwas, Christianity is unintelligible without witness, that is, without people whose practices exhibit their committed assent to a particular way of structuring the whole. Christianity is much more than an idea. Rather, it is a bodily faith that must be seen to be believed, in Stanley Hauerwas and Jean Vanier, *Living Gentle in a Violent World: The Prophetic Witness of Weakness* (Downers Grove, IL: IVP Books, 2008), 17.

becoming Christian is to become part of the Church. By faith
we become joined with the body of Christ, which involves
our participation and emersion in the daily practices of the
Christian Church: prayer, worship, admonition, feeding the
hungry, caring for the sick, etc. so we are transformed over
time to participate in God's life.[637]

Transformation or sanctification is a key theme in Hauerwas' discourses.
Hauerwas differs widely from the rest of Protestant theologians who pay more
attention to justification other than sanctification.

In what can be considered one of his greatest works, *Sanctify Them in the
Truth*, Hauerwas presents his greatest teaching about discipleship. For him,
a person who claims to be a disciple but whose life does not conform to the
Gospel is no disciple at all. In his theology, being a disciple is synonymous with
"performing" the faith. He states,

I have always hoped that my work might exhibit Cardinal
Suhard's claim: to be a witness does not consist in engaging in
propaganda nor even in stirring people up, but in being a living mystery. It means to live in such a way that one's life would
not make a sense if God did not exist.[638]

The theme of discipleship in Hauerwas' theology runs across his theological
writings and can be regarded as his greatest contribution, not only in the world
of ethics but also in theology in general. He is a challenge to both the Protestant
communion as well as to the Catholic world. His teaching of discipleship criticizes the relativistic liberal ethics as an ethics that comes from nowhere and
goes nowhere, and ethics without a head or tail.[639] Hauerwas presents Christ
as head of the church, and in this position, he sets the rules and the code of
conduct, which his disciples are obliged to follow. The following or discipleship
has a higher goal other than the earthly goal of liberal ethics, which is peaceful
living. His ethics of discipleship is eschatological in nature.[640]

Hauerwas' contribution with regard to discipleship is the bottom line on
which he builds his theology. It is what defines him among the universities
where he has lived most of his life, in the academia, in the church, and in the
world. He believes that this is the only way man can live a moral life in the true
sense of the word. "The various attempts by theologians in modernity to 'do'

---

[637] Hauerwas, *In Good Company*, 193.
[638] Hauerwas, *Sanctify Them in the Truth*, 19.
[639] Hauerwas, *Sanctify Them in the Truth*, 19.
[640] Ibid., 19.

ethics from the 'bottom up' has amounted to nothing less than an apologetic strategy which is bound to fail. They confirm modernity's presumption that God is, at best, something 'added on' to the moral life."[641] This theme leads to his other great contribution, namely, the centrality of Christ and the church in the world.

7.2.4 The Centrality of Christ and the Church in the World

One characteristic of Hauerwas that has endeared him to so many, and at the same time caused him to be hated by so many, is his strong stand on Christ and the church as necessary in society. He refers to himself as a terrorist,[642] meaning that he is not willing to negotiate, just like a terrorist, with anyone who dismisses Christ and the church from the world. He actually says that most of what he is doing is resistance.[643] However, his resistance is nonviolent. His contribution in this perspective is his selfless pushing forward of the idea of the dominion of God's rule and lordship over creation. He does not hesitate to make statements like: "Indeed God's 'grace-gull' dominion is embodied most pre-eminently in human form: the fleshly person of Jesus of Nazareth, the prolongation of whose earthly life finds embodiment in the Church."[644]

Hauerwas has been at the forefront in the battle to show to the world that Christ and the church are not a creation of man, but rather the revelation of God and divine institution respectively. And since Jesus is God-made-man, he is necessary in the world, and his institution, the church is also necessary and its mission crucial and central in the world. He opposes relativists who claim that the idea of God and Christianity is an illusion imposed on humanity. Hauerwas thinks this mentality must be confronted by living the Christian message radically. His appeal to the Christians is to live this Christian message of love as sent by the Lord. He elucidates,

Christians have been sent out into a world of war to challenge

---

[641] Ibid., 43.

[642] Hauerwas thinks he is a terrorist—a peaceful, nonviolent terrorist, a Christian fanatic. He gives reasons: "As a pacifist I obviously think that war and terrorism are not compatible with christen discipleship. Christian nonviolence, therefore, cannot help but appear as fanatical just to the extent it challenges the assumed normality of war and violence. We are not radicals because we assume a radical stance on this or that issue that the world understands as radical, but because ant stance we assume must be witness to the God of Jesus Christ. Therefore, Christian nonviolence is a form of terrorism" in Hauerwas, *Sanctify Them in the Truth*, 178.

[643] *Interview with Hauerwas* on Friday, January 28, 2011, at Divinity School, Duke University, cf. appendix.

[644] Hauerwas, *Sanctify Them in the Truth*, 45.

the necessity of war armed only with the weapon of love. Christians are first and foremost called to be witnesses by necessity. That Christians must resist such temptations is not because violence may not seem to provide peace, but because the peace provided is not the peace of Christ.[645]

He calls upon all Christians to share in this resistance of a culture that disregards God's lordship over creation. Both his theology and anthropology are ecclesiological—they can only be comprehended within the church. He sees the church as a necessary institution in the world as the new Israel, the people of God, in which God's kingdom reigns. And according to him, the kingdom of God must rein on earth. He explains,

> The kingdom of God is not a human utopian project, but is a reality established by God. The kingdom of God is historically and socially embodied in the community of the Christian Church, even though God's reign is wider than the Church and even through the Church often has been and is unfaithful. Without the kingdom ideal, the Church loses its identity-forming hope; without the Church, the kingdom ideal loses its concrete character.[646]

Hauerwas advocates for a church that is "the primary locus for a new politics, an alternative *polis* or *civitas*; the counter story that interprets the world's politics."[647] He re-echoes the Augustinian city of God. He wants Christians to belong to this new polis that has the Gospel as its constitution. This is a very dominant teaching in Hauerwas' writings and merits to be one of his greatest contributions to theology and Christian living today.

Conclusively, it is only fair to avow that both Joseph Ratzinger and Stanley Hauerwas have made great contributions toward the recovery of a Christian-forming culture in response to relativism. Their position is that, first and foremost, there is a God who is the source of all things, the Lord of nature, governing and sustaining all creation. Second, man is a creature—created by a living God, and not a result of natural accidents with mysterious beginnings. Third, this god is a living god who continuously governs and sustains nature and humanity. God is not dead; he is not like a watchmaker who, after making the watch, never takes care where it is located or about its functionality. He is

---

[645] Hauerwas, *Sanctify Them in the Truth*, 187.
[646] Hauerwas, *In Good Company*, 186.
[647] Ibid., 188.

instead a hands-on governor, unceasingly watching over creation. This god governs creation by his eternal law—a universal law—binding to every human being. This law was given to us through his Son, Jesus Christ, the head of the church, who rules the earth by the power of his spirit. Fourth, this law of God, the truth, is found in the scriptures and in the tradition of the church. Through this law, man is saved. Therefore, this makes the church necessary in the world. A relativistic way of looking at reality is a lie. It takes man back to Egypt and back into slavery.

We ought to realize that what is at stake is the anthropology gone bad. Therefore, to overhaul the relativistic tendencies, there is need to recollect this anthropology. This is going to be the task of the next chapter.

Chapter Eight

8.0 Toward a Better Theological Anthropology

8.1 Man: His Nature: Body and Soul

Man can be defined as "a rational animal; a substance, corporeal, living, sentient, and rational. A member of the species *Homo Sapiens* or all the members of this species collectively, without regard to sex."[648] It continues to elucidate that

> a bipedal primate mammal [*Homo sapiens*] that is anatomically related to the great apes but distinguished especially by notable development of the brain with a resultant capacity for articulate speech and abstract reasoning, is usually considered to form a variable number of freely interbreeding races, and is the sole living representative of the hominid family; broadly: any living or extinct hominid.[649]

Man's animality is distinct in nature from his rationality, though they are inseparably joined, during life, in one common personality. "Man's animality is rational"; for his "rationality" is certainly not something superadded to his "animality." Man is one in essence.

The *Second Vatican Council* reiterates this, thus:

> Though made of body and soul, man is one. Through his bodily

---

[648] "Man" in Merriam-Webster, http://www.merriam-webster.com/dictionary/man (accessed on March 2, 2012).

[649] Ibid.

composition he gathers to himself the elements of the material world; thus they reach their crown through him, and through him raise their voice in free praise of the Creator. (6) For this reason man is not allowed to despise his bodily life, rather he is obliged to regard his body as good and honorable since God has created it and will raise it up on the last day. Nevertheless, wounded by sin, man experiences rebellious stirrings in his body. But the very dignity of man postulates that man glorify God in his body and forbid it to serve the evil inclinations of his heart.[650]

From the above considerations, it becomes clear that man is not merely an animal. He has something extra that qualifies him to be a human being and not merely an animal as such. This "extra" is the soul. It is this soul that completes the essence of man, for his essence is body and soul.

Maximus the Confessor understands man as a created being, created both body and soul. According to him, the body and soul coexist and were created simultaneously without one being in existence prior to the other.[651] He states,

> Man's co-existence is in two ways: as both an initial and a continuing co-existence. All has been created according to God's foreknowledge, and the λόγοι of all that exists pre-exist in God. . . . The body and soul cannot exist separately, for there is always a relation [σχέσις] between soul and body and they are by necessity bound to each other.[652]

---

[650] GS 14. Two other councils had in fact pronounced themselves on the matter. The Council of Vienne stated, "We reject as erroneous and contrary to the truth of the Catholic faith and doctrine or opinion which asserts that the substance of the rational and intellectual soul is not truly and of itself [per se] the form of the human body, or which calls this into doubt. In order that the truth of the pure faith may be known to all, and the path to error barred, we define that from now on whoever presumes to assert, defend, or obstinately hold that the rational and intellectual soul is not of itself and essentially the form of the human body, is to be censured as heretic." In ND 405, Council of Vienne (1311–1312). The fifth Lateran Council confirmed it: "We condemn and reprove all those who assert that the intellectual soul is mortal or that it is one and the same in all human persons, or who raise doubts in this matter. The intellectual soul is not only truly, of itself and essentially, the form of the human body, but it is also immortal and, according to the number of bodies in which it is infused, it can be, has been and will be multiplied in individuals." In ND 410, The Fifth Lateran General Council (Bull Apostolici Regiminis—1513).

[651] Thomas Aquinas agrees with him. According to Aquinas, "The intellectual soul is created by God at the end of human generation, and this is at the same time sensitive and nutritive, the pre-existing forms being corrupted." In Summa Theologica, q. 118, a. 2.

[652] Lars Thunberg, Microcosm and Mediator: The Theological Anthropology of Maximus the Confessor, 2nd ed. (Chicago, IL: Open Court Publishing Company, 1995), 95–97.

According to him, both the independence and the union of body and soul, for which there exists no preexistence of one in relation to the other but only co-existence, "are based on pre-existence λόγος of both in God."[653] Maximus goes ahead to state that the unity of body and soul in man is analogous with the unity of divine and human nature in Christ.[654] However, Maximus also claims that the human unity of body and soul is not hypostatic, as in the divinity and humanity in Christ, but natural. For him, "Hypostatic union allows that both elements are perfect substances, while natural union implies that their completeness is in the end related to the whole as one species."[655] Man is not therefore, according to Maximus, a unity of two independent substances, but rather a composite nature.

At this point, we can already deny with certainty, the ideas of separately or double creation of body and soul and the Gnostic claim labeling flesh as bad or evil and spirit or soul as good. The objection is rooted in the act of creation itself. If both body and soul are simultaneously created, and created by the one good God, then one cannot be bad and another good. As a matter of fact, scripture says, "God saw everything that he had made, and indeed, it was very good (καὶ εἶδεν ὁ θεὸς τὰ πάντα ὅσα ἐποίησεν καὶ ἰδοὺ καλὰ λίαν καὶ ἐγένετο ἑσπέρα καὶ ἐγένετο πρωὶ ἡμέρα ἕκτη)" (Gen 1:31). Thus, man, body, and soul, by virtue of creation, share the goodness of all creation in equal measure. But man enjoys even one more attribute than the rest of creation. He created, as scripture says, in the image of God, "So God created humankind in his image, in the image of God he created them; male and female he created them (καὶ ἐποίησεν ὁ θεὸς τὸν ἄνθρωπον κατ' εἰκόνα θεοῦ ἐποίησεν αὐτόν ἄρσεν καὶ θῆλυ ἐποίησεν αὐτούς)" (Gen 1:27).

8.1.1 Microcosm and Mediator

Maximus understands man as not only a being, a microcosm, who reflects the constitution of the created universe, but also as a being—a mediator—created in the image of God, whose task it is, in Christ, to reconcile the spiritual

---

[653] Thunberg, *Microcosm and Mediator*, 98.

[654] "For man as a person cannot be isolated from the fact that human nature has its hypostasis in the Logos, and thus is itself enhypostasized. Which is to say that a personal relationship to God cannot be excluded from human nature and is identical with fully realized human existence. Man has full freedom, but his freedom is not fully realized until it finds its end in God. Divine and human nature are strictly kept apart and are yet—in that very separation—deeply interrelated" in Thunberg, *Microcosm and Mediator*, 106.

[655] Thunberg, *Microcosm and Mediator*, 101.

and the sensible into one homogeneous unity.[656] This teaching is re-echoed in St. Augustine's teaching. He states,

> Thou hast given gladness in my heart. Christ has his dwelling place in a man's heart. It rests with such a man to contemplate the truth, since our Lord has told us: "I am the truth." It was He too who spoke by the mouth of the Apostle. "Do you seek a proof of Christ," he asked, "that speaketh in me?" obviously Christ was speaking not audibly, but in his inmost heart, in that secret place where we are to pray (Ps 4:8).[657]

Jesus Christ is the mediator between God and man, as the apostle put it, he is "the image of the invisible God (ὅς ἐστιν εἰκὼν τοῦ θεοῦ τοῦ ἀοράτου, πρωτότοκος πάσης κτίσεως)" (Col 1:15). If this image of the invisible God dwells in man's heart, then man also becomes a sharer in the role of the One who dwells in him. Man therefore has some degree of divinity in him. According to Thomas Aquinas, man shares in the divinity of God by participation. He states,

> God is in all things; not, indeed, as part of their essence, nor as an accident, but as an agent is present to that upon which it works. For an agent must be joined to that wherein it acts immediately and touch it by its power; hence it is proved in Phys. vii that the thing moved and the mover must be joined together. Now since God is very being by His own essence, created being must be His proper effect; as to ignite is the proper effect of fire. Now God causes this effect in things not only when they first begin to be, but as long as they are preserved in being; as light is caused in the air by the sun as long as the air remains illuminated. Therefore as long as a thing has being, God must be present to it, according to its mode of being. But being is innermost in each thing and most fundamentally inherent in all things since it is formal in respect of everything found in a thing, as was shown above (Question 7, Article 1). Hence it must be that God is in all things, and innermostly.[658]

---

[656] Thunberg, *Microcosm and Mediator*, cf. back cover. Vatican II resuscitates this: "According to the almost unanimous opinion of believers and unbelievers alike, all things on earth should be related to man as their center and crown." GS 12.

[657] Augustine, "St. Augustine on the Psalms (*Enarrationes in Psalmos*)" in *Ancient Christian Writers: The Works of the Fathers in Translation*, trans. Dame Scholastica Hebgin and Dame Felisitas Corrigan (Westminster, MD: The Newman Press, 1960), 47.

[658] *Summa Theologica*, q. 8, a. 1.

Like Aquinas, Maximus too believes that the divine and the natural are deeply interrelated; for according to him, "man as a person cannot be isolated from the fact that human nature has its hypostasis in the Logos, and thus is itself enhypostasized, Which is to say that a personal relationship to God cannot be excluded from human nature and is identical with fully realized human existence."[659] And since God exists in all things, including unanimated things, how much more does he exist in man created in his own image? In the section below, we shall discuss the subject of *imago Dei* and *similitudo Dei*.

8.2. *Imago Dei* and *Similitudo Dei*

We shall deliberate this subject beginning with teachings of Maximus the Confessor, St. Augustine, Thomas Aquinas, through the Vatican Council II. The creation story states, "So God created humankind in his image, in the image of God he created him; male and female he created them (καὶ ἐποίησεν ὁ θεὸς τὸν ἄνθρωπον κατ᾽ εἰκόνα θεοῦ ἐποίησεν αὐτόν ἄρσεν καὶ θῆλυ ἐποίησεν αὐτούς)" (Gen 1:27). It is from this scriptural truth that theologians begin to illustrate how this is true to man.

According to Maximus, the *imago Dei* was given to man in the beginning, but the *similitudo Dei* is to be acquired through a spiritual process. Likeness, according him, is related to the divine sonship given to man, and development of this likeness is seen as "a kind of imitation of God, a manifestation of divine virtue and, on the whole, as a moral activity of man."[660] Meanwhile, St. Augustine teaches that we are men made after our Creator's image, which he understands as manifesting itself in love. For Augustine, God is love. He thus stated that "weight is to the body as love is to the soul."[661] Somewhere else, Augustine teaches,

> The light of thy countenance, O Lord, is signed upon us. This light which shines upon the mind, not upon the eyes, constitutes mankind's whole and essential good. It is "signed upon us" like a coin stamped with the king's image. For man was made to God's image and likeness, and defaced it by sin. His true and lasting good therefore is to be stamped anew by regeneration. (Ps 4:7).[662]

---

[659] Thunberg, *Microcosm and Mediator*, 106.

[660] Thunberg, *Microcosm and Mediator*, 126.

[661] Saint Augustine, *The City of God (De Civitate Dei)*, trans. John Healey (Edinburgh: John Grant, 1909), book 11, chapter 28, 335.

[662] Augustine, "St. Augustine on the Psalms (*Enarrationes in Psalmos*)" in *Ancient Christian Writers*, 46–47.

This implies that according to St. Augustine, the *imago Dei* and *similitudo Dei* are sealed in man's nature, and are inert elements of human nature given to man at creation, but which man lost at the fall. This would therefore mean that God dwelt universally in every man at creation, and after the fall, he dwells in those who are regenerated.

Thomas Aquinas addresses the subject in a more profound way. He tends to take Maximus's path; for both distinguish between the *imago Dei* and *similitudo Dei*, whereas Augustine tends to link both together. According to Aquinas, the *imago Dei* is in man in three ways:

> First, inasmuch as man possesses a natural aptitude for under-standing and loving God; and this aptitude consists in the very nature of the mind, which is common in all men. Secondly, inasmuch as man actually or habitually knows and loves God, though imperfectly; and this image consists in the conformity of grace. Thirdly, inasmuch as man knows and loves God per-fectly; and this image consists in the likeness of glory.[663]

This means that according to Aquinas, the *imago Dei* is found in every human being however imperfectly or remotely. This *imago Dei* improves and turns into a *similitudo Dei* with the aid of grace. He believes that "*likeness* may be considered as signifying the expression of and perfection of the *image*."[664] Thus, Thomas distinguishes "likeness" from "image" in the following terms:

> Likeness is not distinguished from image in the general no-tion of likeness [for thus it is included in image]; but so far as any likeness falls short, or again, as it perfects the idea of image. The soul's essence belongs to the image, as represent-ing the Divine Essence in those things which belong to the intellectual nature; but not in those conditions subsequent to general notions of being, such as simplicity. Love of the word, which is knowledge loved, belongs to the nature of image; but love of virtue belongs to likeness, as virtue itself belongs to likeness.[665]

Vatican II resuscitates Maximus's and Aquinas's distinction between *imago Dei* and *similitudo Dei*. The mind of Vatican II is that the "image" is natural

---

[663] *Summa Theologica*, q. 93, a. 4.
[664] Ibid., q. 93, a. 9.
[665] Ibid., q. 93, a. 9.

to man, and it remained so even after the fall. It was the "likeness" that was disfigured from the first sin onward. The council states,

> He Who is "the image of the invisible God" (Col 1:15), is Himself the perfect man. To the sons of Adam He restores the divine likeness which had been disfigured from the first sin onward. Since human nature as He assumed it was not annulled, by that very fact it has been raised up to a divine dignity in our respect too. For by His incarnation the Son of God has united Himself in some fashion with every man. He worked with human hands, He thought with a human mind, acted by human choice and loved with a human heart. Born of the Virgin Mary, He has truly been made one of us, like us in all things except sin.[666]

This means that Jesus alone possesses the perfect likeness of God. In us humans, this likeness was damaged by sin and we regain it by the grace of Christ through whom we are regenerated.[667] Second, the image of God in human nature was not lost by sin; otherwise, Jesus would have been contaminated when he took on our human nature. It was the "likeness" of God in us that was disfigured; and through the grace of Christ, we begin a journey toward renewal and perfecting this likeness of God in us. This takes us to yet another subject, that is, grace and nature.

8.3 Grace and Nature

8.3.1 Augustinian vis-à-vis Thomist Tradition

The book of Genesis clearly states that after the fall, man lost his original justice.[668] "Therefore the Lord God sent him forth from the garden of Eden, to

---

[666] GS 22.

[667] "As an innocent lamb He merited for us life by the free shedding of His own blood. In Him God reconciled us to Himself and among ourselves; from bondage to the devil and sin He delivered us, so that each one of us can say with the Apostle: The Son of God 'loved me and gave Himself up for me' (Gal 2:20). By suffering for us He not only provided us with an example for our imitation, He blazed a trail, and if we follow it, life and death are made holy and take on a new meaning. The Christian man, conformed to the likeness of that Son Who is the firstborn of many brothers, received 'the first-fruits of the Spirit' (Rom 8:23) by which he becomes capable of discharging the new law of love. Through this Spirit, who is 'the pledge of our inheritance' (Eph 1:14), the whole man is renewed from within, even to the achievement of 'the redemption of the body' (Rom 8:23)." GS 22.

[668] The Council of Trent clarifies this in the best terms: "If anyone does not profess that Adam, the first man, by transgressing God's commandment in paradise, at once lost the holiness and justice in which he had been constituted; and that, offending God by his sin,

till the ground from which he was taken (καὶ ἐξαπέστειλεν αὐτὸν κύριος ὁ θεὸς ἐκ τοῦ παραδείσου τῆς τρυφῆς ἐργάζεσθαι τὴν γῆν ἐξ ἧς ἐλήμφθη)" (Gen 3:23). Sending Adam out of paradise is the result of Adam losing his original state and justice and can only regain it through the power of grace, through the process of regeneration. The argument of grace and nature has over the years, taken different directions, with some theologians elevating nature to a higher level than it deserves. On the other hand, there have been those who denied the postlapsarian state of human nature, and all was grace. We cannot discuss this subject without mentioning the protagonists of both nature and grace. On the side of nature, the most prominent was Pelagius from whom heretical Pelagianism originated. Pelagius denied original sin and grace. Pelagius regarded

> The moral strength of man's will (*liberum arbitrium*), when steeled by asceticism, is sufficient in itself to desire and to attain the loftiest ideal of virtue. The value of Christ's redemption was, in his opinion, limited mainly to instruction (*doctrina*) and example (*exemplum*), which the Savior threw into the balance as a counterweight against Adam's wicked example, so that nature retains the ability to conquer sin and to gain eternal life even without the aid of grace.[669]

In refutation of Pelagianism, Jansenius went to the other extreme by denying any power of human nature to ascend to God. The following is worth noting about Jansenius:

> His fundamental error consists in disregarding the supernatural order, for Jansenius as for Baius, the vision of God is the necessary end of human nature; hence it follows that all the primal endowments designated in theology as supernatural or preternatural, including exemption from concupiscence, were simply man's due. This first assertion is fraught with grave consequences regarding the original fall, grace, and justification. As a result of Adam's sin, our nature stripped of elements essential to its integrity, is radically corrupt and depraved. Mastered by concupiscence, which in each of us

---

he drew upon himself the wrath and indignation of God and consequently death with which God had threatened him, and . . . the whole Adam, body and soul, was changed for the worse through the offence of his sin, *anathema sit*" in ND 508, "Decree on Original Sin (1546)."

[669] Richard Hanson, *The Search for the Christian Doctrine of God: The Arian Controversy* (Edinburgh: T & T Clark, 1988), 96.

properly constitutes original sin, the will is powerless to resist; it has become purely passive. It cannot escape the attraction of evil except it be aided by a movement of grace superior to and triumphant over the force of concupiscence. Our soul, henceforth obedient to no motive save that of pleasure, is at the mercy of the delectation, earthly or heavenly, which for the time being attracts it with the greatest strength.[670]

St. Augustine, the doctor of grace, cannot be left out of this discussion. He stands in the middle between Pelagius and Jansenius. Augustine, although he is leaning more to the side of the power of grace, accords nature some degree of power to ascend to God. According to Augustine, human nature has the power to seek God. In *The Confessions*, Augustine writes, "You move us to delight in praising You; for You have formed us for Yourself, and our hearts are restless till they find rest in You."[671] Augustine acknowledges the goodness of creation. For him,

If things are deprived of all good, they cease altogether to be; and this means that as long as they are, they are good. Therefore, whatever is, is good. . . . So it became obvious to me that all that you have made is good, and that there are no substances whatsoever that were not made by you. And because you did not make them all equal, each single thing is good and collectively they are very good, for our God made his whole creation very good.[672]

Another figure that cannot be left out of this argument is Thomas Aquinas. Aquinas, though accused of granting more powers to nature that it actually deserves, stands in the middle ground and explains the divisions of grace.[673]

---

[670] "Pelagius and Pelagianism," in *New Advent*, http://www.newadvent.org/cathen/09580c.htm (accessed on March 2, 2012).

[671] Augustine, *The Confessions* (Book I), 21–41.

[672] Augustine, *Confessions*, 145.

[673] "As grace is divided into operating and cooperating, with regard to its diverse effects, so also is it divided into prevenient and subsequent, howsoever we consider grace. Now there are five effects of grace in us: of these, the first is, to heal the soul; the second, to desire good; the third, to carry into effect the good proposed; the fourth, to persevere in good; the fifth, to reach glory. And hence grace, inasmuch as it causes the first effect in us, is called prevenient with respect to the second, and inasmuch as it causes the second, it is called subsequent with respect to the first effect. And as one effect is posterior to this effect, and prior to that, so may grace be called prevenient and subsequent on account of the same effect viewed relatively to divers others. And this is what Augustine says (*De Natura*

215

According to Aquinas, "grace does not destroy nature but perfects it."[674] In other words, grace builds on nature, which means a nature void of grace cannot be conceived.

It is not our aim to exhaustively discuss the topic nature and grace in this paper. For the purpose of this paper, we intend only to highlight the major arguments from the different schools. However, since this paper's main reference theologian, Joseph Ratzinger, addresses the topic, we wish here below to present his full exposé on nature and grace.

8.3.2 Joseph Ratzinger on Nature and Grace

8.3.2.1 *Gratia Praesupponit Naturam* (Grace Presupposes Nature)

In all his vast theological writings, Joseph Ratzinger treats the nature and grace issue only in his title, *Dogma and Preaching*. In this volume, Ratzinger critiques Aquinas's positive concept of nature. According to him, "Thomism rightly became an object of polemical attack by Reformation thought. Thomas should be discussed especially as a contrast to Bonaventure."[675] He identifies two aspects of the problem; the extreme ends of leaning on either nature or grace he suggests lead to a *via media*. The two aspects are as follows:

1. Supernaturalism—theological denial of nature
2. Naturalism—collapses grace into nature; it denies creation and renders grace meaningless.[676]

8.3.2.2 The Problem

Ratzinger accuses the axiom *"Gratia praesupponit naturam"* as the root cause for the theology of "the *analogia entis*, of the great 'catholic' harmony."[677] For Ratzinger, the *analogia entis* is problematic because it binds two realities that are of different natures. He states that this led to the extreme conclusions made by both Karl Barth and Nietzsche, regarding grace as natural and internal and not external to the human condition. He thus states,

---

et Gratia xxxi): "It is prevenient, inasmuch as it heals, and subsequent, inasmuch as, being healed, we are strengthened; it is prevenient, inasmuch as we are called, and subsequent, inasmuch as we are glorified" in *Summa Theologica*, q. 111, a. 3.

[674] *Summa Theologica*, q. 1, a. 8.

[675] Benedict XVI, *Dogma and Preaching: Applying Christian Doctrine to Daily Life* (San Francisco: Ignatius Press, 2011), 143.

[676] Ibid., 144.

[677] Ibid., 147.

Karl Barth was affected by Nietzsche's revolutionary pathos—acknowledging a nature in which the grace of Christ "is internal and not external, natural and not foreign." But man does not live in his true nature; instead, an unnatural state has become his nature. To continue and perfect that state would mean to accomplish the self-destructive conclusion of man. For this sort of man, grace cannot be continuation or perfection but only disruption.[678]

8.3.2.3 Elements of Answer

Ratzinger faults theologians who are in support of the teaching of the analogy of being. He believes they are erroneous because they believe in a pure nature without artifice and as it was at creation, which according to him, does not exist because he believes that all human "nature" has become artifice. "Nature in the world-friendly theology of the analogy of being, is the opposite of artificial and man-made things and, thus, what is original and in keeping with creation."[679]

8.3.2.4 Original Understanding of Scholastic Axiom

Joseph Ratzinger says that for Bonaventure,

> "*Gratia praesupponit naturam sicut accidens praesupponit subjectum*" (Grace presupposes nature as an accident presupposes a subject). "*Ubi melior est natura, frequenter minor est gratia et qui hodie minor est in merito, cras fortassis erit major*" (Where nature is better, there is always less grace, and someone who is less meritorious today will perhaps be the greater tomorrow).[680]

He asserts that the scholastics realized that someone who is richly endowed in "natural" gifts can fail in God's sight, that his natural strength can also become for him an obstacle that bars him from the threading on the way to the humility of faith. In Bonaventure's view, for example, the human soul is entirely beyond the realm of mere nature. "A merely natural soul is inconceivable. Spirit

---

[678] Benedict XVI, *Dogma and Preaching*, 147.
[679] Ibid., 149.
[680] Ibid., 150.

surpasses pure nature."[681] Rather, according to Ratzinger, natural law, after God spoke with the patriarchs, was surpassed by the entirely new level of direct dialogue with God, as this occurs preeminently in grace.[682] He thus makes the following conclusion; "if we observe nature from its true point of reference, from God's perspective, it becomes evident that in the end all nature is 'grace'—'*hoc totum quod fecit, fuit gratia*' (all this that he made was grace)."[683]

8.3.2.5 Nature and Grace in Scripture

Ratzinger's central scripture defense is taken from St. Paul's Letter to the Ephesians. "We were by nature children of wrath, like everyone else" (Eph 2:3). For the Jew, this was an unheard-of and positively nonsensical statement. Ratzinger argues that "by nature," on account of their birth, the others, the non-Jews, are children of wrath. "Paul now declares to the race of the redeemed: Not only the others are by nature children of wrath, but we are too. All are."[684] Therefore, for Ratzinger, merely natural existence, in and of itself, is in any case without salvation. This means that concrete nature, as it is in fact bestowed on man in his birth, is not a salvific order. Man receives true enlightenment about his being not from "nature," but rather from his encounter with Christ in faith. "Nature can very well be the sign of the Creator, but it is not so with perfect clarity, because it is also the expression of man's highhandedness."[685]

8.3.3 Synthesis

Ratzinger makes the following conclusion:
Gratia praesupponit natura is correct and fully biblical in saying that grace does not destroy what is truly human in man but, salvages and fulfills it. This genuine humanity of man, the created order "man," is completely extinguished in no man; it lies at the basis of every single human person and in many different ways continuously has its effects on man's concrete existence, summoning and guiding him. But of course in no man is it present without warping or falsification; instead, in every individual it is caked with the layer of filth.[686]

Ratzinger minimally subscribes to the doctrine of *analogia entis*. He seems to have fears that its use grants humankind attributes that are above his nature. It tends to make a comparison between God and man—elevating man to a level

---

[681] Ibid., 153.
[682] Ibid., 154.
[683] Benedict XVI, *Dogma and Preaching*, 154.
[684] Ibid., 157.
[685] Ibid., 158.
[686] Ibid.

of a god, the same way relativism does. However, this should be understood in the sense the angelic doctor uses it, namely, that man's being is only understood in the way it participates in the Creator's being. Failure to use it creates a deficiency in such a way that man receives a separated being apart from the Creator's. Man would be disconnected from his creator if he did not participate in his being. And yet man was created in the *imago Dei.*

Therefore, Ratzinger elucidates that the way grace travels to reach man has to pass through the "second nature," breaking open the hard shell of vainglory that covers the divine glory within him. And that means that there is no grace without the cross. On the basis of a robust Chalcedonian Christology, he is able to affirm: only the humanity of the Second Adam is true humanity. The cross is not the "crucifixion of man" at all, as Nietzsche thought, but rather his true healing. "The humanity of God is indeed the true humanity of man, the grace that fulfills nature."[687]

Stanley Hauerwas holds quite a different position. First and foremost, Hauerwas rejects natural theology (and therefore rejects natural law as well). His thesis is that "natural theology is impossibly abstracted from a full doctrine of God."[688] According to him, natural theology would equate to a natural science without our reference to or reliance on any supposed special exceptional or miraculous revelation.[689] Insofar as Hauerwas objects to the use of reason alone to describe the nature of God, he is right. Revelation is the indispensable basis for knowing God. However, this does not mean that nature is devoid of grace. For, as Ratzinger illustrates above, also human postlapsarian nature is endowed with grace—with the desire to seek God. Thus, the second nature of humankind fulfills that to which human nature is ordered toward from the beginning, namely, God. Further, Hauerwas does not seem to be consistent with his position as he later tends to base his ecclesiology on political and existential arguments.

Despite his critique of natural theology, rendering it a mere humanism, Hauerwas turns around and unwittingly tends to lean actually more toward the humanistic side. His ecclesiology tragically betrays his anthropology because in it, Hauerwas portrays an "acting" church, i.e., a people who live by acting, fighting, and resisting evil, a community within a community—resident aliens— very much like the great humanists, such as Henry David Thoreau or Mahatma Gandhi have advocated. Rather than one allowing God's strength and grace to work through Christians, Hauerwas' Christians resort to their own human devices. Such people would be little different from humanists who struggle for

---

[687] Benedict XVI, *Dogma and Preaching,* 159–161.
[688] Stanley Hauerwas, *With the Grain of the Universe: The Church's Witness and Natural Theology* (Grand Rapids, MI: Brazos Press, 2001), 10.
[689] Ibid., 26.

only establishing a kind and caring society. But the psalmist says, "Unless the Lord builds the house, those who build it labor in vain. Unless the Lord guards the city, the guard keeps watch in vain (ᾠδὴ τῶν ἀναβαθμῶν τῷ Σαλωμων ἐὰν μὴ κύριος οἰκοδομήσῃ οἶκον εἰς μάτην ἐκοπίασαν οἱ οἰκοδομοῦντες αὐτόν ἐὰν μὴ κύριος φυλάξῃ πόλιν εἰς μάτην ἠγρύπνησεν ὁ φυλάσσων)" (Ps 127:1). This makes Hauerwas a tragic figure: an existentialist whose anthropology actually contradicts his revelational and theological concerns.

8.4 Conclusion

In conclusion, as stated above, what is at stake, and the root cause of all relativism, is a deficient anthropology; that is, man has misunderstood himself and misused his position as a created being. Man therefore needs to reorient himself and find once again, his proper position, and his relationship with both God and the universe. This chapter has tried, briefly, to restate man's position as a creature whose relationship with God is characterized with receivability instead of makability. All is gift, and it is upon this realization that man finds and acts right. This is better articulated in Ratzinger's than in Hauerwas' theological anthropology. We can therefore conclude that Ratzinger stands in a better position to combat relativism. However, this is not to render Hauerwas' ideas superfluous. We are only stating an obvious fact that to arrive at the right goal, the means to it must also be right, i.e., in agreement with the human nature. The predicate "correct" can more appropriately be prefixed to Ratzinger's than Hauerwas' theological anthropology.

PART IV:

Epilogue
Means by which Sub-Saharan African
Culture can ward off Relativism

Chapter Nine

9.0 The Contribution of the
Ganda Culture to Christianity

Time has come to consider not only an African theology, but also an African Christianity. Christianity has existed on the African continent since the first centuries of Christianity (in North Africa),[690] and for over four centuries in the sub-Saharan Africa.[691] However, there is so little written on African theology and so little on African Christianity. To many (both believers and nonbelievers)

---

[690] The *Encyclopedic Dictionary of Religion* states, "Christianity probably came to Africa from Rome at the end of the first century, but the earliest records are the acts of the Scillitan martyrs (180) and the passion of SS. Perpetua and Felicity (203). Tertullian (197–220) said that the population of the cities was almost entirely Christian and that even the small towns had bishops. By the time of St. Cyprian, there were over 100 bishops. In the second and third centuries the African Church was using a Latin version of the Scriptures and of the liturgy, although Greek was still the official language of the Church of Rome," in Paul Kevin Meagher, et al., eds., *Encyclopedic Dictionary of Religion* (Washington, DC: Corpus Publications, 1979), s.v., "Africa, Early Church in Roman," by J. H. Satterwhite.

[691] "African Christianity is one of the most massive and variegated responses to the Christian faith in the history of Christian missions. After the extinction of the Church in North Africa by the year A.D. 1000, Roman Catholic mission began south of the Sahara early in the 16th century; Protestant missions began three centuries later. After 1800 almost every variety of European and North American Christianity was introduced somewhere onto the African scene and left its imprint. By the year 1900 missioners had begun work with about 400 of the 750 tribes south of the Sahara and had translated the New testament into about 1000 vernacular tongues. The Christian population in sub-Saharan African grew from virtually zero in 1800 to about 98 million in 1974, about 34 million Catholics in 315 dioceses, about 46 million Protestants in 600 national Churches or missions, 6 million Orthodox [almost entirely in Europe], and 8 million adherents of the African Independent Church Movement," in Paul Kevin Meagher, et al., eds., *Encyclopedic Dictionary of Religion*

223

sub-Saharan Africans, Christianity has remained Western and foreign.[692] Due to this foreignness of Christianity to the African, there has been a syncretistic practice of Christianity in many societies of Africa. There has also been a great exodus back to traditional religious practices[693] by many Africans who failed to realize or appreciate the truth of Christianity.

In the meantime, while the local church struggles to enlighten and deepen Christian roots among African believers, there has come a treacherous culture that threatens the very essence of the Christian truth. With the advent of such a culture, the ordinary African Christian is thrown into confusion. First and foremost, his Christian roots are still frail, and now a new contradictory culture focuses. The African is then left in a dilemma, not knowing the way forward.

The intention of this section is therefore to attempt bring into question, the fate and future of Christianity in Africa amid the fast-infiltrating relativistic culture. As an African theology student and pastor, I felt it necessary to make myself relevant to the people I serve by highlighting the truth of Christianity, but also the dangers of relativism. This chapter will clarify the cause of the conflicting cultures and attempt to provide a remedy, as well as pointing out the areas of intersection between Christianity and African religions.

This chapter will also make a road map for the African as to where he can make recourse for possible solutions. Last but not least, in this chapter, we shall attempt to illustrate that traditional African religious practices can offer a great deal to the universal Christianity, particularly in regard to baffling relativism. We shall also make it clear that even if both Hauerwas and Ratzinger's writings are a great help to fighting relativism, Ratzinger offers a better deal for the African and universal Christian in general.

9.1 The History and Geographical Location of the Ganda People

The Ganda people, commonly known as the Baganda,[694] make part to the Bantu-speaking people of east and southern Africa. As in their traditional

---

(Washington, DC: Corpus Publications, 1979), s.v., "African Christianity (Contemporary)," by J. H. Satterwhite.

[692] John Mary Waliggo, "Ganda Traditional Religion and Catholicism in Buganda, 1948–1975," *Christianity in Independent Africa* (Bloomington, IN: Indiana University Press, 1978), 414.

[693] Ibid., 420–421.

[694] "The people of Buganda are referred to as *Baganda* [the singular form is *Muganda*], their language is referred to as Luganda, and they refer to their customs as *Kiganda* customs. Sometimes the generic term *Ganda* is used for all the above [especially by foreign scholars]. Buganda is home to the nation's political and commercial capital, Kampala; as well as the

title, "Ganda,"[695] the Baganda are believed to be a composition of various small groups of people that originated from central Africa. They were organized into one strong political group referred to as Buganda Kingdom by their first king (*Kabaka*) called Kintu about eight centuries ago.[696] The Buganda Kingdom is located in the south-central religion of the country known today as Uganda.[697] Before Uganda became to be, Buganda Kingdom was. Uganda as a country was coiled out of Buganda. The colonial masters first settled in Buganda and used the Baganda to extend their rule to other neighboring kingdoms and chiefdoms. This explains the resentments the other tribal people in modern-day Uganda have toward the Baganda. They perceive them as allies of the colonialists.

> Uganda [Swahili for "Land of the Ganda"] was the name used by the Arab and Swahili traders on the East African coast to refer to the kingdom of Buganda, deep in the interior of Africa. These traders first arrived in Buganda in the mid-nineteenth century in search of slaves, ivory, as well as other merchandise. When the European colonialists eventually extended their hegemony over Buganda and the surrounding territories at

---

country's main international airport, Entebbe," (http://www.buganda.com/bugintro.htm (accessed on May 9, 2011).

[695] Ganda etymologically comes from a compound pronoun "Buganda" which literally means "small bundles of things," in "Buganda Kingdom," http://www.buganda.or.ug/index.php/olulimiebyobuwangwa-nennono-language-culture-a-norms (accessed on May 9, 2011).

[696] "Buganda was one of the several small principalities founded by Bantu-speaking people in what is now Uganda. It was founded in the late 14th century, when the Kabaka, or ruler, of the Ganda people came to exercise strong centralized control over his domains, called Buganda. By the 19th century Buganda had the largest and most powerful kingdom in the region. The local chiefs of conquered areas ruled as personal appointees of the Kabaka, who had a sizable army at his disposal," (http://www.britannica.com/EBchecked/topic/83725/Buganda (accessed on May 9, 2011).

[697] "About 500 B.C. Bantu-speaking peoples migrated to the area now called Uganda. By the 14th century, three kingdoms dominated, Buganda [meaning "state of the Gandas"], Bunyoro, and Ankole. Uganda was first explored by Europeans as well as Arab traders in 1844. An Anglo-German agreement of 1890 declared it to be in the British sphere of influence in Africa, and the Imperial British East Africa Company was chartered to develop the area. The company did not prosper financially, and in 1894 a British protectorate was proclaimed. Few Europeans permanently settled in Uganda, but it attracted many Indians, who became important players in Ugandan commerce. Uganda became independent on Oct. 9, 1962. Sir Edward Mutesa, the king of Buganda [Mutesa II], was elected the first president, and Milton Obote the first prime minister, of the newly independent country. With the help of a young army officer, Col. Idi Amin, Prime Minister Obote seized control of the government from President Mutesa four years later," in "Uganda," http://www.infoplease.com/ipa/A0108066.html (accessed on May 9, 2011).

the end of the nineteenth century, they used the Swahili term Uganda to refer to the new colony. Today, Uganda is made up of almost 40 different ethnic groups with the Baganda being the largest group at almost 20% of the total population. On a visit to the country, the late Winston Churchill was so taken by its beauty, he called it the **"Pearl of Africa"**; a fitting moniker that has stuck to this day.[698]

The favorable and strategic geographical location of Buganda gave the Baganda an edge over the tribal people around them. They live on the shores of Lake Nalubaale or Lake Victoria Nyanza[699] (named Lake Victoria by John Hanning Speke[700] in honor of the Queen of England), which is the source of livelihood in Uganda. They lived in settlements, unlike most of their neighbors who were predominantly pastoralists. Because of its settlement and communitarian nature, Buganda developed a leadership structure similar to civilized societies in the world. Their style of life and organization eased their cooperation with the Arab traders, the colonialists, and later the missionaries. Of all the interior communities of Eastern Africa, the alien groups first collaborated with the Buganda Kingdom people. It was from Buganda that they extended their influence to cover all eastern and central Africa.

9.2 The Culture and Religion of the Baganda

As stated above, the Baganda lived in a community and on farms, on which they grew food and raised animals, such as cows, goats, pigs, and chickens. To date, residents among the Baganda are referred to as *Bataka*.[701] Owing to their settlement in a particular location, the Baganda developed a culture that can

---

[698] "Buganda: Introduction," *Buganda.com*, http://www.buganda.com/bugintro.htm (accessed May 9, 2011).

[699] "Lake Victoria, also called Victoria Nyanza, is the largest lake in Africa and chief reservoir of the Nile, lying mainly in Tanzania and Uganda but also bordering with Kenya. Among the freshwater lakes in the world, it is exceeded in size only by Lake Superior in North America, its area being 26,828 square miles (69,484 square km)," http://www.britannica.com/EBchecked/topic/627661/Lake-Victoria (accessed on May 9, 2011).

[700] "John Hanning Speke (1827–1864) accompanied Richard Francis Burton on his 1854–5 Somali Expedition, then again on the 1857–9 East Africa expedition, which aimed to find the sources of the Nile. The expedition discovered Lake Tanganyika in 1858, and explored part of its extent. Speke supposed that Lake Victoria, which he discovered and named, while off on a foray of his own to the north of the chief route of the expedition, was the source of the Nile," http://burtoniana.org/speke/index.html (accessed on May 9, 2011).

[701] *Ttaka* means earth or soil. *Bataka* are those people who own land (usually who have stayed for decades). But it is also used to designate clan heads because these took care of ancestral

be considered as relational. They related to each other in a family-like order—depending on each other for their survival. The Baganda were unlike their neighboring nomadic people. Their relational culture was both vertical and horizontal.

9.2.1 The Vertical-Relational Ganda Culture

"Africans are notoriously religious."[702] This statement is believed to be John Mbiti's most expressive statement about Africans that cannot be disputed. It confirms the truth about the African peoples. Africans are, without doubt, deeply religious. Mbiti continues, "Each people has its own religious system with a set of beliefs and practices. Religion permeates into all the departments of life so fully that it is not easy or possible always to isolate it."[703] The Baganda are no exception. Their lives are entirely encompassed in a religious veil to the extent that their cultural and religious values, though distinct, cannot be separated. They did not perceive their lives apart from an ultimate source. This was the beginning of their relational culture. They realized that there is a being, supreme and greater than themselves, from whom all come to be and to whom all return. Thus, the bottom line of their life is creation. They perceived themselves as creatures.

The Baganda had a creation story that was very unique and amazingly very similar to the biblical one, particularly the Fall. The story survived in their oral culture long before their encounter with Christianity. The edited and a paraphrased story runs as below:

> Long long ago, Kintu was the only person on the earth [created by *Katonda/Gguluddene*—God]. He lived alone with his cow. Ggulu the creator of all things lived up in heaven [Ggulu also means heaven/the skies] with his many children and other property. From time to time, *Ggulu*'s children would come down to earth to play. On one such occasion, *Ggulu*'s daughter *Nambi* and some of her brothers encountered Kintu in Buganda. *Nambi* was very fascinated with Kintu and she felt pity for him because he was living alone. She resolved to marry him and stay with him. She decided to return to heaven with Kintu and ask for her father's permission for the union. After

---

homes for clan members (http://www.buganda.or.ug/index.php/olulimiebyobuwangwa-nennono-language-culture-a-norms (accessed on May 9, 2011).
[702] John Mbiti, *African Religions and Philosophy* (Oxford: Heinemann Educational Publishers, 1969), 1.
[703] Ibid.

Ggulu decided to allow the marriage to proceed, he advised *Kintu* and *Nambi* to leave heaven secretly and that on no condition were they to return to heaven even if they forgot anything. This admonition was so that *Walumbe*, one of *Nambi's* brothers should not find out about the marriage until they had left, otherwise he would insist on going with them and bring them misery [*Walumbe* means that which causes sickness and death]. Among the few things that *Nambi* packed, was her chicken. They set out for earth early the next morning.

But while they were descending, *Nambi* remembered that she had forgotten to bring the millet that her chicken would feed on. So, she returned to fetch the millet, but on her way back, she suddenly met *Walumbe* who asked: "My sister, where are you going so early in the morning? Filled with curiosity, *Walumbe* insisted on going with her. Therefore *Kintu* and *Nambi* were forced to go to earth together with *Walumbe*. It did not take long for *Kintu* and *Nambi* to get children. One day, *Walumbe* went to *Kintu's* home and asked his brother-in-law to give him a child to help him with the chores in his [*Walumbe's*] house. But remembering *Ggulu's* warning, *Kintu* would not hear of it. *Walumbe* became very angry with Kintu for refusing him the simple favor he had asked. That very night, he went and killed *Kintu's* son. Kintu went back to heaven to report *Walumbe's* actions to *Ggulu*. *Ggulu* rebuked *Kintu*, reminding him of the original warning he had disregarded. *Kintu* blamed *Nambi* for returning to get the millet. Ggulu then sent another of his sons, *Kayikuuzi*, to go back to earth with Kintu and try to persuade *Walumbe* to return to heaven or if necessary return him by force.

On reaching earth, *Kayikuuzi* tried to persuade *Walumbe* to go back to heaven but *Walumbe* would not hear of it. *Kayikuuzi* decided to capture *Walumbe* by force, and a great fight broke out between them. But as *Walumbe* was about to be overpowered, he escaped and disappeared into the ground [*Ttanda*]. *Kayikuuzi* [means he who digs holes] went after him and when Kayikuuzi got to where he was hiding, *Walumbe* run back out to the earth. Further struggle between the brothers ensued and went on for several days. *Kayikuuzi* went and talked to *Kintu* and *Nambi* and instructed them to stay indoors together with their children, and to strictly enjoin their children not to make a sound if they see *Walumbe*. *Kintu* and *Nambi* went into their house, but some of the kids did not go in. After a struggle, *Walumbe* came back out to the surface with *Kayikuuzi* in pursuit. *Kintu*'s children who were outside at the time saw *Walumbe* coming and screamed in terror. On hearing the screams, *Walumbe* went underground once again. *Kayikuuzi* was furious with Kintu and Nambi for not having followed his instructions. He told them that if they did not care to do the simple thing he had asked of them, he was also giving up the fight. *Kayikuuzi* then went back to heaven. *Ttanda*, where the fight between *Walumbe* and *Kayikuuzi* allegedly took place is figuratively referred to as the place of death [i.e., *Walumbe*'s place]. So that is the legend of creation, and how sickness and death started.[704]

The Baganda therefore had faith in one supreme God whom they gave the name *Ggulu*. He was adored and worshiped in his many attributes including *Katonda/Mutonzi* (creator), *Mukama* (lord/master), *Namugereka* (chief designer; one who apportions), *Nyinibyonna* (owner of all), *Luwanga* (chief architect), *Liisoddene* (the all-seeing), *Lugaba* (giver), *Ddunda* (supreme leader), *Nantalemwa* (almighty), *Kagingo* (master of life), *Ssewannaku* (the eternal), *Ssebintu* (master of all things), *Gguluddene* (the gigantic one), *Kiwamirembe* (giver of peace), etc.[705] They did not approach him directly, because they thought of him as unapproachable due to his transcendence. H. P. Gale mentions this in his book *Uganda and the Mill Hill Father*. He stated,

> The Baganda had believed in One Supreme Being, that same "*Ggulu*" or Lord of Heaven who had, be means of *Nambi*, given them life and being, and whom they had also called "*Katonda*" (Creator) or "*Mukama*" (Master). They offered no worship to him, as they considered him too exalted to pay any regard to mankind.[706]

---

[704] "The Legend of *Kintu—Bugandan* Tradition," *Rasta Livewire*, http://www.africare-source.com/rasta/sesostris-the-great-the-egyptian-hercules/the-legend-of-kintu-bugan-dan-tradition/ (accessed May 11, 2011)

[705] "Katonda," *Oxford Dictionary of Mythology*, http://www.answers.com/topic/katonda (accessed on May 11, 2011).

[706] H.P. Gale, *Uganda and the Mill Hill Fathers* (London: MacMillan and Co. Limited, 1959), 4.

Their worship and sacrifices were offered through intermediaries/mediators. Of these, the highest in rank were the semi gods (*Balubaale*) who were in charge of various needs. Some of these were *Ddungu*—god of hunting; *Muwanga*—god of rain; *Mukasa*—god of the sea (particularly Lake Victoria); *Kibuuka*—god of war, *Kitaka*—god of the earth and underworld, *Walumbe*—god of death, Musoke—god of rainbow, *Kiwanuka*—god of lightning.[707] These were deceased kings or humans that exhibited extraordinary skills in their respective fields, which they were delegated to be in charge of. As a result, they were perceived as the gods that actually controlled those activities.

Second in rank were the *Mizimu*, who were the spirits of the dead kings. Because the Baganda believed in a life after death, they believed that those who pass from this life only change in form (*bafuuka*—they change).[708] They change from their material forms to spiritual beings; from living in this world to living in another world (*Magombe*—the netherworld). These people are still part of the community and are still active in life here. They (good spirits) can bless or harm (bad spirits). The good spirits were petitioned for blessings, and the bad ones were appeased to avoid trouble or death. To show that the dead stilled lived, the Baganda (up to date in some traditional communities) performed libation.[709] Before a person took a drink, for example, he first poured some on the ground for those in the netherworld to share.

John Roscoe recounts that the Baganda gathered regularly in the compounds of the priests and diviners to worship and offer sacrifices to the gods. At every special event or occurrence in the community, there was a celebration

---

[707] John V. Taylor, *The Growth of the Church in Buganda* (London: SCM Press Ltd, 1958), 201.

[708] "Up to date, the burial time in Buganda is 2:00PM for adults, 12:00PM for children, and 4:00PM for chiefs and those with special and privileged positions in society, e.g. the *Ssalongos* [Men with twins] and *Nnalongos* [Women with twins]. The reason for this was that some adults commit offences during their life time; hence worthy of punishments by the spirit in the other world. They are thus, buried at 2:00 PM—during time for siesta after lunch. Lunch hour in Buganda is around 1pm and after lunch elders usually had time for siesta. It was believed that at that time the harsh spirits who would punish these adults on arrival, would be in siesta, so they could escape punishment if they arrive during this time. The kids were innocent souls and on top of that, they needed to be fed. They therefore had to be buried before lunch so as to arrive in time for the meals lest they starve. The Chiefs and other respected people had to be receive in honor by all the spirits. They were thus buried after siesta when everyone was awake and ready to receive them in glory," in "The Legend of Kintu—Bugandan Tradition," *Rasta Livewire*, http://www.africaresource.com/rasta/sesostris-the-great-the-egyptian-hercules/the-legend-of-kintu-bugandan-tradition/ (accessed May 11, 2011).

[709] John Roscoe, *The Baganda: An Account of Their Native Customs and Beliefs* (London: Macmillan Publishers, 1911), 427.

and sacrifice to the gods and the *Bajjajja*[710] or spirits. Events that drew lengthy celebrations were such as the installation or death of a king, the birth of twins, before and after a war, harvest times and plagues, or unique and prolonged sickness of a family member. On all such occasions, people gathered in places of worship and were led by a diviner/priest where they invoked the gods for intervention.[711] John Taylor to acknowledged this, thus:

> Modern Western, or Westernized, man, having surrendered to the scientific specialist the duty of giving the explanation for so many phenomena, is prepared to take a great deal for granted. Assuming a mechanical causation in every event, he can afford to let a multitude of incidents pass as accidental without any sense of insecurity or wonder. Not so the African peasant. For him, any occurrence may be significant for his personal well-being, and therefore needs to be explained. There is no such thing as accident. It has been said that the African conception of the universe is just as rational as the European, but while the European idea of causation deals with the question "how?" the African idea of causation deals with the question "why?" Birth of twins was an example of such omens. It was regarded with a mixture of joyous pride and fear, and is celebrated with complicated rituals. The Ganda expressed an attitude toward every event and they frequently offered sacrifices at almost every stage in life to that element of personal being inherent in all existence.[712]

The Baganda believed in the existence of a supreme being and in the fact of their creaturedness—that their being and existence originating from outside themselves. Even in things they performed, such as healing and other things that involved professionalism, the Baganda acknowledged that power to act was not invested in human beings, but in some higher power through mediators. John Taylor confirms this in his statement.

---

[710] "Bajjajja are ancestors whom the Baganda believed to have power and influence in the living community. Jjajja is the Luganda word for Grand Father of Grand Mother. But these bajjajja who were invoked were not the living grand fathers and grand mothers, but rather the dead," in "The Legend of Kintu—Bugandan Tradition," *Rasta Livewire*, http://www.africaresource.com/rasta/sesostris-the-great-the-egyptian-hercules/the-legend-of-kintu-bugandan-tradition/ (accessed May 11, 2011).

[711] Roscoe, *The Baganda*, 427.

[712] Taylor, *The Growth of the Church in Buganda*, 193.

There were two professional experts; the *mulogo*, or sorcerer, dealing mainly in destructive medicines or poisons, and the *muganga*, a doctor who dealt mainly in antidotes and protection against spells. But there were also the *musawo* who was generally a herbalist. However, even when these were experts, they did not do it as ultimate source of power and healing. The actual power of the "medicines" seems to reside not in themselves as physical objects, but in what might almost be called an attached spirit.[713]

The modern society is dismissive and rude toward traditional world views, labeling them as primitive and outdated, unresearched and an ignorant way of looking at reality. However, one reality must be borne in mind that truth endures forever; it is simple, indivisible, and eternal. We cannot affirm a truth at one time and deny it at a later date. If something is proven as true, it will remain so for all eternity. For example, we cannot claim that at one time there was a god from whom all things came to be, and at a point in time this god ceased to be. If there was a god that set reality into being years ago, he will still be many years to come. Circumstances and ways of relating to him may change, but the fact of his existence and the fact of our being creatures remains. The Ganda traditional culture, like many other traditional cultures, affirms a reality of the unmoved mover.[714] If this is true, then however much the prevailing culture denies it, it will still remain true. Therefore, turning away from truth and acting as if we are no creatures is a contradiction of the very reason the relativistic culture employs to deny God's existence. A Protestant writer, John Taylor, stated, "Even when the practice of the old ways comes to an end, the world-view which lies behind them remains."[715]

The Baganda understood very well and rightly, as John Mbtiti put it, that "an ontological balance must be maintained between God and man, the spirits and man, the departed and the living. When this balance is disrupted, people experience misfortunes and sufferings."[716] Is this different from what we read in the scriptures; when at the Fall (Gen 3) man decided to go his separate ways from God? Indeed, the upset of this ontological order by the first parents are the cause of all suffering, and the godliness of the relativistic culture cannot and will not result in any good or freedom, as it may be hoped for, but rather in more slavery and suffering.

---

[713] Taylor, *The Growth of the Church in Buganda*, 195–196.
[714] Thomas Aquinas, *Summa Contra Gentiles*, 1, 9–14.
[715] Taylor, *The Growth of the Church in Buganda*, 192.
[716] Mbiti, *African Religions and Philosophy*, 59.

9.2.2 The Horizontal-Relational Ganda Culture

The Ganda people's relational culture was not only on the vertical praxis; it was even more vividly lived on the horizontal praxis. The entire society was and lived as one big family. Everyone was related to the other—from the king to the least peasant. In fact, to date, the Baganda still refer to themselves as *Baana ba Kintu* (sons and daughters of *Kintu*, the first king of Buganda).[717] This family environment was made possible and realized through the clan systems. The king was the head of the family (the clan system), assisted by the clan heads who administered individual clans. Under each clan, there were other structures running down to the individual.

9.2.2.1 The Structural Organizations of Baganda Clans[718]

Kabaka (king)
Katikkiro (prime minister)
Kasolya (rooftop—clan head)
Ssiga (stone/pillar)
Lunyiriri (lineage)
Mutuba
Luggya (homestead)
Nnyumba (home)

"Like many other African ethnic groups," Immaculate Kizza notes, "the Baganda have a very keen sense of community responsibility and the benefits of being a member of a community."[719] Their clan systems helped them to realize

---

[717] Elliot Green, *Ethnicity and Nationhood in Pre-Colonial Africa: The Case of Buganda* (London: London School of Economics Press, 2010), 6.

[718] "Each clan is structured on six pillars or sub-chieftainships: i) Nnyumba (home) and its head, possibly a father and his immediate family, then ii) Luggya (compound or homestead) headed by a grandfather leading up to other increasingly bigger groupings of families known as iii) Mutuba iv) Lunyiriri (lineage), v) Ssiga and vi) Kasolya (roof or top) which is the apex of the clan hierarchy, connecting up to the Kabaka through the Katikkiro. Sociocultural governance and arbitration are exercised at each of those levels from the bottom to the top. Unsettled matters can then be pushed up to the Kabaka's arbitration through his court of appeals (Kisekwa) composed of the respective top heads of the various clans. The most common cases at that level tend to relate to estate inheritance or replacement of a clan chief in cases of death or incapacity," in Jones Kyazze, "The Ganda Clan System," *Ggwangamujje.com*, http://ggwangamujje.com/content/docs/TheGandaClanSystem.pdf (accessed June 2, 2011).

[719] Immaculate Kizza, *The Oral Tradition of the Baganda* (Jefferson, NC: McFarland & Company, Inc., Publishers, 2010), 77.

this because they were all linked as relatives and members of the same family with the same father (*Kintu*) and mother (*Nambi*).[720] Among the Baganda, everyone is related to another as brother, sister, uncle, aunt, grandfather, grandmother, in-law.

As a matter of fact, the Baganda refer to the children of their uncles as brothers and sisters and not their cousins; and paternal uncles and maternal aunts are not called uncles and aunts, but rather fathers and mothers respectively. This explains how strong the idea of brotherhood and family is among the Baganda. The Baganda have no term for stranger. Everyone is family, and everyone who comes to the house is welcome to share with the family. There is a common saying, "*Mu nnyumba temuba kkubo*" loosely translated as "there is no way through a homestead." Therefore, whoever comes to the house is a guest and friend.

The culture and wisdom of the Baganda can be summed up in the many epigrams and figures of speech they employed to communicate and safeguard the community. It is important to explore a few of these epigrams to understand the Ganda culture. Below are sets of the selected few—one from each section. Nine epigrams are selected. The first five epigrams show a concrete relationship of the Ganda culture, and the last four are abstracts.

9.2.2.1.1 Parenthood

Okuzaala kuba kuzuukira (Parenthood makes one immortal). The Baganda shared a belief with many African ethnic groups that a parent does not die; one lives on in one's children. Consequently, if a person did not beget children, that person would go into oblivion when after death and would be totally forgotten.[721]

9.2.2.1.2 Friendship

Omukwano gutta bingi (Friendship resolves many issues). This proverb promotes friendships as a means of coexistence.[722]

9.2.2.1.3 Relatives

Atakwalize nganda akulaga bifo (One who does not want you to have extended family relatives shows you places instead of introducing you to these

---

[720] Kizza, *The Oral Tradition of the Baganda*, 77.
[721] Ibid., 65.
[722] Ibid., 58.

place's owners). The Baganda thrived in extended families. They valued kinships, so it is important for one to know as many of one's relatives as possible. Also related to that explanation is advice to parents to introduce their children to as many of their relatives as they possibly can before such people die. It is not good to show your children places where their relatives used to live but such relatives are no longer there, let alone taking them for funerals of relatives they never knew they had.[723]

9.2.2.1.4 Community

Musajja gy'agenda gyasanga banne (A man finds friends wherever he goes). The proverb illustrates the Baganda's belief that all humans are inherently good and communal creatures. Therefore, one does not have to fear or be apprehensive going to unfamiliar places because there are no people there one knows. One should be able to find friends wherever one goes; "the word 'stranger' is not in their language."[724]

9.2.2.1.5 Strangers

Mu nnyumba temuba kkubo (There is no road going through a house/home). This demonstrates the Baganda's hospitality. Everyone who came to the house was treated as a guest and friend, expected to be served with all there could be in the house. Young couples are reminded of this proverb as they set up their homes.[725]

9.2.2.1.6 Knowledge/Wisdom/Truth

Amagezi luwombo (Knowledge is like sauce prepared in banana leaves). "Traditionally the Baganda make their most delicious dishes in tender, delicate banana leaves. When you are served sauce in such banana leaves and you finish what you can see at the top, you can check under the lawyers for more."[726] In other words, knowledge is layered, and you must check all layers to get the whole truth. Also, knowledge is precious and should be handled with care, which is why it would be stored in tender banana leaves. Last, tender banana leaves used as dishes are not supposed to leak, so one cannot lose one's knowledge if it is stored safely.[727]

---

[723] Kizza, *The Oral Tradition of the Baganda*, 72.
[724] Ibid., 78.
[725] Ibid., 69.
[726] Ibid., 76.
[727] Ibid.

9.2.2.1.7 Fairness/Judgment

Tosala gwa kawala nga tonnawulira gwa kalenzi (Do not pass judgment based on the lady's side of the story before hearing the man's). In domestic conflicts, according to the traditional Ganda culture, a woman is often the first to approach her in-laws with her complaints, and there is a tendency to feel sorry for her or to be swayed to her side before the in-laws get a chance to hear from the husband. This proverb warns against passing judgment before thoroughly examining both versions in a conflict, since there are always going to be two or more sides to each story. One should hear all versions before taking action.[728]

9.2.2.1.8 Providence

Tosekerera ajeera ffenna omugabi y'omu (Never laugh at those less fortunate than you because we all have the same provider). This is caution against arrogance as well as reminder of how transient material things can be. Since we all have the same provider, we can be lucky today and totally unlucky tomorrow, depending on our mutual provider's plans for each of us.[729]

9.2.2.1.9 Authority

Ezenkanankana n'ebisiki tezaaka (Two equal pieces of wood side by side cannot make a fire). This proverb reminds people to acknowledge authority wherever they might be—home, work, school and so on—to ensure a functionary society. Leadership and authority were very respected and obeyed without question. This ensured harmony, civility, productivity, and accountability in society.[730]

9.2.3 Synthesis

The above and other Baganda epigrams are proof that in the beliefs and cultures of the Baganda, human life is relational, which has to be lived on both vertical and horizontal praxes. The Ganda culture is not a culture of only dependence but rather of interdependence. Much as they realized that they could not survive without depending on *Katonda*—the Supreme God—they also believed that they had a part to play as human beings. They did not have to sit

---

[728] Kizza, *The Oral Tradition of the Baganda*, 79.

[729] Ibid., 73.

[730] Ibid., 68.

back and wait for *Katonda* to provide, but instead, they played a participatory role—cooperating with God.

Another epigram states, *"Lubaale mbeera; nga n'embiro kw'otadde"* (Help me God, but continue running).[731] They understood that God acts through many mediations, many of which were human mediations. So they sought for their (mediators) help, hence the interdependence. The relativistic culture of the contemporary times turns this upside down. Man today wants to run the course by his own power—depending on neither God nor on one another. The prevailing culture is a culture of extreme individualism.

9.3 The Encounter with Christianity

The Ganda culture first encountered Christianity in the late nineteenth century with the pioneers being the Anglican missionaries. They arrived in Buganda on June 30, 1877, followed with Catholic missionaries arriving on February 17, 1879.[732] Even if Islam had come to Buganda earlier, it did not make as much impact as Christianity did. This, according to many scholars, was due to the many similarities between the Baganda's traditional religion and the new White Man's religion. Gale testifies to this in his reflections on the Mill Hill Mission in Uganda. He states,

> In actual fact, the religious problem of evangelizing the Baganda was anything but simple. For centuries the Baganda had been living within the circle of their ancient paganism, at the centre of which was their divine monarchy, which both controlled religion and was itself religion. Islam first broke into the circle, and many of the Baganda embraced it. Some indeed showed such readiness for a more satisfying religion than paganism. Then came Protestantism, accompanied by powerful white men who seemed linked to great political power; next followed Catholicism, taking up the heritage of earlier Roman Missions.[733]

Monsignor Gorju said that the Baganda were Christian in origin.[734] The story of the Ganda religion, particularly in their mythological story, has very

---

[731] Ibid., 68.

[732] Taylor, *The Growth of the Church in Buganda*, 34.

[733] H.P. Gale, *Uganda and the Mill Hill Fathers* (London: MacMillan and Co. Limited, 1959), ix–x.

[734] Ibid.

significant parallels to the Bible's Adam and Eve story, a version which the Baganda were not familiar with before the onslaught of Christianity in the eighteenth century. Parallels can be identified as:

- Ggulu—Yahweh (God/Creator)
- Kintu—Adam
- Nimbi—Eve
- Walumbe—Serpent
- Kayiikuzi—Jesus
- Kintu's children—Descendants of Adam
- Ttanda—Netherworld
- Buganda—Garden of Eden.[735]

These similarities made it easy for the Baganda to assimilate Christianity within a very short period. Both the Protestants and Catholic missionaries aimed at converting as many Baganda as possible, each to their respective denominations, which they performed in a rather jealous and competitive manner. Even though the missionaries at many points were driven by their political motives, and even if Muteesa[736] also had a political motive for inviting the missionaries, they nevertheless taught the faith to a readily available community.

Jean Brierley acknowledged that "the missionaries had followed trade and pestilence along the trade routes and gathered together their flocks in Buganda with a success that was rare elsewhere in pre-colonial eastern Africa."[737]

---

[735] Kizza, *The Oral Tradition of the Baganda of Uganda*, 37.

[736] "Muteesa I was the King [Kabaka] of Buganda at the time the first missionaries arrived in Buganda. He actually invited them. It was believed that he had a political motive behind this invitation because he was being pressured by mightier political powers who were a threat to his kingdom. So, he wanted a superior political power to lean on. Taylor thus writes: 'There are strong grounds to believe that Muteesa looked upon the white man simply as the most powerful all against Egyptian aggression and the source of that technical mastery which promised untold power.' Mackay, one year after his arrival in Buganda, records how Muteesa asked him one day why the missionaries came. He replied that it was in response to Kabaka's appeal to Stanley. But Muteesa answered that he understood that they came to teach his people how to make powder and guns, and what he wanted was men who would do so. Yet, this does not appear the whole of the truth. There is a strong tradition among the Baganda themselves that early in Muteesa's reign there was a widespread loss of confidence in the old structure of paganism," in John Taylor, *The Growth of the Church in Buganda* (London: SCM Press Ltd, 1958), 29–30.

[737] Jean Brierley and Thomas Spear, "Muteesa, The Missionaries, and Christian Conversion in Buganda," in *The International Journal of African Historical Studies*, 21, 4 (1988), 612.

Therefore, the missionaries and Christianity found a prolific atmosphere in Buganda. John Taylor put it in simple terms:

> In the palace of the Kabaka and in the great households of the nobility, were already gathered together the groups of men and women and young boys who were soon to be the living cells of the Body of Christ. Here were almost all the leaders of the future; here were the martyrs; the very form and structure of the Church had been prepared in advance.[738]

The unhealthy competition between the Protestant and Catholic missionaries was not good news. Sooner or later, the competition became a stumbling block to the king's conversion and later persecution of all converts to Christianity, as Taylor narrates,

> Muteesa's first reaction was to make the choice on behalf of his kingdom. He became a regular member of Lourdel's catechism class and, in spite of sending envoys to Queen Victoria, sounded the French fathers about the possibility of placing his country under the protection of France. Meeting in them a natural hesitation, he decided for the Protestants, and asked Mackay for baptism. This was refused him until he could demonstrate a change of heart by giving up witchcraft, polygamy and other practices. The following month he made the same request of Lourdel and was given virtually the same reply.[739]

Fast forward, the successor and son of Kabaka Muteesa, Kabaka Mwanga, later put so many believers to death.[740] Among those were twenty-two Catholic

---

[738] Taylor, *The Growth of the Church in Buganda*, 34.

[739] Ibid., 40.

[740] "On 3 June 1886, thirty-two young men, pages of the court of King Mwanga of Buganda, were burned to death at Namugongo for their refusal to renounce Christianity. In the following months many other Christians throughout the country died by spear or fire for their faith. These martyrdoms totally changed the dynamic of Christian growth in Uganda. Introduced by a handful of Anglican and Roman missionaries after 1877, the Christian faith had been preached only to the immediate members of the court, by order of King Mutesa. His successor, Mwanga, became increasingly angry as he realized that the first converts put loyalty to Christ above the traditional loyalty to the king. Martyrdoms began in 1885. Mwanga first forbade anyone to go near a Christian mission on pain of death, but finding himself unable to cool the ardor of the converts, resolved to wipe out Christianity," in "The Martyrs of Uganda," *Bibliographical Sketches of Memorable Christians of the Past*, http://justus.anglican.org/resources/bio/176.html (accessed June 8, 2011).

martyrs and twenty-five Anglican martyrs. The names of the Catholic Uganda martyrs are Charles Lwanga (their leader), Mathias Kalemba Mulumba, Mukasa Kiriwawanvu, Andrea Kaggwa, Yosefu Mukasa Balikuddembe, Anatoli Kiriggwajjo, Mbaaga Tuzinde, Pontiano Ngondwe, Yakobo Buuzabalyawo, Dinozio Ssebuggwawo, Atanansi Bazzekuketta, Adolf Muksa Ludigo, Gonzaga Gonza, Amblozio Kibuuka, Akileo Kiwanuka, Bruno Sserunkuuma, Luka Baanabakintu, Kizito, Mugagga, Gyaviira, Noowa Mawaggali, and John Maria Muzeeyi.[741]

Most of these martyrs can be identified in a historical picture taken with some of the missionaries.

A picture showing some of the Catholic Uganda martyrs.

[741] Uganda martyrs' names, their dates of birth, their hometowns, and their dates of death are kept in the Uganda martyrs archive as below:
"Joseph Mukasa Balikuddembe (1860, Buganda–November 15, 1885, Nakivubo)
Anderea Kaggwa (year of birth unknown, Bunyoro–May 26, 1886, Munyonyo)
Ponsiano Ngondwe (year of birth unknown, Buganda–May 26, 1886, Ttakajjunge)
Denis Ssebuggwawo (year of birth unknown, Buganda–May 26, 1886, Munyonyo)
Antanansio Bazzekuketta (year of birth unknown, Buganda–May 27, 1886, Nakivubo)
Gonzaga Gonza (year of birth unknown, Bugosa–May 27, 1886, Lubowa)
Matiya Mulumba, a.k.a. Matthias Murumba Kalemba (year of birth unknown, Bugosa–May 27, 1886, Old Kampala)
Nowa Mawaggali (year of birth unknown, Buganda–May 31, 1886, Mityana)
Charles (Carl or Karoli) Lwanga (1865, Buganda – June 3, 1886, Namugongo)
Lukka Baanabakintu (year of birth unknown, Buganda–June 3, 1886, Namugongo)
James Buzabaliao (1857, Buganda–June 3, 1886, Namugongo)
Gyavire (year of birth unknown, Buganda–June 3, 1886, Namugongo)
Ambrosio Kibuuka (year of birth unknown, Buganda–June 3, 1886, Namugongo)
Anatoli Kiriggwajjo (year of birth unknown, Bunyoro–June 3, 1886, Namugongo)
Mukasa Kiriwawanvu (year of birth unknown, Buganda–June 3, 1886, Namugongo)
Achileo (Achilles) Kiwanuka (year of birth unknown, Buganda–June 3, 1886, Namugongo)
Kizito (1872, Buganda–June 3, 1886, Namugongo)
Adolofu (Adolphus) Mukasa Ludigo (year of birth unknown, Toro–June 3, 1886, Namugongo)
Mugagga (year of birth unknown, Buganda–June 3, 1886, Namugongo)
Bruno Sserunkuumba (year of birth unknown, Buganda–June 3, 1886, Namugongo)
Mbaga Tuzinde (year of birth unknown, Buganda–June 3, 1886, Namugongo)
John Maria Muzeyi (year of birth unknown, Buganda–January 27, 1887, Mengo)," in http://wau.org/archives/article/the_uganda_martyrs (accessed on December 1, 2011).

(1) Mukasa Kiriwanvu (2) Anderea Kagwa (3) Yozefu Mukasa (4) Anatoli Kirigwajjo (5) Mbaaga Tuzinde (6) Ponsiano Ngondwe (7) Yakobo Buuzabalyawo (8) Dionizio Ssebuggwawo (9) Atanansi Bazzekuketta (10) Adolf Mukasa Ludigo (11) Gonzaga Gonza (12) Ambrozio Kibuuka (13) Karooli Lwanga (14) Akileo Kiwanuka (15) Bruno Sserunkuma (16) Matia Mulumba (17) Luuka Baanabakintu (18) Kizito (19) Muggagga (20) Gyaviira.[742]

The martyrdom of Christian converts was a blessing in disguise, as Tertullian once asserted, "the blood of the martyrs is the seed of Christianity."[743] As a matter of fact, Buganda and Uganda became the center of Catholicism in sub-Saharan Africa in modern times. Kevin Ward writes, "Christianity came late to Uganda compared with many other parts of Africa. Missionaries first arrived at the court of Kabaka Muteesa in 1877, almost a century after the missionary impetus from Europe had begun. And yet within 25 years Uganda had become one of the most successful mission fields in the whole of Africa."[744] The witness of these young neophytes, who walked to their deaths singing hymns of praise and praying for their enemies, inspired many of the bystanders that they began to seek instructions from the remaining Christians. Isn't this true of the biblical truth: "Amen, I say to you, unless the grain of wheat falls to the ground and dies, it remains just a grain of wheat, but if it dies, it produces much fruit" (Jn 12:24).

---

[742] Tina Sheila and Panta Babinaga, "Sainthood—Why June 3 Is Important to All Uganda," (June 2, 2011), *The Red Pepper*, http://redpepper.co.ug/welcome/?p=10256 (accessed on June 8, 2011).

[743] Robert D. Sider, *Christian and Pagan in the Roman Empire: The Witness of Tertullian* (Washington, DC: The Catholic University of America Press, 2001), 69.

[744] Kevin Ward, "Buganda and Christianity: Buganda in the 19th Century," *Dictionary of African Christian Biography*, http://www.dacb.org/history/a%20history%20of%20christianity%20in%20uganda.html (accessed June 8, 2011).

9.3.1 The Ganda Traditional Worldview and Catholicism

In addition to the similarities between Ganda traditional religion and Christianity, the Catholic teaching appealed more to the Baganda because of its closeness to the Ganda traditional worldview. This explains why the faith that came after both Islam and the Anglican faith attracted more converts, and to date, the Catholic faith enjoys the biggest number of Christians in Uganda.[745] John Taylor, an Anglican theologian, admitted this fact and provided reasons as to why this was the case. He argues,

> The Catholic Church enjoys the majority of Christians in Uganda today for one simple reason. Despite being secondary to Anglican Faith—at least in terms of time in Buganda—and being sidelined by the Anglican Colonial masters, it pulled more crowds. This one thing was the fact that it had systems that appealed to the Baganda, i.e. visible or visual aids which people could identify with and relate to in daily lives, other than a transcendent God taught by the Anglicans and other denominations. This transcendent God failed to appeal to the senses of the people. Things like the statues of saints [particularly of Mary] and the teaching of a good Mariology and saints, served well for the Baganda. They identified more with these— who had been human as they were. This made recourse to their idea of their traditional gods and spirits. The only danger with this was that some people, with inadequate catechism, would go to the extreme of idolatry.[746]

On the other hand, Taylor gives reasons for a slow progress of the Anglican faith in Buganda. He believes that the message, upon which Anglican faith in Buganda was founded, was primarily news about the transcendent God— *Katonda*, the unknown and scarcely heeded creator.

> "This God," Taylor continues, "was proclaimed as the focus of all life, who yet lay beyond and above the closed unity of all existence. Considered historically and sociologically, the

---

[745] "According to the census of 2002, Christians made up about 84% of Uganda's population. The Roman Catholic Church has the largest number of adherents (41.9%), followed by the Anglican Church of Uganda (35.9%). The next most reported religion of Uganda is Islam, with Muslims representing 12% of the population," in http://exploredia.com/uganda-population-2011/ (accessed on June 8, 2011).

[746] Taylor, *The Growth of the Church in Buganda*, 252.

proclamation of the gospel is a matter of culture contacts; theologically it is more than that. The revelation of a transcendent, personal and righteous God was not relevant, but revolutionary, to the Baganda, yet that was the Word which they heard."[747]

Arthur Gakwandi concurs with Taylor. According to him, the majority of the people in Buganda and Uganda as a whole were converted to Christianity, and yet some revert to traditional practices whenever need arises. Gakwandi suspects that one of the reasons for this syncretism is that the latter and former are not always incompatible. For example, many foreign religions recognize a supreme being. They also recognize some lesser deities, such as the angels and saints. He asserts that "the Ganda traditional religions attach importance to ancestral worship, which can also be compared to intercession by saints in Christianity. Ritual practice in traditional religions include offering of sacrifices, chanting, offering prayers, forms of eating and drinking, just as in some foreign religions."[748]

As stated earlier in this chapter, the Baganda traditional culture could not be separated from religion, much as they were distinct. Every activity in the traditional Baganda culture was related to God and man and the world. For the Baganda, culture and religion were intertwined. Jean Brierley believed that like most African religions, Ganda traditional religion was "essentially this-worldly, designed to and control both social and natural occurrences, so that what appeared to be magico-religious elements of the foreign religions, especially prevalent in the rural folks variants common among the missionaries, were readily accepted and assimilated."[749] The Baganda found ready parallels between their ancestral spirits and the Christian saints or angels. They also saw the Catholic catechism, which they learned to sing rhythmically, as similar to traditional invocations in which the words themselves conveyed spiritual power.[750] Brierley further affirms,

> The rosaries worn by the White Fathers were seen as alternatives to Kiganda charms. The Kiganda presence of sense of the presence of mystical forces was easily confirmed by prayers designed to invoke protection against devils and spirits, the

---

[747] Ibid., 253.

[748] Arthur Gakwandi, *Uganda: Pocket Facts* (Kampala, Uganda: Fountain Publishers Ltd., 1999), 34.

[749] Brierley and Thomas Spear, "Muteesa, The Missionaries, and Christian Conversion in Buganda," 613–614.

[750] Ibid.

Parables, or the Catholic Mass. In short, there was much that was familiar, promising, and potentially powerful in the messages preached by the foreigners, more than those foreigners could expect, much less accept.[751]

The god of the Baganda is a living god—active in the day-to-day events of life. He sustains life, rewards the good, and punishes the bad. Their god is one who provides and protects his creatures and continually gets involved in all their activities. He has a hand in all that goes on in this world and in the next. For them, a god that is detached from the society's life is a hopeless god. This is why they did not relate as much with the supreme god, Katonda. They instead built immediate relationship with the mediators whom they believed to be acting on behalf of the supreme god. Even if, in many occasions, this led to idolatry, the idea behind it was not idolatrous, but rather they believed in the advocacy and the intercessory role of the mediators.

The rejection of mediation by most Protestant preachers, with their more political-leaning motives, led many Baganda converts to either desert them and join Catholicism, or turn to their traditional religions where they encountered God in their daily lives. John Mary Waliggo,[752] probably the greatest Muganda Catholic theologian ever, wrote this:

> The traditionalist movement which exists in the Buganda Church today began to regroup itself in 1948. The Church and the colonial rule had become inseparable in the eyes of

---

[751] Ibid., 613–614.

[752] Fr. John Mary Waliggo (July 18, 1942–April 19, 2008) is believed to be one of the greatest of theologians in Uganda. He served both the church and state because of his intellectual capacity. Much was written about him after his death, and as his legacy, a paragraph read, "He wanted the human person to be liberated holistically. He rejected any form of dualism and dichotomy, believing that people had to be liberated according to their nature as complex beings at the physical, spiritual, and supernatural levels. This also called for holistic evangelization, in which every dimension of the human person has to be evangelized. All aspects of society and all peoples were to be evangelized as well, without discrimination. As a researcher, Waliggo was able to pioneer many projects, but his great achievements were in the articulation of his ideas, and in the development of a vision for the Church and the nation in the area of holistic development. In his own words he said: 'The honest and serious attempt to make Christ and his message of salvation evermore understood by peoples of every culture, locality and time. It means the reformulation of the Christian life and doctrine into the very thought patterns of each people. It is the conviction that Christ and his Good News are even dynamic and changing to all times and cultures as they become better understood and lived by each people. It is the continuous endeavor to make Christianity truly 'feel at home' in the cultures of each people.'" (http://www.dacb.org/stories/aa-print-stories/uganda/waliggo_john.html (accessed on June 14, 2011).

the people in exactly the same way as the Church had identified Mwanga's supporters as rebels not only against the British
administration but also against the Christian Churches.[753]

This political orientation, mostly fueled by Protestant missionaries, plus
a god, so far removed from his people as portrayed by the Anglican faith,
drew more and more people away from Anglican faith. In other words, both
Christianity and the traditional Ganda religion are mediated religions. The
role of mediation is vital and is well laid in the scriptures. All the prophets and
priests of the Old Testament were sent for this. In the New Testament, Jesus
instituted another mediatory structure in the church. It is through adherence to
this mediation that God draws us closer to him. Therefore, the greatest weapon
man has today to defeat relativism is to return to the roots.

9.4 A New Invading Culture: Relativism in Buganda

For the last 134 years (since 1877), Christianity has been preached across
Buganda and Uganda. To date, Uganda is over 85 percent Christian.[754] Even
if Islam arrived in Buganda before Christianity, the Baganda embraced
Christianity more than Islam. For Christianity to win over 85 percent of the
population in only one hundred years, during a period characterized by slow
development and poor communication, was rather remarkable as the harvest
was abundant. With a greater percentage being Christian, we cannot expect
an unadulterated Ganda traditional culture to be still in existence anymore.
What we have today can best be described as Ganda Christian culture. Every
day, the traditional Ganda culture continues to vanish into the *Zamani*,[755] as a
result of the impact exerted by the Christian culture. Christianity took Buganda
by storm and soon dominated its members' lives. There are no regrets about
this.

---

[753] John Mary Waliggo, "Ganda Traditional Religion and Catholicism in Buganda, 1948–
1975," *Christianity in Independent Africa* (Bloomington, IN: Indiana University Press,
1978), 414.

[754] "The National Census of October 2002 resulted in the clearest and most detailed information ever given on the religious composition of Uganda. According to the Census,
Christians of all denominations made up 85.1% of Uganda's Population. The Catholic
Church has the largest number of adherents (41.9%) followed by the Church of Uganda - a
local Anglican denomination- (31.9%). Minor Christian groups include Pentecostals (4.6%)
and SDA followers." ("Uganda: Religion," *Global Oneness*, http://www.experiencefestival.
com/a/Uganda_-_Religion/id/5556320 (accessed June 14, 2011).

[755] "*Zamani* is a Swahili African concept of time that covers the 'past-period'—a remote
past," in John Mbiti, *African Religions and Philosophy* (Oxford: Heinemann Educational
Publishers, 1969), 21.

Unfortunately, another now dangerous and fast-paced wave is overwhelming Buganda, Uganda, and the rest of Africa. This wave is nothing other than Western relativism. It is treacherously packaged in unpredictable but attractive ways. It uses quite different and modern means of "evangelization." Unlike Christianity, which employed missionaries as agents of evangelization, who evangelized in a slow but systematic manner, the prevailing culture makes use of fast modern means and powerful technical agents. This wave will probably cover a wider and larger percentage of the population in a shorter period than Christianization did. This new wave has de facto both a de-Christianization of and more generally a removal of religion from Africa as its implicit but prime aim.

9.4.1 A New Anthropology

There seems to be a new anthropology developing based on two essential questions: (1) What does it mean to be a human being? (2) What is our position in this universe?[756] Answers to these questions given by the postmodern society are ushering in what can be referred to as a new anthropology. Driven by the unreflected dynamics of technical scientific development, many different groups and people the world over are pressing for a redefinition and transformation of the human situation. There seems to be something fundamentally out of balance in the world we live in. Humankind seems to have lost a sense of orientation and direction on its cosmic journey.[757] Hans Schwarz thinks that the root cause of this lack of orientation is the loss of a firm metaphysical foundation on which to build our lives. He states,

> The firm foundation on which to build our lives has disappeared from our sight. Our world is in turmoil and our lives are threatened by the impact of technology that made our lives more changeable than ever and increased the pace in modern living to such an extent that truly "our years come to an end like a sigh" (Ps 90:9). We have domesticated the world in an unprecedented way, but we have lost our souls and each other in the process. At no point in history have we had so much knowledge about the world that surrounds us and so

---

[756] Hans Schwarz, *Our Cosmic Journey: Christian Anthropology in the Light of Current Trends in the Sciences, Philosophy and Theology* (Minneapolis, MN: Augsburg Publishing House, 1977), 13.
[757] Ibid.

little insight into our own place in this world and so little understanding for each other.

According to Schwarz, contemporary technological civilization is responsible for a profoundly changed worldview and a radically altered self-understanding of the human being and his position in the universe. For him, this civilization has managed to put everybody into a splendid, though rigorous isolation.[758] Surely, an isolated living can easily lead to a subjectivistic perspective forcing upon oneself relativism. And this is *nolens volens* the kind of life situation present man finds himself in. Contemporary man, whether in Europe, the Americas, Asia, or Africa, is facing the same fate—that is, a culture of isolation where, as Schwarz puts it, each phase of life is self-contained and without much interaction with other brackets of age and income.[759]

Without his own consent, the African is posited now in a predicament: in anguish he sees his ancestral community-based life being inescapably torn apart. Older forms of life are eventually waning away and new ones are arising that promote anonymity. He experiences accelerated transitoriness[760] to such a degree that his very cultural existence is threatened. He is now part of the global society in transit, in which nothing can be taken for granted and everything is in uncontrollable, constant flux. The following appropriately illustrates the current trends in society and holds true also in sub-Saharan African society in particular:

> Traditions that served as a guide for our attitude towards family structures, religion, etc., more and more rapidly lose their binding character, and no longer are replaced by other traditions, but by steadily varying trends. It is not only that old foundations are shaking but that new ones are not built with the same strength and duration. We become more and more uncertain which way to move. Our own identity becomes increasingly uncertain, since the more possibilities there are to pursue the future, the more choices we must make and the more we realize that in making them there is nothing to rely on except our own self.[761]

The theologian Jürgen Moltmann agrees with Schwarz. He envisages this

---

[758] Schwarz, *Our Cosmic Journey*, 14.
[759] Ibid.
[760] Ibid., 15.
[761] Ibid.

world as a changed world, living essentially in rootlessness.[762] For him, the new world order is an order of veiled interests and of struggles for power, and of frightening manipulation of men. "The new world order is an order of the 'man without qualities in a world of qualities without man.'"[763] According to Moltmann,

> Modern society is called a pluralistic society because in it a multitude of views and interests, groups and associations are competing with one another. In it man experiences himself too as a pluralistic being, who must live at the point of intersection of often very different claims, standards and expectations, which can no longer be brought under the common denominator of a single personality which is at peace with itself, and of a consistent picture of life.[764]

Now the Sub-Saharan African society, a largely faithful "consumer" of foreign influences, particularly from the West, has most probably fallen victim to this rootlessness, manipulation, and inconsistence more than any other society. Africa is the society that, in matters sociopolitical, economic, and religious, is truly tossed about by "every wind of teaching"[765] as Pope Benedict XVI observes in general concerning modern-day relativism. As a consequence, the supposedly firm African Christian roots are becoming uprooted gradually but relentlessly. Thus, the African Christian finds himself in a vacuum and crisis of faith not of his own making. He seems to be at a crossroads and encounters great difficulty with regard to the choice which way to go. Below, we shall attempt to shed some light on prevailing trends.

9.4.1.1 Resorting to Old Standards

The Ganda culture has a historical past and a dynamic present. The historical past was characterized with a very static existence and static values. With the encounter with Christianity and Western civilization, the Baganda renounced the static existence of their forefathers and embraced a transitory existence. The former Ganda culture was transformed into a largely Ganda Christian culture. Before the Christian culture was firm enough, the Ganda

---

[762] Jürgen Moltmann, *Man: Christian Anthropology in the Conflicts of the Present* (Philadelphia, PA: Fortress Press, 1971), 86.
[763] Ibid., 87.
[764] Moltmann, *Man*, 87.
[765] John F. Thornton and Susan B. Varenne, eds., *The Essential Pope Benedict XVI: His Central Writings and Speeches* (New York: HarperCollins Publishers, 2007), 22.

are now confronted with a new culture that disintegrates the former, rendering it superfluous and obsolete. Perplexed by the turn of events, many among the Baganda are turning back, resorting to old standards, proving what Schwarz's statement that "to arrive at an answer to these vexing issues, one is sometimes inclined to resort to old standards and reinforce them with rigor."[766]

There is a significant and strong movement back to traditional beliefs and practices among the Baganda. More people today boldly and publicly declare themselves as, for example: *abasamize*[767] (worshippers of traditional gods), *abalaguzi* (diviners), and *abalogo* (witch doctors). The greatest of absurdity is the return of human sacrifices as a result of the movement. There are disturbing findings about child sacrifices in Uganda.

According to a *BBC News* report on child sacrifice in Uganda published on published on 7/1/2010, the situation is worse than what the media or the authorities will disclose. Quote:

> A BBC investigation into human sacrifice in Uganda has heard first-hand accounts which suggest ritual killings of children may be more common than authorities have acknowledged. One witch-doctor led us to his secrete shrine and said he had clients who regularly captured children and brought their body parts to be consumed by spirits. Meanwhile, a former witch-doctor who now campaigns to end child sacrifice confessed for the first time to having murdered about 70 people, including his own son. The Ugandan government told us that human sacrifice is on the increase, and according to the head of the country's Anti-Human Sacrifice Taskforce the crime is directly linked to rising levels of development and prosperity,

---

[766] Schwarz, *Our Cosmic Journey*, 16.

[767] These traditional gods' worshippers have formed an association currently under the leadership of Sylvia Namutebi (a Catholic) commonly known as Maama Fiina. She is a professed traditional gods' worshipper but does not feel ashamed or hesitate to admit that despite this, she is a Catholic Christian. One Uganda newspaper, *The Weekly Observer*, once wrote about her: "Here is a woman who does not shy away from acknowledging she practices witchcraft. Unlike her colleagues, Maama Fiina brags about helping ministers, MPs, CEOs, managing directors and corporate people secure a job, jump conviction in court, get promoted, elected or appointed ministers," in Shifa Mwesigye, "Corporates Practice More Witchcraft than the Lowly—Maama Fiina," (September 1, 2010), *The Weekly Observer*, http://www.observer.ug/index.php?option=com_content&task=view&id=9931& Itemid=70, Wednesday, September 1, 2010, accessed June 15, 2011).

and an increasing belief that witchcraft can help people get rich quickly.[768]

Some people in society have dismissed connections of such acts with worship, but rather as acts endemic to poor and desperate communities struggling to ascend the ladder of development. Yet others speculate that those who trade in human body parts for transplants are the cause. However, there are also many pointers toward a religious orientation. Brandon Thorp wrote the following on the subject:

> One murdered child was found in the brush with his organs removed. Sick? Obviously. Witchcraft? Probably not. At least in the U.S., most child killers, even the very weird ones, act more out of deranged psychosexual compunction than out of any impulse toward mysticism, and I can only assume the same is true in Uganda. Human nature doesn't change much from place to place, and most folks, even atavists, will balk at killing children in the service of the spirit world. That's why God took such a shining to Abraham: He was uniquely cuckoo.[769]

The reason for discussing this subject here is not to turn this paper into a kind of a sociological research, nor is it meant to support, in any way, what takes place in these atrocities. Rather we intend to bring it to the awareness of society, particularly the Baganda and Africans, that the problem is and has far-reaching dire consequences than what appears.

What is exactly fascinating about sacrifice? Most societies would agree that there is a deeply inherent trait of salvation that is attached to sacrifice. The Baganda, in particular, strongly believed in the salvific nature of sacrifice. Their concept of sacrifice holds great similarities with the Jewish concept that runs through the scriptures, from Abraham to Zechariah, which were substituted by the greatest sacrifice of the Savior. The first missionaries to Buganda condemned the Baganda ritual sacrifices, without initially trying to comprehend their significance. The church only needs to take this as an opportunity to explain and embed the supreme importance of Jesus's sacrifice into the culture. Because the Catholic faith and liturgical celebrations have sacrifice at

---

[768] Tim Whewell, "Witch-doctors Reveal Extent of Child Sacrifice in Uganda," (January 7, 2010), *BBC News, Uganda*, http://news.bbc.co.uk/2/hi/programmes/newsnight/8441813. stm (accessed June 15, 2011).

[769] Brandon Thorp, "Child Sacrifice in Uganda" (January 9, 2010), *James Randi Educational Foundation*, http://www.randi.org/site/index.php/swift-blog/829-child-sacrifice-in-uganda.html (accessed June 15, 2011).

the center,[770] it was one reason it attracted following than any other churches or faiths in Buganda.

One of Buganda's prominent Catholic theologian-priests, John Mary Waliggo, stated that the reasons people gave for the backtracking of Baganda Catholics into traditional beliefs and practices was attributed, to a greater degree, to the weaknesses within the church herself.[771] According to him, priests are criticized for failing to pay regular and long visits to catechist centers to get to know the people, and of doing away with the religions sodalities of men, women, girls, and boys through which people's faith was strengthened and useful discussion held. They are also accused of weakening the former Christian substitutes for the deep-rooted traditional rites. The practice of blessing pregnant and newly delivered women is disappearing, the use of holy water to dispel evil forces is declining, and the popularity of religious processions is withering away. The vacuum created by the removal of the former Christian substitutes, older Catholics argue, has been to the advantage of the growth of traditional religion.[772]

Waliggo goes further and states,

> The fundamental mistake of the Church has been failure to understand the nature and force of traditional religion, failure to come to the rescue of Christians who live in two world views that conflict, failure to see the diversity of traditional religion which varies according to ethnic groups, traditional skills, geographical settlements and the length of time Christianity has been in the area. There has also been a lack of creativity in proposing experiments that attempt to answer the present needs of the people. The Church has continued to use disciplinary measures against those who divert from the defined positions, without understanding enough their fears and anxieties. It has failed to discover or work out a theology of the "weak" who cannot or frequently fail to reach the ideal. It has finally failed to start a meaningful dialogue with the ordinary Christians at the grass-root level of the catechist centres on this vital issue.[773]

People returning to traditional religions marks one form of de-Christianization of Africa, to which Waliggo in conclusion suggests that a successful

---

[770] CCC 1324.
[771] Waliggo, "Ganda Traditional Religion and Catholicism in Buganda, 1948–1975," 420.
[772] Ibid.
[773] Ibid., 420–421.

marriage between Christianity and traditional religions and cultures must take a long time to be planned before it is consummated. "Short-lived experiments cannot provide useful conclusions. Instead of driving away people from sacraments, we need a new approach that will invite them back. Instead of a theology of the 'ideal' and for the ideal, we need one for the 'weak.'"[774]

9.4.1.2 The Overwhelming Nature of Social Relativism

Another form of de-Christianization more hazardous than the above is the invading Western relativistic culture. To many, relativism is a Western problem. Many consider talking about relativism in Africa is stretching it too far. However, the analysis below proves otherwise. As previously noted, Christianity (and Western civilization) was preached throughout Africa and it traversed across the second largest continent, in less than fifty years. This occurred during a time when the flow of information was by far slower compared to the present day. If Christianity was spread this fast by word of mouth, how much faster would de-Christianization spread in the age of fast technology? Today, information is received or shared simultaneously across the globe.

Geographical boundaries have been broken. For example, it is not uncommon for international students here in the United States to follow the media (TVs, radios, newspapers, etc.) from their respective countries by means of the Internet. Under such circumstances, many have learned about issues happening in their neighborhoods, first from African media. Because of Africa's economic dependence on the West, Africa's business world feeds on more Western information than their local countries'. Such people, and the number is increasing every passing day, appreciate more and actually live according to foreign/Western cultures. Even if Africa still has a different material culture,[775] its ideological culture is slowly merging with the West.

The drums of relativism are sounding louder and louder in Buganda and elsewhere in Africa, and the message is spreading like a wildfire. The relativistic culture is infiltrating Africa via different forms but with one goal. It comes in form of human rights activism, freedoms, born-again (liberal) Christianity, political liberalism, economic independences, etc.; all these are disguises. Instead of freeing the African, they isolate him from another, so that there is no longer a community, no communion with either God or fellow men but an individual.

---

[774] Waliggo, "Ganda Traditional Religion and Catholicism in Buganda, 1948–1975," 424–425.

[775] The "inferior" and different material culture of Africa is fast changing into Western styles. About 130 years ago, there were no modern infrastructures in Africa (at least similar to Western standards). Today, most townships have a Western look. In the next fifty years, the story will be different. Africa's material culture too will merge with the West.

The former Uganda minister of *Ethics and Integrity*, James Nsaba Buturo, wrote a critical article at the end of his tenure (June 24, 2011). He stated,

> The quest to construct a Uganda which is egalitarian, free, stable and prosperous and founded on impeccable moral credentials is underway. Although our expectations are high, there is an ongoing conspiratorial undercurrent threatening them. In the rush to propel our nation to modernity, it would be unwise to ignore this undercurrent. The undercurrent in question is the new agenda which secularists are championing against Uganda under the banner of "human rights." The following are its main elements: removing God from our education system and schools in particular and society in general, reducing parental authority over their children, encouraging youth to rebel against the status quo, destroying traditional family structure, making sex free and abortion legal, making divorce easy, misleading society into believing that anal sex is at par with heterosexual sex and using the media to promote and change both our mindset and value system.[776]

The minister held office for five years. He had grappled with all these forces, and at the end of his term in office, he made a kind of prophecy. He believed that the ultimate goal of the secularists or relativists is "to have a one-world government, a one-world economic system and a one-world religion."[777] He acknowledges that progressively Ugandans are distancing themselves from God, abandoning their time-honored *valkuesin* favor for secular ones. He continues to affirm the new culture when he says that this culture targets the young generation, particularly those school-going youth. He wrote the following on the subject:

> Schools are becoming a repository of fashion wear, indecent dance styles, pornographic material and promiscuity. School authorities are promoting comprehensive sexuality and sex education programmes as never before. As a result, sexual immorality and sexual experimentation are on the increase and leading to early and unwanted pregnancies, sexually transmitted diseases, abortions and associated health problems that

---

[776] James Nsaba Buturo, "Secularists Leading Us Astray," (June 24, 2011), *The New Vision Uganda*, http://www.newvision.co.ug/D/8/20/758456 (accessed June 18, 2011).
[777] Ibid.

impair the wellbeing of the youth. Sexual experimentation includes masturbation, exploring one's sexuality with friends of either sex, sharing erotic fantasies and instructing students about homosexuality, bisexuality, inter-sexuality, *transgenderism* as well as a variety of other deviant practices. The effort to sexualize our society as well as popularize human sexuality is being done under the deceptive banner of "human rights." Here, our marketing and media industries have become the main propagating agents.[778]

What bothers the minister is that this culture does not respect the local people's sovereign rights and religious and cultural values. They are undermining the institution of the family and community. By not accepting other people's views and values, this new culture constitutes itself into a dictatorship, according to Joseph Ratzinger, a "dictatorship of relativism."[779]

The minster concludes his article by cautioning the public that some Ugandans are acquiescing to these pressures—increasingly accepting it as the new agenda. He ends by calling upon all Ugandans to "refuse to tread the road they [secularists] want them to take."[780]

An article written by a high-profile government official, who was directly involved with the ethic fabric of the state, speaks volumes. Nothing more is needed to prove the reality of the culture of relativism in Uganda. Like the high priest during the trial of Jesus, we can also ask, "What more proof do we need?" We all have heard it from the man in charge. More information would only be examples adding to the depth of the problem.

What seems to be at stake is the sociological question of human existence, each individual and group trying to find their position in the universe. Schwarz says that the age-old sociological questions "What does it mean to be a human being? What is our position in this universe?" are being asked with renewed strength and intensity today.[781] He says that minority groups (mistreated in most cases) "are pressing for a redefinition, nay, even a transformation of the human situation."[782] The subjective and uncompromising voices of such groups have taken their fight to Africa. These groups fight for their rights and position in the world regardless of the existing social norms and religious values.

---

[778] Ibid.

[779] Thornton and Susan Varenne, *The Essential Pope Benedict XVI*, 22.

[780] James Nsaba Buturo, "Secularists Leading Us Astray," (June 24, 2011), *The New Vision Uganda*, http://www.newvision.co.ug/D/8/20/758456 (accessed June 18, 2011).

[781] Schwarz, *Our Cosmic Journey*, 13.

[782] Ibid.

Examples of such groups are the pro-choice group, the gay activists, women activists, people with disability activists, children rights activists, etc.

The gay activists have exerted themselves more emphatically in the recent past. The practice, however, is foreign to the African culture, and in Uganda, it was resisted forthwith. Its condemnation and rejection[783] attracted a global attention and reaction. Its condemnation brought into light those behind its spread. A group of seventeen organizations[784] came to its defense and denied any cultural, social, or religious values against it. Other groups have also penetrated the society in a significant manner. In the process, they erode the Christian culture of its foundational values. On July 5, 2011, Paul Kasolo, a Uganda education analysis wrote,

> All the traditional schools in the country [Uganda], if you notice were all religious-founded. This reminds me of what someone said: "Education without God, simply makes someone a clever devil"—but not educated. The more we pull God out of our education, the worse we degenerate morally, spiritually, academically and discipline wise. You cannot talk of discipline and morals without God. We are leaving in days where we are saying truth is relative, we cannot have sound

---

[783] Homosexuality is foreign to African society. The Ugandan society sought to restrict its spread via a prohibitive law drafted in 2009 in what they termed as The Anti-Homosexuality Bill 2009 with its principle stating, "The object of this Bill is to establish a comprehensive consolidated legislation to protect the traditional family by prohibiting (i) any form of sexual relations between persons of the same sex; and (ii) the promotion or recognition of such sexual relations in public institutions and other places through or with the support of any Government entity in Uganda or any non-governmental organization inside or outside the country." in *The Anti Homosexuality Bill 2009*, http://wthrockmorton.com/wp-content/uploads/2009/10/anti-homosexuality-bill-2009.pdf (accessed on July 8, 2011).

[784] "Akina Mama wa Afrika (AMwA), Amnesty International, ARC International, Article 19, Center for, Women's Global Leadership, COC Netherlands, Committee for the International Day against Homophobia and Transphobia, Egale Canada, Human Rights Watch, International Commission of Jurists, International, Foundation for the Protection of Human Rights Defenders (Front Line), International Gay and Lesbian, Human Rights Commission (IGLHRC), LAMBDA Mozambique, Swedish Federation for Lesbian, Gay, Bisexual and Transgender Rights (RFSL), Uganda Feminist Forum (UFF), Unitarian Universalist Church, United Nations Office, The World AIDS Campaign." The president of the United States of America, Barrack Obama, referred to the bill as "odious" and the secretary of state, Hillary Clinton, made a call to the Ugandan president urging him not to pass it into law. in "Uganda: 'Anti-Homosexuality' Bill Threatens Liberties and Human Rights Defenders" (October 15, 2009), *Human Rights Watch Organization*, http://www.hrw.org/en/news/2009/10/15/uganda-anti-homosexuality-bill-threatens-liberties-and-human-rights-defenders (accessed July 8, 2011).

education. Today, most people are popularizing the notion of our country being a secular nation, a situation similar to our education and every sphere of influence in our nation. Secular means devoid of God. So how can we declare our nation and education being devoid of God, while at the same time claim that our motto is "For God and my Country," that is what the Bible calls hypocrisy, and the Bible promises that if we are neither hot nor cold, God will spit us out of his mouth.[785]

The writer expresses the facts in the Ugandan society that many people, especially those in positions of authority, would not care talk about (perhaps due to Western donor influence). Every time someone defends cultural-religious values against treacherous traditions, the donor community responds with threats of reduced foreign aid. It appears the poor African and Christian cultures must sacrifice their identities and values in exchange for a noxious culture disguised in foreign aid, which many organizations christen as charity. The writer of the article concludes by expressing his wishes, which are fit to be the wishes of the society.

I am longing for a time when schools will again teach our children that God, created the universe. I am longing for a time when our children will learn from school, that God makes a bean seed grow, other than moisture, water and warmth alone. I long for times where what is learned in school is in agreement with what is learned in Church and home. That is my passion and. Do not think of me as a prophet of doom, but we shall continue to see this degeneration, not only in our schools but in the society if we do not turn back to God as the source of our life.[786]

As stated earlier, these are just a few examples of how this strong culture is cutting across Africa with powerful people and strong and influential organizations supporting and promoting it.

---

[785] Paul Kasolo, "Have Schools Ignored God?" (July 5, 2011), *The New Vision Uganda*, http://www.newvision.co.ug/D/9/35/759408 (accessed July 10, 2011).
[786] Paul Kasolo, "Have Schools Ignored God?" (July 5, 2011), *The New Vision Uganda*, http://www.newvision.co.ug/D/9/35/759408 (accessed July 10, 2011).

9.4.1.3 Religious Relativism

Let us now explore yet another form of relativism. This is a disguised Christian faith/religion. With it, the church and Christianity is assaulted on two fronts: both from without and from within. This religious relativism is in form of evangelical or Pentecostal faiths that are mushrooming everywhere in Uganda. Since Buganda is the economic center of Uganda, it also has the biggest share of this. Kampala city and townships are full of churches built in many forms—homesteads, clublike dilapidated structures, market places, shades, etc.—where anyone who can read can become a pastor. An analyst wrote,

> Anyone with some knowledge of the bible, a booming voice, a good translator and the ability to move large crowds with words can start a Church any day. While the traditional Churches have oversight institutions and are governed by the Trustees Incorporation Act, many of the Pentecostal Churches are a power unto themselves and only answerable to God and their pastors.[787]

According to the *Pew Forum on Religion and Public Life*, Pentecostalism is almost overtaking, at least numerically, the mainstream religions in Africa. On October 5, 2006, they wrote,

> Pentecostalism has become an increasingly prominent feature of Africa's religious and political landscape. The movement's growth has been particularly dramatic since the era of decolonization in the 1950s and 1960s. According to recent figures from the World Christian Database, Pentecostals now represent 12%, or about 107 million, of Africa's population of nearly 890 million people. This includes individuals who belong to classical Pentecostal denominations, such as the Assemblies of God or the Apostolic Faith Mission, that were founded in the early 20th century, as well as those who belong to Pentecostal denominations or Churches that have formed more recently, such as the Deeper Life Bible Church in Nigeria. Charismatic members of non-Pentecostal denominations, who in Africa are drawn mainly from Catholic and Protestant Churches and

---

[787] Eunice Rukundo, "Lies, sex and hypocrisy in Pentecostal Churches in Uganda," (June 1, 2009), *Majimbo Kenya*, http://majimbokenya.com/home/2009/06/01/lies-sex-and-hypocrisy-in-pentecostal-Churches-in-uganda/ (accessed July 8, 2011).

African Instituted Churches (AICs), number an additional 40 million, or approximately 5% of the population. As recently as 1970, Pentecostals and charismatics *combined* represented less than 5% of Africans.[788]

They provided the statistics below:[789]

CHRISTIANITY IN AFRICA

	1990		190		1990		2006	
	In millions	As % of total population	In millions	As % of total population	In millions	As % of total population	In millions	As % of total population
Christians	10	9%	144	40%	276	45%	411	46%
Catholics	2	2	45	13	91	15	147	17
Protestants, Anglicans and Independents	2	2	53	15	162	26	253	29

Source: *World Christian Encyclopedia* (2001) and World Christian Database (2006)

Although the figures above may not be very accurate due to lack of statistical data in most of these communities (and there are most likely to be exaggerations for strategic reasons), the fact remains that Pentecostal form of Christianity is the fastest growing form in Africa, Uganda not excluded. The forum continues to state that "Pentecostalism has penetrated important sectors of African public life. In Uganda and Kenya, for example, Pentecostals and other evangelicals control numerous radio and TV stations."[790] It is true; there is an upsurge of Pentecostalism on the African continent and a proliferation of Pentecostal news. They have the best marketing strategy, and their voice tends to be more appealing, especially to the young generation.

The concern for this paper is the philosophy behind this movement. Many of these churches take advantage of desperate and unsuspicious peasants, majority of whom are duped with sham and pretentious miraculous acts to extract money from them. Their philosophy seems to be the extreme version of the Lutheran *Solar Fidei* and *Sola Scruptura*. The subjectivity in these formulae is the real folly. Their teaching does not appeal to any authority or tradition. The follower has only to believe biblical truths following a personal interruption.

---

[788] "Overview: Pentecostalism in Africa" (October 5, 2006), *The Pew Forum: On Religion and Public Life*, http://pewforum.org/Christian/Evangelical-Protestant-Churches/Overview-Pentecostalism-in-Africa.aspx (accessed July 8, 2011).

[789] Ibid.

[790] Ibid.

Therefore, there are as many teachings as there are pastors, and thus, as many truths as there are preachers. In the end, everyone who reads will uncover their own truth. Their philosophy is what is intrinsically implied in their title "Pentecostalism."[791] Each individual acts as one experiences the "spirit."

Some Catholics downplay the magnitude and seriousness of the movement, referring to them as confused people, moneymaking conjurors, who cannot constitute a serious threat to the church. However, the reality could be different. They are present in all corners, and their voice is becoming louder. Culture is a repetitive action or tradition developed over time and something that usually one learns in their early years. Any experiences a person encounters in their later years can hardly become that person's culture. Therefore, if the young generation grows up in this, even if it collapses later, the damage will have been done. Such people will never feel at home with the teachings they embrace in their advanced years. Christianity is a culture that needs to be lived right from childhood.

9.5 Summary Observations

While the Baganda, and Africans in general, do not have to revert to a static existence, they cannot, as a solution, embrace a constantly changing existence without roots. They need something to cling to on their journey, a point of orientation, and a point of reference. This is especially necessary at a time when most of the traditional points of reference have become unreliable and obsolete. But how can they orient themselves? Schwarz suggests that "one way of achieving this is to relate us humans to the phenomena by which we are surrounded, or to the human matrix."[792]

Confronted with the immense turmoil in which the Baganda find themselves, their essence, place, and destiny as human beings must then be defined in relation to the items which give origin and form to humanity and which enclose it. Schwarz continues to teach that "a human self-definition would be of no avail to solve our existential anxieties, since we are neither our own boundaries nor our own creators."[793] Therefore, the divine is the ultimate matrix in which man finds fulfillment, for there is evidently a restless and a yearning in

---

[791] "The Pentecostal movement within Protestant Christianity places special emphasis on gifts of the Holy Spirit, as shown in the Biblical account of the Day of Pentecost. Pentecostalism is similar to the Charismatic Movement, but developed earlier and separated from the mainstream Church. Charismatic Christians, at least in the early days of the movement, tended to remain in their respective denominations," (http://christianity. wikia.com/wiki/Pentecostalism [accessed July 10, 2011]).

[792] Schwarz, *Our Cosmic Journey*, 16.

[793] Ibid.

man that remains unfulfilled unless it results in union between man and his creator.[794] By alienating ourselves from our creator, we have estranged ourselves from each other and from our environment. Moltmann says that "if man lives in and of the world, he does not live from and in God. He has fallen into the hands of the powers of this world and their law."[795]

In this chapter, we have tried to briefly describe the Baganda traditional culture and religion vis-à-vis their newfound Christian faith as faced with a new and rapidly spreading culture of relativism. This culture seems to be undeflectable. However, the Baganda have both the resources and ability to obstruct it. These are embodied in their traditional Christian culture. Ugandans, Africans, and the church have plenty to learn from the Ganda culture. The Baganda have a contribution to make toward the faithful living of Christianity amid the prevailing relativism. We also endeavored to illustrate that the Ganda culture is congenial with the culture and that it can help Catholic Christianity to flourish. By remaining loyal to their natural cultural Baganda values, the Ganda not only become receptive to the Catholic faith, but are also capable of defending Christianity against Western relativism.

John Taylor's words constitute a very appropriate conclusion for this section:

> There are many who think feel that the spiritual sickness of the West, which reveals itself in the divorce of the sacred from the secular, of the cerebral from the instinctive, and in the loneliness and homelessness of individualism, may be healed through a recovery of the wisdom which Africa has not yet thrown away. The world Church awaits something new out of Africa. The Church in Buganda, and in many other parts of the continent, by obedient response to God's calling, for all its sinfulness and bewilderment, may yet become the agent through whom the Holy Spirit will teach His people everywhere how to be in Christ without ceasing to be involved in mankind, how to be bound in the bundle of life, yet at one with the Lord their God.[796]

---

[794] Ibid., 18.
[795] Moltmann, *Man*, 94.
[796] Taylor, *The Growth of the Church in Buganda*, 259–260.

General Conclusion

When we were beginning this project, all was fear and trembling. The minds were filled with uncertainly and our minds were asking tons of questions but with very possible answers. At the conclusion, we have less fears, and anxiety has diminished, though more questions have been raised, and answers to such will take perhaps a lifetime. We have managed to go through the rigorous exercise. It has been a process of learning. Along the way, more doors have been opened and more insights were obtained. This project has closed one chapter and opened another of a lifetime search for answers, and a commitment to faithfully follow into the paths of the Gospel.

We started this project at the STL level with the topic: "Evangelization of Cultures in the Theology of Joseph Ratzinger." It proved a worthwhile project for STD, but with a broader perspective and scholarly activity. The questions raised in the initial project became the foundation to quest for more. We are happy with what we have discovered, and we look forward to more wisdom to help us fulfill the Lord's command to take his word to the ends of the earth.

The first part of this paper was a review of the church's ageless mandate to evangelize. It meant to refute, at the very start, the claim of the relativism that the mandate of church and the Gospel was accomplished in the past centuries; that we are now living in a post-Christian era, in which everyone is his own legislator of the good and bad, the right and wrong. In this part, we restated the church's mission as not only her own but the Lord's, and God's word is everlasting. This reaffirmation of the church's mandate provided the basis for this paper and sustained the argument throughout the paper. In brief, the base of this paper is that Christianity is a revealed message through the second person of God who handed it over to his church, and that the church's mission, sustained and guided by the Holy Spirit, is to keep the faith and pass it on to generations to come. What the church teaches therefore is not its own but Christ's. This is what St. Paul meant when he said,

For the word of the cross is foolishness to those who are perishing, but to us who are being saved it is the power of God. For it is written, "I will destroy the wisdom of the wise, and the cleverness of the clever I will set aside." Where is the wise man? Where is the scribe? Where is the debater of this age? Has not God made foolish the wisdom of the world? For since in the wisdom of God the world through its wisdom did not *come to* know God, God was well-pleased through the foolishness of the message preached to save those who believe. For indeed Jews ask for signs and Greeks search for wisdom; but we preach Christ crucified, to Jews a stumbling block and to Gentiles foolishness, but to those who are the called, both Jews and Greeks, Christ the power of God and the wisdom of God. Because the foolishness of God is wiser than men, and the weakness of God is stronger than men. For consider your calling, brethren, that there were not many wise according to the flesh, not many mighty, not many noble; but God has chosen the foolish things of the world to shame the wise, and God has chosen the weak things of the world to shame the things which are strong, and the base things of the world and the despised God has chosen, the things that are not, so that He may nullify the things that are, so that no man may boast before God. But by His doing you are in Christ Jesus, who became to us wisdom from God, and righteousness and sanctification, and redemption, so that, just as it is written, "let him who boasts, boast in the lord."[797]

Hence, the Christian faith is mistakenly identified (by relativists) with older outdated human systems. Robert Barron denies that Christianity is a system. For him, "atheists write off religion as primitive, premodern nonsense. Aquinas, Augustine, Paul, Teresa of Avila, Joseph Ratzinger, and Edith Stein—in all their intellectual rigor—struggle against this dismissive atheism."[798] He instead calls it the Infleshment of God. He explains,

What makes Catholicism, among all of the competing philosophies, ideologies, and religions of the world, distinctive? I stand with Blessed John Henry Newman who said that the great principle of Catholicism is the Incarnation, the infleshment of

---

[797] 1 Cor 1:18–31.
[798] Robert Barron, *Catholicism: A Journey to the Heart of the Faith* (New York: Image Books, 2011), 7–8.

God. What do I mean by this? I mean, the Word of God—the mind by which the whole universe came to be—did not remain sequestered in heaven but rather entered into this ordinary world of bodies, this grubby arena of history, this compromised and tear-stained human condition of ours. "The Word became flesh and made his dwelling among us" (Jn 1:14).[799]

Barron helps us clarify the confusion of relativism. He shows how in many of the philosophies of modernity, God is construed as a threat to human well-being. He says that "in their own ways, Marx, Freud, Feuerbach, and Sartre all maintain that God must be eliminated if humans are to be fully themselves."[800] In so doing, these relativistic systems aim at killing God and replacing him with themselves—turning themselves into gods.

This paper concurs very well with Barron in refuting these claims. However, it does not stop at disproving the secular relativists, but most important, it rules out as false, the claims of religious relativists. Therefore, a great emphasis has been put to the reaffirmation of the Catholic doctrine against the relativistic doctrines that developed especially beginning with the Reformation period. The Reformers, particularly Martin Luther, John Calvin, and Zwingle, contributed a great deal to the relativistic teaching of the faith. It all began with their subjective interpretation of the scriptures and all their theologies and anthropologies were twisted toward a relativistic understanding—replacing truth with fragments of truths.

The paper also reminisces what we considered prominent religious relativists of the modern times, namely, Friedrich Schleiermacher and SØren Kierkegaard. We chose these particularly because, unlike their counterparts in the same period—the likes of Kant, Hegel, Marx, and Nietzsche—these two were more of theologians than philosophers. They preached a religious relativism distinct from the secular relativistic philosophies. They stood in the footsteps of the Reformers of the sixteenth century and presumptuously promoted their ideas to greater heights. With their teachings, religious relativism surfaced more clearly and yielded dire consequences to the Christian faith.

We against attempted to distance the Catholic faith from such relativistic ideas by restating and reaffirming the Catholic teaching—giving the totality of doctrine as left to the church. Barron can once again help us to summarize what we have been trying to explain—what the Catholic faith stands for:

The incarnation separates Christianity from the other great world religions, but how does it distinguish Catholicism from

---

[799] Ibid., 1.
[800] Ibid., 2.

the other Christian Churches? Don't Protestants and the Orthodox hold just as firmly to the conviction that the Word became flesh? They do indeed, but they don't embrace the doctrine in its fullness. Essential to the Catholic mind is the prolongation of the Incarnation throughout space and time, an extension made possible through the mystery of the Church—seeing God's continued infleshment in the oil, water, bread imposed hands, wine, and salt of the sacraments; appreciating it liturgy; savoring it in debates of theologians; sensing it in governance of popes and bishops; loving it the struggles of saints; knowing it in catholic writings and architects. All this discloses the ongoing presence of the Word made flesh, namely Christ.[801]

The incarnation of Christ relativizes all relativism and asserts that truth has dwelt among us. Relativism attacks the incarnation of Christ and the Christological doctrines of the first centuries. Both Ratzinger and Hauerwas rebut relativism, arguing that if God became incarnate, then I can no longer live as if God did not exist. Incarnation therefore denies atheism and agnosticism any right to uphold relativism. No human being can argue to be ignorant of ethical and spiritual truth after the mystery of the incarnation. The incarnation becomes the architect of spirituality; but without Christianity, truth and religion become privatized and everyone develops his own virtue and moral standards. This is too much for any human to achieve alone. Therefore, he is condemned to become a victim of prevailing political, ecological, social, and religious ideas.

Anthropology hinges on Christology. If Chalcedon says Jesus became fully human,[802] then it means that it is only in Jesus that we learn to be fully human. In ultimate analysis, if the incarnation of the Lord is ignored, human rights remain hollow. The question is "What religion is able to redeem the dignity of human being?" This begs the second question: "In what religion but Christianity has God become a human being?"

A godless world appears to be the best idea to humanity today, because then there would be no bother from promptings of the law and the lawgiver. The greatest craving for man, it so seems to be, is to be a self-legislator. However, the

---

[801] Robert Barron, *Catholicism: A Journey to the Heart of the Faith* (New York: Image Books, 2011), 3.

[802] ND 614, Council of Chalcedon, AD 451: "Our Lord Jesus Christ, the same perfect in divinity and perfect in humanity, the same truly God and truly man." Cf. Vatican II Council: "He who is the 'image of the invisible God' (Col 1:15), is himself the perfect man who has restored in the children of Adam that likeness to God which had been disfigured ever since the first sin. Human nature, by the very fact that it was assumed, not absorbed, in him, has been raised in us also to a dignity beyond compare." GS 22.

end result of this is a replacement of the truth with slavery (for true freedom lies in the truth) and the good with the bad, the wrong, the evil, the unjust, and at the end of the line, death. Away from God, man finds himself naked and afraid. Adam and Eve found themselves in such a circumstance because they were away from God's presence. The tempting voices that tend to offer freedom and sweeter life are serpentry, which will abandon humanity after leading it away from its creator, just as the serpent deserted Adam and Eve (Gen 3).

In conclusion, we realized in this book that relativism strives to empty faith of its essence, that is, truth. It drains the society of the reality of God. Its goal is to make faith a private affair. It has therefore been a key point of this paper to negate that faith is a private affair, but rather reaffirm faith as a revelation that is given to a community, lived in and by the community and sustained in the community. With the church as the body of Christ, we can realize God's presence in our midst—not necessarily in our personal lives. Therefore, we cannot talk of truth without mentioning church—the mystical body of Christ.

Let the last words of this paper come from one of our heroes, Joseph Ratzinger, for he seems to have a high grasp of the phenomenon under discussion in this book. He poses questions which impel us to reflect more and search for more and better ways of combating the threat of relativism, which has been the aim of this paper. Ratzinger elucidates,

> Once more, we have to say: How far we are from a world in which people no longer need to be taught about God because he is present within us! It has been asserted that our century is characterized by an entirely new phenomenon: the appearance of people incapable of relating to God. As a result of spiritual and social developments, it is said, we have reached the stage where a kind of person has developed in whom there is no longer any starting point for the knowledge of God. Whether that be true or not, we would have to admit that our distance from God—the obscurity and the dubiousness surrounding him today—is greater than ever before; indeed, that even we who are trying to be believers often feel as if the reality of God is being withdrawn from between our hands. Do we not ourselves often begin to ask where he is amid all the silence of this world? Do we not ourselves often have the feeling that, at the end of all our thinking, we have only words in our grasp, while the reality of God is farther away than ever before?[803]

---

[803] Joseph Ratzinger, *What It Means to be a Christian* (San Francisco: Ignatius Press, 2006), 24–25.

Appendix

An Interview with Professor Stanley Hauerwas

Date: Friday, January 28, 2011—Feast of St. Thomas Aquinas

Time: 9:15–10:15 a.m.

**Place: Hauerwas' office at Divinity School—
Duke University, Durham, North Carolina, USA**

Fr. Ssenyondo:
Nice meeting you. Let me first introduce myself briefly. Of course you know my name. I am Charles Ssennyondo, a Catholic priest from Uganda. I have been a priest for eight years as of this year in August. Before I came to Chicago, I was teaching in a high school seminary in Uganda for four years. My bishop sent me to the University of St. Mary of the Lake. I may go back to teach in the seminary. I completed my master's degree, and I am now working on my doctoral program. My dissertation topic is "Christianity and the Contemporary Culture of Relativism." My main references are Stanley Hauerwas' and Joseph Ratzinger's theological anthropologies.

Hauerwas:
It's humbling to be compared to Joseph Ratzinger (laughter). He is a wonderful theologian.

Fr. Ssenyondo:
Stanley, in brief, how do you describe yourself?

Hauerwas:

I am first and foremost a theologian. I hope to be in service to the church, and I come from an American working-class background. That makes a lot of difference because I have never felt at home in a university. Universities in America are not working-class institutions. But I have a wonderful wife, and I thank God for the life that I have been given. My father and mother were brick layers. And they had trouble becoming pregnant, and my mother had a stillborn child and had heard the story of Samuel and Hannah. So she prayed that if God gave her a son, she would give that son to God. She had to tell me this when I was sick. I think that set my life, and it has been a wonderful life on my side.

Fr. Ssenyondo:
Beautiful description of you. Now, Stanley, you said that you're basically a theologian. In your career as a theologian, what has been your inspiration?

Hauerwas:

My deepest inspiration has been the life of my parents. They were hardworking good people. And if I have any deep commitment to make, it is to make such lives significant for the future of the church. I also have a number of intellectual influences. The work of Karl Barth is special to me. Philosophers like MacIntyre are crucial to me, but the lives of my father and mother have been the most determinant.

Fr. Ssenyondo:
In many of your writings, you refer to yourself as a pacifist and at some point as a terrorist. How do these two get along?

Hauerwas:

In that specific article, "A Non-violent Terrorist," I used MacIntyre's account of the Impeachment Crisis to suggest that what Christians are all about is calling into question that life isn't intelligible without God. And so, terrorism means that I understand my work being a challenge to those people who think that you can put the world together without the worship of the just God. I am not terrorizing them (laughter), not in the sense of creating pain, though I create a sort of intellectual and moral pain. That's why I call in question that the only way the world can be governed is through violence; and so, nonviolence becomes a kind of terror insofar as we call in question from the fundamental presuppositions by which the world is ruled. And that is what I mean by being a nonviolent terrorist.

Fr. Ssenyondo:
That brings me to the fact that radicalism breeds intolerance, violence, and sometimes terrorism. What is your take on this?

Hauerwas:
I am not quite intolerant because I regard tolerance as a virtue sprung on a liberal political arrangement which presupposes that I am tolerant, but you are not and so, I am superior to you. And I take that to be a proposition that leads to be called into question. The question, virtue is not tolerance; it is humility in which we expect to hear how God speaks to us in the person of the stranger. And so, we must display a kind of humility that comes from believing that we must be ready to receive from others pain and joy. I also think, in terms of how to respond to terrorism, that people think that to respond to terrorism, people only need to have no response. But I do not believe that is the case. I believe the first thing you have to do is first of all, not to respond to terrorism with more terrorism. And this has to be done one person at a time. And that, unfortunately, we Christians have too often not had the patience that is necessary to respond to people's agony with the kind of care that avoids violence. And these are very deep problems. It is very interesting how John Paul II responded to the man that tried to assassinate him. He responded with reconciliation. I think that is what Jesus wants us to do—to seek reconciliation. Without reconciliation, we (and oftentimes have) kill those that we love. But you don't make things better by killing again.

Fr. Ssenyondo:
Jesus said when someone hits you on the right cheek, you turn the other as well (laughter).

Hauerwas:
Yes, and it doesn't mean that he may not hit the other too (prolonged laughter). It is not a way of trying to control the person.

Fr. Ssenyondo:
You are a citizen of one of the most significant democracies in the world. And democracy means tolerance and listening to each other's ideas in a way to find a common ground. How would you reconcile democracy and the truth of Christ?

Hauerwas:
Well, the democratic-minded [people] have criticized me and MacIntyre and Milbank of being new traditionalists, of calling into question the presuppositions that make democracy impossible. I don't think America is a democracy. I

think America is an autocracy. And that means that it is run by money. To call it democracy is a mystification. One of the problems of calling it democracy is making it legitimate for a very strong state who is uncontrolled just because it is a democracy. You are Ugandan. Americans feel that you are not democratic. So I am very committed to local forms of conversation to which people are respectful of one another and able to discover the goods in common without being a democracy. Democracy is just a mystification, because no one is very specific about what they mean by that. As a result, we let ourselves be manipulated in ways that are disastrous to ourselves and to other people. I tried to address this in a book, *The Radical Ordinary: Christianity, Democracy and the Radical Ordinary*. That book answers most questions of democracy.

Fr. Ssenyondo:
Do you think democracy can really breed true peace in the world?

Hauerwas:
No (strong no). One of the last things Immanuel Kant wrote was about perpetual peace. He thought that if you established democratic/autonomous systems to make up forms of republican governments, then the world would live in peace, because democracy doesn't go to war against democracy. I just don't think that is true. I think that while it is good to have social orders that are responsive to the interactions between people—the discovery of the good as I said—I don't think that will give you a more peaceable world. A more peaceable world will occur when people think that by following Christ, they are able to live as Christ would like them to live nonviolently, and that means that you may have to watch the innocent suffer for your conviction. It is a harsh and incredible world. But we believe that that way, God will rule the world. For me, I don't think very much about how to make peace possible between nations. I worry much more at the local level about how we can be a people of peace in a way that makes the world where I live peaceful.

Fr. Ssenyondo:
What is your view of the church?

Hauerwas:
I have a very conventional view. The church is where the word is proclaimed, the sacraments are enacted, and the people of God are holy. I do think for example that Matthew 18 is very important concerning our ability to confront one another with our hands and in ways that we can seek reconciliation. That is impossible for the church. What I make of the questions of the places of bishops, for example, I think bishops are necessary; and I think in every church,

whether they call them bishop or not, something like this, their pastoral office is to make sure that Eucharistic assemblies are not isolated from one another. I think the role of the bishop is very important for the catholicity of the church, and I believe deeply in the catholicity of the church. You and I have something to talk about even though I am an American and you are Ugandan. And we are united in a common faith, and I think that is church. And I praise God for that. I think church is Emmanuel's[804] brother helping his people in Uganda have clean water, providing good schooling, etc. That is church, and it is everyday work. Fundamentally, the church is the worship of God. Eucharistic celebration is at the center of it—it is the bottom line.

Fr. Ssenyondo:
Talking about the Eucharist reminds me. At one time, you wrote that you encourage your church to celebrate the Eucharist more often. I wonder what you understand by the Eucharist.

Hauerwas:
My understanding is very traditional, normally that this is the rite in which we are made part of the body of Christ; the transformation of this bread into the bread and body of Christ. At the conclusion of our worship (in the book, *Common Prayer*), we [Methodists] pray, "Eternal God, Heavenly Father, you gracious accepted us as living members of your Son, Our Savior Jesus Christ and you have fed us with spiritual food in the sacrament of body and blood. Send us now to the world and give us peace. We pray this through Christ our Lord." Now that prayer says everything of what happens in the Eucharist. We are sent out to be the body and blood of Christ for the world. And that what happens every time we share in the body and blood of Christ. We are unified with Christ, with one another for the world.

Fr. Ssenyondo:
So the Eucharist is a communion?

Hauerwas:
Exactly.

Fr. Ssenyondo:
You seem to admire Bonheoffer, especially his nonviolent resistance. Do you think resistance can combat liberalism?

---

[804] Emmanuel Katongole is a Catholic priest and associate professor of theology teaching at the Divinity School of Duke University.

Hauerwas:

I think people are wrong when they think that Bonheoffer was cooperative in killing Hitler. I don't think there is evidence to that regard. It is important to resist bad regimes and systems, but the question is how you resist them. Remember, Hitler had his army—largely Christian. They should have said no, but they did not know how to say no. This way, they lost their identification with the people. Bonheoffer understood all that. The problem is that Christians do not know how to say no. In fact, they thought they were good Germans. Likewise, American Christians think they are good Americans. American Christians don't know how to say no. Most of what I do is resistance.

Fr. Ssenyondo:

Many people have been resisting bad regimes, people like Nelson Mandela, Mahatma Gandhi. How different can your Christian resistance be in contrast to the mentioned people above?

Hauerwas:

I admire Mandela very much in terms of how he conducted his resistance. There was a lot of violence against him, and how he handled it comes into question. I take it that it was one of the great achievements of Mandela to have practically overthrown apartheid with nonviolence. It is one of the great achievements as John Paul II says in *Centesimus Annus*, that the Soviet domination of Eastern Europe was ended nonviolently.[805] I think that was a great achievement. I mean, people forget that Martin Luther King was a pacifist. He extraordinarily resisted evil systems of segregation. Those kinds of people—Gandhi, Luther—were extraordinary. That's what Bonheoffer wanted to do.

Fr. Ssenyondo:

Truth is one and unchangeable/immutable. You claim to stand for the revealed truth of Christ. But today, the Christian faith has hundreds of institutions/sects/denominations. Why push forward for the same truth on different fronts? Does that mean there are many truths?

Hauerwas:

Well, I tend to use the language of truthfulness. You begin to know how to get to the truth by knowing how not to lie. I think that the truth can be a kind of a loosely twined subject to the extent of underwriting that this proposition has those kinds of facts. Truth has a practical character. I have just been taking

---

[805] John Paul II, *Centesimus Annus*, Libreria Editrice Vaticana, 2003, http://www.vatican.va/edocs/POR0067/_INDEX.HTM (accessed on February 5, 2012).

a class on Immanuel Kant that influenced me. According to Kant, practical knowledge is the cause of how to understand. So that means that what signs we make as Christians, they are transformative for us to be people capable of making that claim. So now lying is the beginning of how to know what is being said has truthfulness. And that means that to discover the truth is an ongoing process of a community that doesn't feel it. I think the church is quite remarkable over the centuries of always being open about what God will teach us, about how we have not been as truthful as we need to be. And that has a lot to do with interacting with other people who say it differently.

Fr. Ssenyondo:
When we look at the early church, we realize that the apostles had a creed (Apostles' Creed), a set of beliefs consisted in the *Didache*—containing the truth that was handed to them by the Lord. At that time, we can point at what we can call the Christian doctrine. Can we still talk of Christian doctrine or Christian doctrines?

Hauerwas:
Well, we do not only have the Apostles' Creed. We also have the Nicene, the Constantinopolitan, and the Chalcedonian creeds. I think all those are absolutely crucial for helping us to say what we know to be true. Newman wondered whether the Nicene Creed, which was promulgated under Emperor Constantine, is still normative for the church. Yes it is, but then, does it say everything that need to be said? According to Newman, we don't know yet. So the Apostles' Creed says much of what need to be said but does not say everything that need to be said. We don't know yet, because the spirit hasn't given up on us. I think Newman's discovery of the development of doctrine is very astute of how it is a fresh articulation of how to say what was necessary that was there, but we didn't know was there. I have a progressive view of doctrine, but I have the view that we become better to say what we believe over time.

Fr. Ssenyondo:
What do you make of ecumenism?

Hauerwas:
I think I am a living ecumenical movement (big laughter). I am deeply committed to Christian unity. And I am a Methodist. Methodism was a movement that accidentally became a church. And therefore I long and hunger for Christian unity. The ecumenical movement is not the same as the desire to Christian unity. I certainly desire and hunger for the day when you and I will share the same Eucharistic meal. In the meantime, we have to have the pain of our

separation. I hate the pain, but it reminds us of what it means to be divided and yet long for unity. Where I started is not where the church needs to be one, but that Christians learn not to kill one another because we are Christians. That is where I deeply think the unity has to start. If we learn not to kill one another, we might learn that we need to share the same Eucharistic feast. Christian unity has always been at heart of what I care about.

Fr. Ssenyondo:
Say something about Joseph Ratzinger's theology.

Hauerwas:
I can't say that I have read everything that he has written, but I take Ratzinger's work to be at the heart of Vatican II. Insofar as I read Vatican II, I think that he is doing a recovery of the Christological center of the Catholic faith. I am much more sympathetic with Ratzinger than I am with Rahner. Rahner seems to me, at least in some of his theological expressions, a representative of a theorization of Christian faith. And Ratzinger is much more Christological-centered and has a more profound understanding of liturgy in particular—the centrality of worship. I am on Ratzinger's side on that regard. I think he was right to say that he and Rahner were on different planets. I am quite sympathetic with his theology—we are on the same planet.

Fr. Ssenyondo:
What are your views about relativism?

Hauerwas:
My view is that the problem is not about relativism but the epistemological conceit that gives you the problem of relativism. My views about relativism are very similar to MacIntyre's. Now once you have left behind the fundamentals of the Christian project, which gives you relativism, because you think that people of different traditions should necessarily know how to defeat the other tradition, and if you can't defeat it, as a matter of fact, you are promoting relativism. I think those foundations or notions are just wrong. What you face is a world of diversity; and you must discover how your tradition might put in question the other tradition, which MacIntyre calls an epistemological crisis. In that article, you mentioned about the "nonviolent terrorist" is an article about relativism. It shows how the very effort to defeat relativism only reproduces it. I am just not in a position to argue in general that I know what I am talking about. And that is why it is not a problem for me because you are going to find that disagreements are possible, and that is a great achievement. Many times we will discover that we don't even know what the other is talking about. And that is

why Christianity is ready to listen to the other person. Listening and knowing that disagreements can occur is the beginning of how to defeat relativism.

Fr. Ssenyondo:
What do you consider to be your legacy?

Hauerwas:
Hahahaaa! That is an invitation to self-deception (prolonged laughter). I think the most important thing I have done is trying to make graduate students care about the theological formation of how to think about moral life; and that is a better contribution to an ongoing formation of the church. People may say he is the one who started the recovery of virtue, recovery of narratives. I think the centrality of Christ and the church and Christ in the world have been crucial for me. I think that is my lasting contribution.

Bibliography

I. General Reference Section

Brenton, Lancelot. *The Septuagint with Apocrypha: Greek and English*. London: Hendrickson Publishers, 1951.

Britannica Concise Encyclopedia. http://www.answers.com/topic/john-wesley.

Brown, Raymond E. Brown. et al., eds. *The New Jerome Biblical Commentary*. Garden City: NY: Prentice Hall Inc., 1990.

Carson, Thomas and Joann Cerrito, eds. *New Catholic Encyclopedia*. New York: The Gale Group Inc., 2003.

Catechism of the Catholic Church. 2nd edition. Vatican City: Libreria Editrice Vaticana, 1997.

Denzinger/Hünermann, *Enchiridion Symbolorum Definitinum et Declarationum de Rebus Fidei* et Morum, 37th edition. Freiburg i. Br.: Herder, 1991.

Flannery, Austin. Ed. *Vatican Council II: The Conciliar and Postconciliar Documents*. Northport, NY: Costello Publishing Company, 1996.

Landau, Sidney and Paul Heacock. eds. *Cambridge Dictionary of American English*. New York: Cambridge University Press, 2000.

Neuner, Joseph and Jacques Dupuis. *The Christian Faith in the Doctrinal Documents of the Catholic Faith*. 7th edition. New York: St. Paul's, 2001.

Stanford Encyclopedia of Philosophy. http://plato.stanford.edu/entries/kierkegaard/.

The Holy Bible: New Revised Standard Version. Catholic Edition. New York, NY: HarperCollins Publishers, 1991.

The New American Bible. Trans. Members of the Catholic Biblical Association of America. New York: Catholic Book Publishing Co., 1968.

Wildman, Wesley, ed. *Boston collaborative Encyclopedia of Western Theology*. Boston, MA: Boston University Press, 1994.

II. Primary Sources

1. Joseph Ratzinger

a. Books

Benedict XVI. Dogma and Preaching: Applying Christian Doctrine to Daily Life. San Francisco: Ignatius Press, 2011.

_____. *Light of the World*, trans. Michael Miller and Adrian Walker. San Francisco: Ignatius Press, 2010.

_____. *Volk und Haus Gottes in Augustins Lehre von der Kirche.* München: K. Zink, 1954.

Ratzinger, Joseph (Pope Benedict XVI). *Christianity and the Crisis of Cultures.* San Francisco: Ignatius Press, 2005.

_____. *Jesus of Nazareth, Part Two.* San Francisco: Ignatius Press, 2011.

Ratzinger, Joseph and Marcello Pera. *Without Roots: The West, Relativism, Christianity. Islam,* New York: Basic Books, 2006.

Ratzinger, Joseph, and Vittorio Messori. *The Ratzinger Report: An Exclusive Interview on the State of the Church.* San Francisco: Ignatius Press, 1985.

Ratzinger, Joseph. *Church, Ecumenism and Politics.* New York: Crossroad, 1988.

_____. *Credo for Today: What Christians Believe.* Trans. Michael Miller. San Francisco: Ignatius Press, 2009.

_____. *Eschatology, Death and Eternal Life.* Translated by Michael Waldstein and edited by Aidan Nichol, OP. Washington DC: CUA, 1988.

_____. *God and the World: Believing and Living in Our Time.* San Francisco: Ignatius Press, 2000.

_____. *Gospel, Catechesis, Catechism: Sidelights on the Catechism of the Catholic Church.* San Francisco: Ignatius Press, 1995.

_____. *Handing on the Faith in an Age of Disbelief.* San Francisco: Ignatius Press, 1983.

_____. *Introduction to Christianity.* San Francisco: Ignatius Press, 1968.

_____. *Milestones: Memoirs: 1927–1977.* San Francisco: Ignatius Press, 1998.

_____. *Pilgrim Fellowship of Faith: The Church as Communion.* San Francisco: Ignatius Press, 2002.

_____. *Principles of Catholic Theology: Building Stones for a Fundamental Theology.* San Francisco: Ignatius Press, 1987.

_____. *The Feast of Faith.* San Francisco: Ignatius Press, 1981.

_____. *The Spirit of the Liturgy*. San Francisco: Ignatius Press, 2000.

_____. *The Theology of History in St. Bonaventure*. trans. Zachary Hayes. Chicago, IL: Franciscan Herald Press, 1971.

_____. *Truth and Tolerance: Christian Belief and World Religions*. San Francisco: Ignatius Press, 2003.

_____. *Values in a Time of Upheaval*. San Francisco: Ignatius Press, 2006.

Thornton, John and Susan B. Varenne, eds. *The Essential Pope Benedict XVI: His Central Writings and Speeches*. New York: HarperCollins Publishers, 2007, 22.

b. Articles

Ratzinger, Joseph and Tarcisio Bertone. "Defending Orthodoxy." *Inside the Vatican*: (October 1997), 66–69.

Ratzinger, Joseph. "Address to the German Public Authorities." *Janet—97*: (2005): 893–897.

_____. "Christian Faith as 'The Way': An Introduction to Veritas Splendor." *Communio* 21: (1994): 199–207.

_____. "Difficulties in Teaching the Faith Today." *International Catholic Journal, Communio* 12: (1983): 259–267.

_____. "Experience and Belief." *International Catholic Journal, Communio* 9: (1980): 58–70.

_____. "Faith in the Context of Contemporary Philosophy." *International Catholic Journal, Communio* 31: (2002): 267–273.

_____. "Faith Is a Communion of Life with Jesus." *Osservatore Romano*: (Nov. 3, 1999): 1615–1617.

_____. "Freedom and Truth." *International Catholic Journal, Communio* 24: (1995): 527–542.

_____. "Introduction to Christianity: Yesterday, Today, and Tomorrow." *International Catholic Journal, Communio* 31: (2004): 481–495.

_____. "Jesus Christ Today." *International Catholic Journal, Communio* 17: (1990): 68–87.

_____. "Preserve Your Christian Roots." *Inside the Vatican*: (March 2002): 72–75.

_____. "Report on the Situation of Faith." *Materials of the Denomination Service Ethnography Institute Bensheim* 36: (1985): 15.

_____. "Tradition and Progress." *Theological Yearbook*: (1979): 189–203.

_____. From the Trust in the Divine Initiative and Human Response." *Order of Message*—48: (2009): 79–83.

_____. The World through the Eyes of the Creator's View." *Religious Messages*—49: (2010): 56–59.

_____. Uncompromisingly Proclaim the Primacy of God." *Religious Messages*—47: (2008): 70–73.

Thavis, John. "The New Danger, Ratzinger Says, Is Relativism." *National Catholic Reporter:* (Oct. 18, 1996): 32.

2. Stanley Hauerwas

a. Books

Hauerwas, Stanley and Jean Vanier. *Living Gently in a Violent World: The Prophetic Witness of Weakness.* Downers Grove, IL: IVP Books, 2008.

Hauerwas, Stanley. *A Better Hope: Resources for a Church Confronting Capitalism, Democracy, and Postmodernity.* Grand Rapids, MI: Brazos Press, 2000.

_____. *A Cross-Shattered Church: Reclaiming the Theological Heart of Preaching.* Grand Rapids, MI: Brazos Press, 2009.

_____. *After Christendom: How the Church Is to Behave if Freedom, Justice, and a Christian Nation Are Bad Ideas.* Nashville, TN: Abingdon Press, 1991.

_____. *Christian Existence Today: Essays on Church, World, and Living in Between.* Durham, NC: Labyrinth Press, 1988.

_____. *Cross-Shattered Christ: Meditations on the Seven Last Words.* Grand Rapids, MI: Brazos Press, 2004.

_____ *Dispatches from the Front: Theological Engagements with the Secular.* Durham, NC: Duke University Press, 1994.

_____. *Hanna's Child: A Theologian's Memoir.* Grand Rapids, MI: Wm. B. Eardmans, 2010.

_____. *Hannah's Child: A Theologian's Memoir.* Grand Rapids, MI: William B. Eerdmans Publishing Company, 2010.

_____. *In Good Company: Church as Polis.* Notre Dame, IN: University of Notre Dame Press, 1995.

_____. *Living Gently in a Violent World: The Prophetic Witness of Weakness.* Downers Grove, IL: IVP Books, 2008.

_____. *Peaceable Kingdom: A Primer in Christian Ethics.* Notre Dame, IN: University of Notre Dame Press, 1983.

_____. *Performing the Faith: Bonhoeffer and the Practice of Nonviolence.* Grand Rapids, MI: Brazos Press, 2004.

_____. *Prayers Plainly Spoken*. Downers Grove, IL: InterVarsity Press, 1999.

_____. *Resident Aliens: Life in the Christian Colony*. Nashville, TN: Abingdon Press, 1989.

_____. *Sanctify Them in the Truth: Holiness Exemplified*. Nashville, TN: Abingdon Press, 1998.

_____. *Unleashing the Scriptures*. Nashville, TN: Abingdon Press, 1993.

_____. *Where Resident Aliens Live: Exercises for Christian Practice*. Nashville, TN: Abingdon Press, 1996.

_____. *Wilderness Wandering: Probing Twentieth-century Theology and Philosophy*. Boulder, CO: Westview Press, 1997.

_____. *With the Grain of the Universe: The Church's Witness and Natural Theology*. Grand Rapids, MI: Brazos Press, 2001.

_____. *Working with Words: On Learning to Speak Christian*. Eugene, OR: Cascade Books, 2011.

b. Articles

Hauerwas, Stanley "Explaining Christian Nonviolence: Notes for a Conversation with John Milbank." *Must Christianity be Violent?* (2003): 172–182.

_____. "In Praise of *Centesimus Annus*." Theology 95: (1992): 416.

_____. "The Importance of Being Catholic: Unsolicited Advice from a Protestant Bystander." *Listening*, 25: (1990): 27.

_____. "Beyond the Boundaries: The Church Is Mission." *Walk Humbly with the Lord*: (2010): 53–69.

_____. "Christians in the Hands of Flaccid Secularists: Theology and 'Moral Inquiry' in the Modern University." *Ethical Perspectives* 4: (1997): 32–44.

_____. "Dietrich Bonhoeffer and John Howard Yoder." *The Sermon on the Mount Through the Centuries*: (2007): 207–222.

_____. "Eliminating People Who Suffer?" (Sept/Oct 1983), *Stauros Notebook*, http://www.stauros.org/notebooks/v02n5a01.html.

_____. "Stanley Hauerwas and the Church as God's New Language." http://jeremyberg.wordpress.com/2010/01/05/essay-stanley-hauerwas-the-church-as-gods-new-language/.

_____. Stanley. "The Christian Difference: Or Surviving Postmodernism." *Anabaptists and Postmodernity*: (2001): 41–59.

_____. "The Church in a Divided World: The Interpretative Power of the Christian Story." *Journal of Religious Ethics* 8: (1980): 55–82.

_____. "The Democratic Policing of Christianity." *Pro Ecclesia* 3: (1994): 215.

Hauerwas, Stanley. "*Veritatis Splendor*: Responses to the Encyclical." *Studies in Christian Ethics* 7: (1994): 16.

_____. "Virtue, Description and Friendship: A Thought Experiment in Catholic Moral Theology." *The Irish Theological Quarterly* 62: (1996): 170–184.

_____. "Why the Truth Demands Truthfulness: An Imperious Engagement with Hartt." *Journal of the American Academy of Religion* 52: (1984): 141–147.

II. Secondary Sources

1. Joseph Ratzinger

a. Books

Corkery, James. *Joseph Ratzinger's Theological Ideas: Wise Cautions and Legitimate Hopes*. New York: Paulist Press, 2009.

de Gaál Gyulai, Emery. *The Theology of Pope Benedict XVI: The Christocentric Shift*. New York: Palgrave Macmillan, 2010.

Jankunas, Gediminas T. *The Dictatorship of Relativism: Pope Benedict XVI's Response*. New York: St. Paul's Press, 2011.

Miller, Michael J., and Adrian J. Walker (translators). *Benedict XVI: Light of the World*. San Francisco: Ignatius Press, 2010.

Nichols, Aidan. *The Thought of Benedict XVI: An Introduction to the Theology of Joseph Ratzinger*. London: Burns & Oates, 2005.

Rowland, Tracey. *Ratzinger's Faith: The Theology of Pope Benedict XVI*. Oxford: Oxford University Press, 2008.

Thornton, John F. & Susan B. Varenne, eds. *The Essential Pope Benedict XVI: His Central Writing and Speeches*. New York: HarperCollins Publishers, 2007.

2. Stanley Hauerwas

a. Books

Berman, John, and Michael Carwright, Eds. *The Hauerwas Reader*. Durham, NC: Duke University Press, 2001.

Jones, Gregory, et al. *God, Truth, and Witness: Engaging Stanley Hauerwas*. Grand Rapids, MI: Brazos Press, 2005.

Katongole, Emmanuel. *Beyond Universal Reason: The Relation between Religion and Ethics in the Work of Stanley Hauerwas.* Notre Dame, IN: University of Notre Dame Press, 2000.

Long, Michael. *Christian Peace and Nonviolence: A Documentary History.* Maryknoll, NY: Orbis Books, 2011.

Thomson, John. *The Ecclesiology of Stanley Hauerwas: A Christian Theology of Liberation.* Burlington, VT: Ashgate, 2003.

b. Articles

Grenz, Stanley J. "Stanley Hauerwas, The Grain of the Universe, and the Most 'Natural' Natural Theology." *Scottish Journal of Theology* 56: (2003): 381–386.

Hartt, Julian. "Reply to Crites and Hauerwas." *Journal of the American Academy of Religion* 52: (1984): 149–156.

Hobson, Theo. "Against Hauerwas." *New Blackfriars* 88: (2007): 300–312.

Jenson, Robert. "The Hauerwas Project." *Modern Theology* 8: (1992): 285.

Koopman, Nico. "The Role of Pneumatology in the Ethics of Stanley Hauerwas." *Scriptura Stellenbosch*: (2002): 4–15.

Mahn, Jason. "Kierkegaard after Hauerwas." *Theology Today* 64: (2007): 172–185.

Mathewes, Charles T. "Appreciating Hauerwas." *Anglican Theological Review* 82: (2000): 343–360.

Webb, Stephen. "The Very American Stanley Hauerwas." *First Things*: (June/July 2002): 14–17.

Welch, Sharon D. "Communitarian Ethics after Hauerwas." *Studies in Christian Ethics* 10: (1997): 82–95.

III. General Sources

1. Books

Aquinas, Thomas. *Summa Theologica*, III. New York: Benzinger Brothers, Inc., 1948.

Armstrong, John. ed. *Understanding Four Views of the Lord's Supper.* Grand Rapids, MI: Zondervan, 2007.

Augustine. *The City of God.* Trans. Marcus Dods. New York: Random House Inc., 1950.

_____ *The Fathers of the Church: Writings of St. Augustine*, vol. 2. New York: Cima Publishing Co., Inc., 1947.

Barron, Robert. *Thomas Aquinas: Spiritual Master.* New York: The Crossroad Publishing Company, 2008.

Berger, Peter. *A Rumor of Angels.* New York: Doubleday & Company, Inc., 1970.

Bourke, Vernon J. *The Essential: Augustine.* New York: The New American Library of World Literature, Inc., 1964.

Brown, Milton. *The Authentic Writings of Ignatius.* Durham, NC: Duke University Press, 1963.

Cahoone, Lawrence. ed. *From Modernism to Postmodernism: An Anthology.* Cambridge, MA: Blackwell Publishers Inc., 1996.

Descartes, René. *Discours de la Methode.* Paris: Librairie Philosophique, 1930.

_____. *Discourse on the Method of Rightly Conducting the Reason and Seeking Truth in the Sciences.* London: Edinburgh Publishers, 1863.

Dillenberger, John. ed. *Martin Luther: Selections from His Writings.* New York: Anchor Books, 1962.

Gakwandi, Arthur. *Uganda: Pocket Facts.* Kampala, Uganda: Fountain Publishers Ltd, 1999.

Gale, H. P. *Uganda and the Mill Hill Fathers.* London: MacMillan and Co. Limited, 1959.

Green, Elliot. *Ethnicity and Nationhood in Pre-Colonial Africa: The Case of Buganda.* London: London School of Economics Press, 2010.

Hanson, Richard. *The Search for the Christian Doctrine of God: The Arian Controversy.* Edinburgh: T & T Clark, 1988.

Hegel, Friedrich. *The Phenomenology of Mind.* trans. George Lichtheim. New York: Harper Torchbooks, 1967.

Kant, Immanuel. *Critique of Pure Reason.* New York, NY: Willey Book Co., 1943.

Kierkegaard, Søren. *Philosophical Fragments: Johannes Climacus.* Princeton, NJ: Princeton University Press, 1985.

Kizza, Immaculate. *The Oral Tradition of the Baganda.* Jefferson, NC: McFarland & Company, Inc., Publishers, 2010.

Lakeland, Paul. *Postmodernity: Christian Identity in a Fragmented Age.* Minneapolis, MN: Augsburg Fortress, 1997.

Law, William. *A Serious Call to a Devout and Holy Life; The Spirit of Love.* New York: Paulist Press, 1978.

Lund, Eric. ed., "The Augsburg Confession," in *Documents from the History of Lutheranism, 1517–1750.* Minneapolis, MN: Fortress Press, 2002.

Mbiti, John S. *African Religions and Philosophy.* Oxford: Heinemann Educational Publishers, 1990.

Möhler, Johann Adam. *Symbolism*. New York: The Crossroad Publishing Company, 1997.

Moltmann, Jürgen. *Man: Christian Anthropology in the Conflict of the Present*. Philadelphia, PA: Fortress Press, 1971.

Murphy, Michael. *A Theology of Criticism: Balthasar, Postmodernism, and the Catholic Imagination*. New York, NY: Oxford University Press, 2008.

Nancy, Jean-Luc. *Dis-Enclosure: The Deconstruction of Christianity*. New York, NY: Fordham University Press, 2008.

Nietzsche, Friedrich. *Basic Writings of Nietzsche*. trans. Walter Kaufmann. New York: Random House, Inc., 1968.

Page, T. E. ed. *Tertullian and Minucius Felix*. New York: G. P. Putnam's Sons, 1931.

Rasmusson, Arne. *The Church as Polis*. Notre Dame, IN: University of Notre Dame Press, 1995.

Roscoe, John. *The Baganda: An Account of Their Native Customs and Beliefs*. London: Macmillan Publishers, 1911.

Ryan, John. *The Confessions of St. Augustine*. New York: Image Books, 1960.

Saint Augustine. *The City of God (De Civitate Dei)*. Trans. John Healey. Edinburgh: John Grant, 1909, Book 11.

Schleiermacher, Friedrich. *On Religion: Speeches to Its Cultured Despisers*, translated by R. Crouter. Cambridge: Cambridge University Press, 1988.

_____. *The Christian Faith*. Berkeley, CA: The Apocryphile Press, 2011.

Schwarz, Hans. *Our Cosmic Journey: Christian Anthropology in the Light of Current Trends in the Sciences, Philosophy and Theology*. Minneapolis, MN: Augsburg Publishing House, 1977.

Sider, Robert D. *Christian and Pagan in the Roman Empire*. Washington, DC: The Catholic University of America Press, 2001.

Söhngen, Gottlieb. *Die Einheit in der Theologie*. Munich: Zink, 1952.

Spalding, John. *Religion, Agnosticism and Education*. Chicago, IL: A. C. McClure & Co., 1902.

St. Augustine on the Psalms (*Enarrationes in Psalmos*) in Ancient Christian Writers: The Works of the Fathers in Translation. Trans. Dame Scholastica Hebgin and Dame Felisitas Corrigan. Westminster, Maryland: The Newman Press, 1960.

Taylor, John. *The Growth of the Church in Buganda*. London: SCM Press Ltd, 1958.

Thunberg, Lars. *Microcosm and Mediator: The Theological Anthropology of Maximus the Confessor*, 2nd ed. Chicago, IL: Open Court Publishing Company, 1995.

Von Balthasar, Hans Urs. *The God Question and Modern Man.* New York: The Seabury Press, 1967.

2. Encyclicals

Benedict XVI. *Charity in Truth, Caritas in Veritate.* Vatican City: Libreria Editrice Vaticana, 2009.
_____. *God Is Love, Deus Caritas Est.* Vatican City: Libreria Editrice Vaticana, 2006.
John Paul II. "Veritatis Splendor": *The Splendor of Truth: Regarding Certain Fundamental Questions of the Church's Moral Teaching;* Encyclical Letter (August 6, 1993).
_____. *On the Permanent Validity of the Church's Missionary Mandate "Redemptoris Missio,"* Encyclical Letter (December 7, 1990).

3. Instructions

The Lord Jesus: Declaration Dominus Jesus on the Unicity and Salvific Universality of Jesus Christ and the Church. The Congregation for the Doctrine of the Faith. Nairobi, Kenya: Paulines Publications Africa, August 6, 2000.

4. Articles

Brierley, Jean and Thomas Spear. "Muteesa, The Missionaries, and Christian Conversion in Buganda." *The International Journal of African Historical Studies:* (April, 21, 1988): 612.
Waliggo, John Mary. "Ganda Traditional Religion and Catholicism in Buganda, 1948–1975," *Christianity in Independent Africa:* (Bloomington, IN: Indiana University Press, 1978): 414.

IV. Consulted but not Cited Sources

1. Books

Allen, John. *Pope Benedict XVI: A Biography of Joseph Ratzinger.* New York: Continuum, 2005
Calvin, John. *Institutes of the Christian Religion.* Grand Rapids, MI: Eerdmans Publishing Co., 1995.
Donald Henry, Matthews. *Honoring the Ancestors: An African Cultural Interpretation of Black Religion and Literature.* New York: Oxford University Press, 1998.

Harnack, Adolf. *What Is Christianity? A Collection of Lectures Given at the University of Berlin, 1899-1900*. Trans. Thomas Bailey. Philadelphia: Fortress Press, 1986.

Hauerwas, Stanley. *A Better Hope: Resources for a Church Confronting Capitalism, Democracy, and Postmodernity*. Grand Rapids, MI: Brazos Press, 2000.

_____. *Naming the Silence: God, Medicine, and the Problem of Suffering*. Grand Rapids, MI: Wm. B. Eerdmans, 1990.

_____. *The State of the University: Academic Knowledge and the Knowledge of God*. Malden, MA; Oxford: Blackwell Pub., 2007.

MacIntyre, Alasdair. *Whose Justice? Which Rationality?* Notre Dame, IN: University of Notre Dame Press, 1988.

Malina, Bruce J. *The New Testament World: Insights from Cultural Anthropology*. Atlanta, GA: John Knox Press, 1981.

Schroeder, H. J. *Canons and Decrees of the Council of Trent*. Rockford, IL: Tan Books and Publishers, Inc., 1978.

2. Articles

Albrecht, Gloria. "Unmasking the Differences: Nonviolence and Social Control." *Cross Currents*: (Spring 2002): 16–27.

Clooney, Francis Xavier. "Relativism in Perspective: Rereading Ratzinger." *Commonweal*: (Jan. 31, 1997): 9–10.

Hauerwas, Stanley. "Abortion, Theologically Understood," *Address given June 14, 1990, at the 1990 meeting of the North Carolina Annual Conference of the United Methodist Church*, Published by Taskforce of United Methodists on Abortion and Sexuality at Dothan, Alabama, February 1991.

_____. "Discipleship as a Craft, Church as a Disciplined Community." *The Christian Century*: (October 1, 1991): 881–884.

_____. "The Testament of Friends." *The Christian Century*: (February 28, 1990): 213–216.

Nwaigbo, Ferdinand. *Church as a Communion: An African Christian Perspective*. Frankfurt am Main: Peter Lang, 1996.

Parratt, John. *Reinventing Christianity: African Theology Today*. Grand Rapids, MI: African World Press, 1995.

Index

violence, 50, 60–61, 122–23, 180, 203–4, 268–69, 272, 297
Violent World, 280

CPSIA information can be obtained at www.ICGtesting.com
Printed in the USA
LVOW07s0907030215

425479LV00001B/155/P